To Da...

With ev...

share 2 ♭ 0 ♮ with
you & the world!

Carol

Called To The Peaceable Kingdom

The Mosaic Covenant of Shalom

The Kingdom of God And Zion

By

Carol Cease Campbell

Little Eagle Publishing
Lamar, MO 64759
www.little-eagle.com

Abstract:

"The dream of a holy city, of a place where the God of Israel reigned has been on the hearts and lips of people throughout the pages of scripture. This dream has inspired people from the very beginning of Judeo-Christian history to this time.

For many Christians, this was dream of a heavenly city; for others, the dream was of an

earthly place where people treated each other with justice and none was denied access to those things necessary for life because the righteousness of God was upheld as the model for human behavior. The people would be of one heart and one mind, living in righteousness with no poor among them. For some, the dream was based on individual salvation. For others although personal response to God was essential, their scripture understanding was that God sought a people, a covenant community, living "The Kingdom" that Jesus preached in their everyday lives.

Although the book is written for a specific faith movement, Community of Christ, the message of this volume is for all within the Judeo-Christian tradition in its emphasis on the importance of community from the biblical witness.

Copyright 2004
Little Eagle Publishing
Ralph Williston, editor
71 S.E. 30th Lane
Lamar, Mo. 64759

Cover: Photographed by Ralph Williston

ISBN 0-9707904-2-2

Printed in the United States of America

Listen to the Voice that echoes across the eons of time and yet speaks anew in this moment. Listen to the Voice, for it cannot be stilled, and it calls you once again to the great and marvelous work of building the peaceable kingdom, even Zion, on behalf of the One whose name you claim.

Doctrine and Covenants 162:1b

Table of contents

Preface

Introduction

Part I The First Testament

Part II The New Witness

Preface

Steppingstones to Zion

The word, Zion, was everywhere in the church of my childhood located in Buchanan, Michigan. Each Sunday, we received little papers called, "Zion's Hope" or "Stepping Stones" with stories and activities – probably designed to keep us quiet during church. I remember the word, Zion, used in other ways like the name for youth groups like Zion's League or Zioneers, a former hymnal called Zion's Praises, and campgrounds or women's groups named for Zion. The word, Zion, became inextricably interwoven with my early church experiences.

Zion was not merely a word, but was connected to some of the most meaningful *experiences* of my youth where I came to more fully know and give my life to Christ. Our family vacation was spent at church camp, usually Park of the Pines in northern Michigan, where we all worked, played and worshiped together as family. We were often told that the week, called reunion, was a *foretaste of Zion* because of the rich spirit of Christian fraternity that we experienced. Youth camps also echoed themes of the connection between God and Christ and Zion. These experiences combined to create a deep longing within my innermost being to not only know Christ, but also to experience life in sacred community that was blessed by the fulfillment of the promises of God.

Stepping Stones was not only the name of a child's Sunday paper. There were people who acted as steppingstones for me. My parents, Glenn and Iona Cease, were wonderful guides and role models. My father held especially passionate belief in Zion as the means of *embodiment* of his faith in the living Christ. He loved scripture and genuinely enjoyed delving more deeply into scriptural questions and problems. I remember hearing him asked if he ever preached about anything other than repentance, stewardship or Zion because it seemed that these topics found their way into every part of his ministry. Like so many others that we knew, New Year's Day was the occasion for filing the annual stewardship accounting following Old Testament examples to determine the tithe. In our family, stewardship was a lifestyle with tithing being paid first, no matter what the financial difficulties were, and the "repression of unnecessary wants" being practiced both so that we could support the church more generously and also in order to be able to do things like attend college[1].

High school years were spent in Middletown, Ohio where I met another steppingstone. Jacob Halb was a retired church appointee missionary who had served the church in Europe while his wife, Addie who was a schoolteacher, sacrificially supported him there during depression years. Brother Halb always gave testimony at midweek services and ended with the summary of Zion from the Book of Mormon, "And surely there could not be a happier people among all the people who had been created by the hand of God[2]. Perhaps the way that I mouthed the words that finished every testimony did not always sense or appreciate the full significance of the words or his life of faithful service, but in his constant repetition of this passage, this description of sacred community became indelibly etched on my mind and heart.

People like Dr. Margaret Barker and Roy Weldon were also steppingstones from youth camps at Cantor's Cave in southeastern Ohio. Dr. Barker (later Booth)

---

[1] Doctrine and Covenants 130:7d and 147:5b.
[2] IV Nephi 1:19.

introduced me to the concept of the stewardship of health - body, mind and spirit - as expressed in the Word of Wisdom, *the abundant life*[3]. As a practicing physician (the first woman that I had ever known in a role like that!!), I was encouraged not only to claim *vibrant* health but also to greatly enlarge the scope of my goals, dreams and aspirations.

I had grown up fascinated by the pictures of the archeological evidences of the Book of Mormon in Meso America when Clair Weldon was our church appointee in Michigan. When his father, Roy Weldon, came to camp, the Holy Spirit bore witness to me of the deeply *spiritual* significance of the Book of Mormon, an additional testimony of Christ. I was challenged to read this book – and did so. I particularly remember reading the promise of the gift and power of the Holy Spirit that would assist those who seek to bring forth Zion in the latter day and the powerful affirmation of that Spirit as I read that promise[4]. Those words still echo in my soul calling me to claim that promise.

There were many steppingstones during college years, but two whose contributions were most significant in terms of Zion were Ed and Joy Browne. I was invited to their home where they not only shared scriptural insights and their dream of Zion but also the important tasks that needed to be done in the cause of Zion. They were not alone in their focus on Zion but were joined by many fine people in the Lawrence, Kansas congregation.

Richmond, Michigan was another congregation that sought to make Zion real among them. This was a small congregation, located in an unpretentious rural community

---

[3] Doctrine and Covenants 86.
[4] I Nephi 3:187-189.

that would never have been considered a place where people might undertake Zionic projects. But they were willing and able to dream big and work hard as a team toward those goals. Initially a small buying club had been formed to purchase pure foods in their desire to live according to teachings of the Word of Wisdom. Only fourteen member families voted to open a store with far less than two hundred dollars worth of stock, fixtures, and equipment. Hard work, ingenuity, great sacrifice and creative utilization of publicity resulted in a viable business that served the community for a number of years. A thrift and resale shop was opened in conjunction with the food cooperative that gave assistance to the poor of the community in many ways. Like the food cooperative, this enterprise was a blessing both to those who worked there and to the community.

Developing and managing the food cooperative opened the door for another steppingstone for me - involvement with the larger cooperative movement by serving on state boards for several organizations. My eyes were opened to the world of cooperative movements that were important, especially in their work with the poor because of the possibility of barter systems, prior to the tax code revision of the 1980s. Many of these organizations that used various systems of profit sharing or barter came from the English Cooperative Movement that is still in existence. Perhaps the best part of the whole cooperative experience was the wonderful feeling I experienced in working together with people from all walks of life for the common good of all.

My first trip to Israel in 1985 was a tremendously important transformative experience, a huge steppingstone, made possible by Reed and Jean Holmes and ViewPax Mondiale, an organization dedicated to the cause of peace. My life was changed in many ways when I came to know not only Jesus the Christ but also Jesus, the true son of Judah and began the journey of finding the golden threads of unity between the Old and New Testaments. It was also a time that provided the means to know and seek greater clarity in understanding the culture, customs and traditions of the people, the soil from which the sacred witness sprang. It was also thrilling to discover the work of Reed Holmes that told the story of people from our movement in the nineteenth century who had been pioneers for Zion in their work in fulfilling prophecy concerning the return of Jews to Palestine, later to become Israel[5].

Steppingstones enable us to move forward. This effort has certainly been blessed by persons who were steppingstones A wise person once said that God sends people into our lives when we need them. I have found this to be so in this work. I am especially indebted to Wesley Theological Seminary professors Bruce C. Birch and M. Douglas Meeks who greatly inspired and challenged me in their ministry of teaching. I am also indebted to Wallace B. Smith, the former leader of my church for taking the time to talk with me, sharing observations and answering my questions. His suggestions and input were of great benefit to me. Thanks are also extended to Anthony Chvala-Smith, Mark A. Sherer and Andrew Bolton who participated in the original work as well as Pam Robinson for proofreading help.

I have found the ministry of helps listed by Paul (I Cor. 12:28) to be an important role not only for this work, but also for the church. I am not sure that I would have completed my initial doctoral work without the help of my friend, Joanna (Joey) Kernstock. There was *serious* enmity between the computer and me – and it was winning the warfare! Her patient guidance and help enabled the

---

[5] Reed M. Holmes, *The ForeRunners, 2nd edition,* Pepperell, MA: Reed and Jean Holmes, 2003

computer and I to become working friends. She also helped with editing. When this book was begun we had moved. God sent another helper who is an excellent detail-oriented reader/editor who loves words. Cleo Barrett has become a wonderful friend as well as a great helper and I am greatly indebted to her for her assistance. Both Joey and Cleo are women of deep faith and conviction in their dedication to Christ who saw their efforts in this project as participation in the movement toward Zion.

As a complete novice in the area of publishing, I am especially indebted to editor and publisher Ralph Williston and his wife Nancy for their encouragement, helpful suggestions and hard work that enabled the publishing of this book.

I am also thankful for the host of people throughout the church for their interest and encouragement in this project, often asking when they would be able to read this book. This work has been blessed by a host of faithful witnesses in many parts of the world that I will never meet whose dedication to God is affirmed in their lives as their brother's keeper and stewards of the gifts of bountiful gifts of creation. Most of all, I thank my husband, Robert E. Campbell for his unfailing encouragement and loving support of my endeavors.

Introduction

On a bright, crisp January day in 1999 while in the doctoral program of Wesley Theological Seminary in Washington, D. C., I eagerly took my place in class. The previous semester I had had courses in theology, economics and the Bible. This class was titled *The Bible and the Poor* and was taught by Bruce C. Birch. As Dr. Birch was explaining the communal organization of the Mosaic community that developed from the post-exodus experience, he drew a large equilateral triangle on the blackboard illustrating the tripartite model of that early biblical communalism. At the apex of the triangle was the righteousness and freedom of God. All meaning and life itself was dependent on and pointed to and from God. The bottom line that connected the two angles represented egalitarian or democratic relationships within the community expressed by equality of access to the goods needed for life – the *economics of equality* – and the just exercise of power, particularly for the vulnerable – the *politics of justice*[1].

As I copied the triangle into my notes, I found myself writing in large letters within the triangle the word, ZION!!! As I did this, I experienced a profound and unmistakable sense of what I have come to know as the confirming power of the Holy Spirit that had touched alive within me a lifetime of dreaming, hoping, working, and longing for Zion. Some of the most competent Old Testament scholars had found the communal, or in our terms *the Zionic, principle at the very beginning of the time when the Lord called a people together and gave them the means to sustain sacred community.*

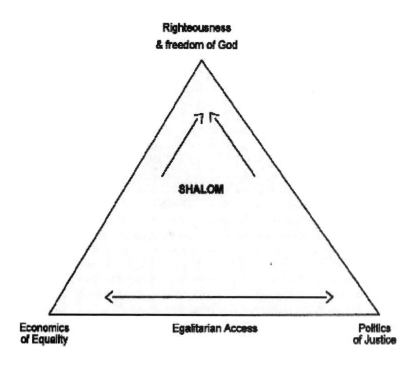

Righteousness
& freedom of God

SHALOM

Economics
of Equality

Egalitarian Access

Politics
of Justice

[1]Walter Brueggemann, *The Prophetic Imagination* (Minneapolis: Fortress Press, 1978), 11-27. Paul D. Hanson, *People Called: The Growth of Community in the Bible* (San Francisco: Harper & Row, 1986), 30-86.

Life in covenant community was an important part of God's desire for the human family from the very beginning.

I then began to wonder if this tripartite scheme, the triangle, could be traced through the Bible and into the Restoration movement's concept of Zion. What difference might it make to our ideas of Zion if we allowed the biblical text to speak to us from Moses through the prophets, the ministry of Jesus, the apostolic communities of all things in common, the Book of Mormon's Golden Age and our movement's rich heritage of community? Would this tripartite model prove sufficient for the exploration? Could this be used to share our belief with others and also deepen our commitment to Zion, shalom?

The word, shalom, is a wonderful way to describe life in sacred community. Shalom does not mean a state of static frozen perfection, but is a vital interplay and movement that allows for growth and development. Shalom is first of all about right relationships, balance and harmony that extend into all facets of life. The first dimension of that balance is the vertical; our individual and corporate lives honor God and strive to keep that relationship open. The next dimension could be the inward axis; there is integrity and health of the physical and emotional parts of our inward being. The outward dimension is tremendously important to shalom as it creates ever-widening circles of harmony and balance. The first area of shalom needs to be harmonious relationships with those closest to us that extends outward to our church or employment relationships, communities and relationships with other nations. The outward dimension also includes our part in the created order with our special responsibility to care for the earth and her creatures. A life of shalom is a life of stewardship that honors God in every aspect of life and because this is so, seeks life-affirming justice for all. It is a life of shared abundance.

Thus, this first community is called the Mosaic Covenant of Shalom in this exploration. From the beginning, the righteousness of the community or individuals was to be determined by their treatment of the poor and vulnerable. There could be no righteousness without justice.

Important understandings were added as the Mosaic Covenant was used through the Bible. The Mosaic Covenant was extended and broadened in adopting some of the understandings of Zion, the place where God dwelt among his people and from which the whole earth was to be blessed. The prophets went back to the original covenant in calling the people to justice and care for the poor and vulnerable. Jesus' teachings about the kingdom of God took the heart of the Mosaic and prophetic tradition and added great spiritual depth that called the apostolic church to form communities of "all things in common". These communities, sometimes called "the primitive church", were the inspiration for many religious movements. One of these movements began when a young teenager prayed in a grove; that simple act was the genesis of the Restoration movement. Almost a year before its formal organization, the people were called to the cause of Zion, not knowing exactly what it meant, but trusting in the power of God's continuing word to them.

Zion is a rich biblical and theological construct that has been an important part of our corporate identity from the beginning of the movement. It identifies salvation as not just the result of our individual response to the grace of God, but as God's intention for life in covenant relationship with God and in community with persons and the entire interconnected created order. This means that all things, including the components of everyday life, can be seen in spiritual terms.

This is a book that speaks the message of the importance of sacred community – past, present, and future. This exploration, which was based on my doctoral project at Wesley Theological Seminary, was finished at the beginning of the year 2000. Thus issues like the change in the church's name from The Reorganized Church of Jesus Christ of Latter Day Saints to Community of Christ from the April 2000 conference or the massive changes in the new Bishopric interpretation of stewardship called the Disciples Generous Response from the 2002 World Conference will not be considered in this work.

Part One

The First Testament

Chapter 1
Creation

"In the beginning, God"[2]
"When God began to create heaven and earth...
God said...And it was so.
And God saw all that He had made,
and found it very good."[3]

The Story of God

The opening sentences of Genesis have been the source of awe, wonder and mystery through the ages introducing the story of God and the creation of life. God alone is sovereign and the source of all goodness and blessing. Genesis is the story of God and assumes that God does not need introduction or explanation. God simply IS. In chapters one through eleven God "creates, blesses, gives laws, judges, grieves, saves, elects, promises, makes

---

[2] Genesis 1:1. Genesis 1-2:4a give the Priestly account of the transcendent Yahweh God who is over, above and superior to creation in every way. Scholars date the first written account from 600 to 500 B.C.E. The Yahwehist account of the immanent God of creation who is intimately involved with creation is found in Genesis 2:4b-25 and thought to have been written in the late tenth century B.C.E.
[3] Jewish Publication Society, *Tanakh, Genesis 1:1, 1:29-31.* (NY: Jewish Publication Society, 1985), 3-4.

covenants, provides counsel, protects, confers responsibility to human beings and holds them accountable"[4]. These stories or myths are foundational to the human story because the God of goodness in creation became the basis of understanding God as redeemer, the source of righteousness. In turn, the human story was shaped by its response to the story of God.

These texts are not only the initial introduction of the God of our fathers but are also the prologue for the story of humans and the earth itself. In the beginning, there was God. All else was chaos. God brought forth order and created all that exists and pronounced it good, very good. This was because the presence of God was extended to all that exists. "All the world is holy, suffused with divine presence."[5] Creation bears the stamp of its creator and continues to be in relationship with that source of being. A characteristic of all creation continues to be a shared finitude, being dependent both on God, the source of all life and also in an interconnected relationship

---

[4] Bruce C. Birch, Walter Brueggemann, Terence E. Fretheim, and David L. Petersen, *A Theological Introduction to the Old Testament,* (Nashville, TN: Abingdon, 1999), 41-42.

[5] Tikva Frymer-Kensky, David Novak, Peter Ochs, David Fox Sandmel, and Michael A. Singer, *Christianity In Jewish Terms.* (Boulder CO: Westview Press, 2000), 149.

[6] Douglas John Hall, *Thinking the Faith – Christian Theology in a North American Context.* (Minneapolis: Fortress Press, 1991), 299-300. Fritjof Capra, *The Turning Point – Science, Society, and the Rising Culture.* (NY: Simon and Schuster, 1982), 303. Capra lists two universal themes throughout all living matter: universal interconnectedness and interdependency and the dynamic nature of reality. Matthew Fox, *Creation Spirituality – Liberating Gifts for the People of the Earth,* (NY: HarperSanFrancisco, 1991), 29. "...a creation story instructs us in the fact that in our origins we are all poor, all born naked and dependent on others, all born gratuitously into this vast cosmic dance; not one of us has earned it."

with the entire created order.[6] The created world is always changing and responding to the forces of nature.

Not only is the good world of God's creation interrelated, existing in a web of mutual relationships of interdependence, it is a world of abundance. The giver of abundant life from chaos was and is also the source of continued blessing to be shared by the inhabitants of earth. The *abundance of God is defined as sufficiency for all.* "There is no conception here that some may have to go without, or that some orders exist only to provide abundance for others."[7] "... for the earth is full, and there is enough and to spare."[8]

The created order bears testimony to God, the source not only of all beginning but also ongoing creative activity. The God of goodness and abundance also pronounced the *Original Blessing,* first upon the entire created order, then to humankind, and finally to the Sabbath.[9] Humans and the world were created to be in relationship with the rest of the

---

[7]Bruce C. Birch and Larry L. Rasmussen, *The Predicament of the Prosperous,* (Philadelphia: Westminster, 1978), 116.

[8] *Doctrine and Covenants,*101:2f. (Independence, MO: Herald Publishing House, 1990.

[9] Genesis 1:22, 28; 2:3.

[10] Genesis 1:22, 1:28 and 2:3. Bruce C. Birch, *Let Justice Roll Down – The Old Testament Ethics, and Christian Life,* (Louisville, KY: Westminster, 1991), 74-79. The Old Testament does not support the idea of *creatio ex nihilo* (creation from nothing) but sees God's creative power as ongoing, bringing order from chaos. Thus God as Creator continues to renew, sustain and speak peace and creative wholeness. God the Creator is also from the beginning, God the Redeemer. Walter Brueggemann, *Theology of the Old Testament – Testimony, Dispute, Advocacy,* (Minneapolis, MN: Fortress, 1997), 529. Brueggemann states that this is the consensus of Old Testament scholarship. Doctrine and Covenants 22:21-23.

created order and also with their creator.[10] This blessing extended to all of creation as divine light that permeates creation.[11]

Not only was the created order relational, blessed and good, *humans are created in the image of God*. Creation in the image of God means that there is something of the divine being, sometimes termed as soul, in each human. Image was not meant as reflection, seeing the face of God mirrored in humans. It had far deeper meaning as the essence of finite personhood that was located in the being of God. Creation in the image of God has three aspects. First, the creation of humans through joint effort indicates the intentionality and cooperation that is to be at the heart of personhood. Persons were created by God for mutuality -- cooperation and community with each other. Second, humans were created to re-present God as agents. This indicates a relationship of dependence upon God but not the ultimate control of God over the human family as robots. Third, human life is to have primacy over that of animals but accountability is required. Humans were allowed to use animals for food, but they were to exercise stewardship in this, being accountable for taking life. Because the image of God is not limited by gender or race and is not dependent on human merit, a critical aspect of creation in the image of God is that no person is to have dominion over another.[12] Creation in the image of God is the basis of human worth, dignity and morality.

---

[11] John 1:1-9. *Doctrine and Covenants,* 83:7b;85:2-3. Fox, Creation, 90, 59. Fox sees salvation as our return to the Original Blessing.

[12] Frymer-Kensky, Novak, Ochs, Sandmel and Signer, 331-333. This concept of the worth of all persons is the bedrock of Judaism and Christianity. Doctrine and Covenants 16:3c-f.

...whatever else is implied by creation in the image of God, it at least suggests that humanity is to represent God's own concern to maintain the goodness of all creation. The commission that follows is to a kind of trusteeship, not a granting to humanity of inherent power to use as humans themselves see fit.[13]

"...faith in the living God enables an apprehension of inviolable worth that enlivens passionate responsibility for the created world and all people."[14] (It must be noted that in the ancient world, the ideals of worth and mutuality associated with personhood were primarily reserved for males.) In the ancient Near East creation in the image of God indicated commission and authority to act for God as trusted stewards charged with responsibility for the bounty of creation.[15] Both in their stewardship of creation and in their social life, humans were to not exploit but to live in harmony with the world, caring for nature so that it can continue to provide sufficiency for all.[16]

Covenant

Yahweh God was never an abstract or capricious being like other gods but a being who desired to know and be known by the good world of his creation. The way that God was known to the human family was in relationship that was marked by God's steadfast love, justice,

---

[13] Birch and Rasmussen, *Predicament,* 113

[14] Frymer-Kensky, Novak, Ochs, Sandmel and Signer, 348.

[15] M. Douglas Meeks, *God, The Economist – The Doctrine of God and Political Economy.* (Minneapolis: Fortress, 1989), 90-91. The image of God can be likened to Near East practice; when an emperor gave a medallion with his image, it constituted authorization to act for the emperor.

[16] Ross Kinsler and Gloria Kinsler, *The Biblical Jubilee and the Struggle for Life.* (Maryknoll, NY: Orbis, 1999) 37. Frymer-Kensky, Novak, Ochs, Sandmel, Signer, 350. The J account, Genesis 2:4b-25.

[17] Frymer-Kensky, Novak, Ochs, Sandmel, Signer, 144.

righteousness and compassion. The Hebrew term for this relationship is covenant. The covenant was based on committed love of an eternal God that was willing to be bound together even in the face of obstacle or failure.[17] God was always the initiator of the covenant as creator and owner of all that exists. Covenant meant that forever would their relationship be changed by the commitments of that agreement.

> For humans to be summoned into covenant...is to be singled out in love; the call to do more and to get closer to God is the content of the experience of election. Only divine self-control and a profound commitment to full human development can motivate God's promise to neither reject nor coerce human beings.[18]

The identification of God with the created order was such that God is never seen apart from creation. And yet, Yahweh was also hidden, completely beyond human grasp or apprehension.[19] While not like us, God was understood as a being who could be known in personal terms. Early names for God included: "Creator of the world, Master of the world, Almighty, Holy One – blessed be He, the Place, the Presence, Merciful, the one whose name cannot be spoken."[20]

> The description of God as a Person is indispensable....whatever else He may be – enters into a direct relation with us in creative, revealing and redeeming acts, and thus makes it possible for us to enter into a direct relation with Him....The concept of personal being is indeed completely incapable of declaring what God's essential being is,

---

[18] Ibid., 142.

[19] Brueggemann, Theology – Testimony, 333-334.

[20] Frymer-Kensky, Novak, Ochs, Sandmel and. Signer, 49.

6

but it is both permitted and necessary to say that God is also a Person.[21]

Shalom

The Hebrew word for God's vision for creation is *shalom*, the meaning of creation in community. Although often translated as "peace," its meaning also includes positive things in wholeness: "justice, unity, well-being, joy, health, relationship and peace."[22] God created life as shalom – harmonious and benevolent well-being for all people, the land and all the created orders of life. God's shalom was cosmic wholeness in relationship with other created beings, the earth and deity. The ancient understanding was that humans and the created world were not separated, but were to live in harmonious relationship called shalom that began with the being of God.[23] "Shalom… affirms that God, our Creator, has been at work from the beginning, bringing order out of chaos, community out of alienation."[24] God created the world for love and communion with it; the whole evolutionary process is an expression of the ongoing nature of the love of

---

[21] Liturgy Committee of the Central Conference of American Rabbis, *Gates of Prayer – The New Union Prayerbook,* (NY: Central Conference of American Rabbis, 1982), 11.

[22] Birch, *Justice,* 83. Harold N. Schneebeck, Jr., *The Body of Christ – A Study of the Nature of the Church,* (Independence, MO: Herald Publishing House, 1968), 67.

[23] Birch and Rasmussen, 118.

[24] J. Milburn Thompson, *Justice And Peace – A Christian Primer,* (Maryknoll, NY: Orbis Books, 1998), 12-13. Birch and Rasmussen, *Predicament,* 147-150.

7

God.[25] "The central vision of world history in the Bible is that all creation is one, every creature in community with every other, living in harmony and security toward the joy and well-being of every other creature."[26]

A graphic description of shalom begins with the vertical dimension, God and the individual being in relationship that includes our caring enough to practice repentance and accepting the gift of healing forgiveness. The second aspect of shalom is within, a closely related word includes the harmony that needs to exist within – physically and mentally. Circles describe the third part of shalom with mutuality and harmony within our families, groups such as church communities, larger governmental units such as nations, between nations and our earth. The last aspect of shalom is our harmonious relationship with the created order, the world around us.

While in the primal paradise of Eden, Adam was given responsibility for the created world. He named the animals which involved an on-going responsibility for them in the ancient sense. He tilled and cared for the land. An implicit understanding was that the first human couple also had responsibility or stewardship for each other. Justice and moral accountability to God are at the heart of humanness and constitute responsible relatedness to all of creation.[27] All of these things were defined as stewardship, responsibility to God for the created world and other persons. This was one of the first and most basic understandings given to the human family. "Stewardship

[25]Robert W. Hamma, *Landscapes of the Soul, a Spirituality of Place,* (Notre Dame, IN: Ave Maria Press, 1999), 147.

[26]Walter Brueggemann, *Living Toward a Vision: Biblical Reflections on Shalom,* (Philadelphia: United Church Press, 1976), 15.

[27]Brueggemann, Theology, Testimony, 338.

[28]Douglas John Hall, *The Steward – A Biblical Symbol Come of Age,* (Grand Rapids, MI: Eerdmans, 1990), 49.

belongs to the most ancient strands of our Judeo-Christian heritage."[28]

Unlike the rest of the created order, humans also had the capacity for deeper thought and hence had the power of choice that could result in obedience or disobedience to God. God's shalom could be broken by the refusal of humans to live as stewards of the bounty of creation.

Sin and Grace

By the third chapter of Genesis, the initial harmony of Eden was broken. Sin began with dissatisfaction and the denial of the goodness of creation, followed by a progression of doubt, distrust, suspicion of the motives of God, selfishness and pride and finally the desire for power beyond creaturely limits. "It is the desire to shift from cooperation to control, and it is a constant aspect of human sinfulness."[29] The role of the steward was negated for the desire to go beyond creaturely limits to know as God knows and to forget that God alone is the creator and giver of all. Humans are part of the created order.

> The temptation, which crouches at the door at the moment of abundance, is to think that what you have belongs to you personally, that the stuff you possess is in fact who you are. The first temptation of sin, as Cain (whose name means "the acquirer") discovered, is always the sin of injustice.[30]

Their covetous desire ended in injustice and the rupture of the existing harmonious relationship resulting in alienation and estrangement, shame, brokenness, fear and

---

[29] Birch and Rasmussen, Predicament, 117.
[30] Frymer-Kensky, Novak, Ochs, Sandmel, and Signer, 309.

guilt.[31] Unfortunately human sin also created havoc for all creation that innocently suffered.

> But in Biblical terms sin is relational. Its character is seen in the brokenness of relationships not in a shift downward on the ladder of being. In Genesis 3 the sinful disobedient act creates a breach in relationship to God, erects barriers between humans one to another, and alienates humanity from the very soil out of which human life was created. Sin is not a matter internal to human life. It breaks the shalom intended by God in creation.[32]

Sin was met with immediate divine judgment. Although there were always painful consequences, God also provided for the healing of relationships. In the midst of that suffering was the healing mercy and redeeming grace of a compassionate creator God. The rupture of the divine human relationship was met with the loving grace of God. When humankind sinned against the heart of God, God acted as Redeemer. The Hebraic understanding of a redeemer was a family member who acted to restore what was lost or mend the breach in relationships. God did not pardon unconditionally but waited for repentance on the part of humans who had sinned. Both being able to repent and receive forgiveness were gifts of God to the human family. "The unconditionality of grace includes repentance as an essential element of reconciliation with God."[33] The

---

[31] Hall, 55-57. The relational sense of sin is Hebraic. Jesus taught this but Greek concepts came to replace clear Hebraic understandings. The Greek idea of sin is not relational but is a personal lack or failure that took away from one's personal moral, spiritual perfection. Because of Greek dualism, preferring the spiritual realm, Jesus' teachings as well as those of the Hebraic witness were not only personalized but also spiritualized, negating interest or concern for others or the physical world itself. Teachings like stewardship also suffered in the process.

[32] Birch and Rasmussen, 121. See also Brueggemann, Theology – Testimony, 452.

[33] Frymer-Kensky, Novak, Ochs, Sandmel and Signer, 318. This statement is by a Christian author.

need was to accept this gift of grace, working with the redeemer toward full restoration of shalom, repentance that is turned toward the repair of the world. "Justice restored is sin redeemed."[34] An essential part of this has always been acknowledgment of sin and the need of forgiveness, healing and restoration.

God's intention for humankind has always been shalom - mutuality, harmony and blessing, not cursing. But curses were pronounced by God. The ancients heard these things as a recitation of things that were somehow wrong. The curses were not what God had intended but a description of life as it became apart from God where dominance, control and submission replaced mutuality, companionship and harmony. Unfortunately humankind adopted the "curse" model of human relationship with dominance and submission that resulted in hierarchies based on gender, power and possession of wealth rather than the original blessing. This was seen as evidence of continuing sin, not the loving grace extended by a redeeming God.[35]

Throughout scripture, God has desired for his creation to come back into a harmonious relationship with each other, the created world and deity, living in shalom. All relationships needed to be made new including the earth and her creatures that had suffered because of the sin of humans. Therefore, God's work of redemption needed to embrace all relationships, including the orders of creation that had been ruptured by sin. The recognition that humans have a role to play in the repair of the world is called *tikkum olam*.[36] Later this would be identified as the new creation or the peaceable kingdom.[37]

---

[34] Ibid. , 301-303, 308.

[35] Birch, Justice, 93-94.

[36] Frymer-Kensky et. al. 143-144

[37] Birch and Rasmussen, 122. Isa. 11:6-9, 55:12-13.

11

Chapter 2

Abraham, Covenant and Blessing

Genesis describes the depth and power of sin over the human family from the first act of rebellion until the call of Abram. The desire of God to redeem and deliver his errant children was not matched by human interest to return to communion with God. God had created a world of shalom where the human family was blessed with capacity to think, discover and create but the intelligence and creativity of humans were used instead in countless forms of rebellion against God.

> After its (Genesis') gloomy portrayal of the intrinsic limitations of human creatureliness and the added deprivations of human rebelliousness, it reaches a turning point when God takes hold of Abraham and his family and declares his intention to make him a model of blessing and thus a means of blessing to the world.[38]

The *Abrahamic covenant,* the first covenant to be considered in this work, was unconditional and everlasting. God who is holy would be known through a particular people not in an abstract sense, but in day-to-day relationship, initiated and guaranteed by the character of God. To share in covenant with God was to be in partnership with God in the work of healing, restoring, redeeming and mending relationship.

---

[38] John Goldingay, *Theological Diversity and the Authority of the Old Testament,* (Grand Rapids, MI: Eerdmans, 1987), 226-227.

The call of Abram in Genesis 12 is considered by many interpreters to be the key to the rest of Genesis and the Pentateuch...The promise to Abraham was not one that was fulfilled instantly. Rather, it began with Abram and continued in the lives of his descendants.[39]

God called a person, Abram, perhaps the first person with such a clearly individual destiny to an open future with God in which all the people of the earth would be blessed.[40] Yahweh God called Abram and talked with him whereby "the power and summons of promise are irreversibly embedded in the life of Israel".[41] The promise of blessing to Abram was threefold: (1) land – a place of home, (2) progeny – children that were a guarantee of the future, and (3) purpose or mission as the chosen people of God. These promises were tied to his willingness to risk everything in complete faith, trust and obedience. He was required to leave wealth, comfort, security and everything that was known and familiar, setting aside his mental and spiritual maps of reality in humility and trust to venture forth to an unknown world with Yahweh.

The essential identity of a person or a people is often more defined during times of great trauma or stress rather than in periods of easy success. In times of difficulty, distractions are easily identified while fundamental values are clarified and affirmed. This was true of Abram's experience as a sojourner who responded in complete

---

[39]Ronald E. Vallet, *The Steward Living in Covenant – A New Perspective on Old Testament Stories,* (Grand Rapids, MI: Eerdmans, 2000), 39.

[40]Thomas Cahill, *The Gift of the Jews – How a Tribe of Desert Nomads Changed the Way Everyone Thinks and Feels,* (NY: Doubleday, 1998), 28.

[41]Walter Brueggemann, *Theology of the Old Testament – Testimony, Dispute Advocacy,* (Minneapolis: Fortress, 1997), 570.

obedience to the call of God and would later be true of Israel's desert experiences or their Babylonian exile. Abram built altars and worshiped Yahweh God on his journey. He paid a tithe of all his possessions when he visited and spent time with Melchizedek, high priest and king of Salem, the city that would later be known as Jerusalem.

Abram personified the difference between a sojourner and a resident that would continue to play a role in the story of the people of Yahweh God. When Abram left Ur, he became a *sojourner*, a resident alien dependent upon the hospitality of the community without full rights of membership. The sojourner's journey was not completed until the promise of God was fulfilled. He lived in complete dependence upon that promise of God while a *resident* lived in possession of the land and hence his destiny. A sojourner looked for deliverance even if that deliverance came by "going into the wilderness" whereas a resident was settled, secure and a part of the status quo.[42] Sometimes it is far easier for a sojourner to respond to God than it is for a resident to do so.

God, the Creator of order from chaos, summoned an individual, asking him to leave all that he knew and follow in complete trust in order to learn another way to understand God and the world. The relationship between Abraham and Yahweh God was to be central to the faith and understanding of Israel. The tremendous faith and courage of Abraham who was willing to venture forth laid the foundations of the great monotheistic religions -- Judaism, Christianity and Islam.

---

[42] Birch, Justice, 110..

Chapter 3

Moses and the Birth Story of a People

The miracle of Exodus is the birth story of the *people* of Israel. This story centered in God who had ultimate freedom to act on behalf of his people in slavery. One of the most powerful images of God is as the deliverer of a group of oppressed Hebrew slaves in Egypt. This God also freely chooses to be in loving relationship and vulnerable to the hurts and cries of his people. For the people of God, Exodus is not so much history as it is God's eternal proclamation of salvation.[43]

> The exodus is...the magnificent and unique act of Yahweh's power, faithfulness, and justice, whereby the descendants of Abraham are freed to serve and acknowledge Yahweh as his own people.[44]

This birth story is unique; nothing like it had happened before. "Yahweh burst into the world as a theological *novum.*"[45] Thus began a revolution that extended to every phase of life, but the most important aspect was that it established the justice of God as its core value. Righteousness would forever after be intrinsically linked with justice for the most vulnerable of the children of God.

This story refuses to be simply about ancestors in the thirteenth century B.C.E. It is about the

---

[43]Birch, Brueggemann, Fretheim, and Petersen, 99.

[44] Goldingay, 11.

[45] Brueggemann, Theology – Testimony 735.

experience of bondage, liberation, covenant community and the presence of God's glory in our midst in every generation of God's people.[46]

Yahweh God was the only power that could have enabled freedom for them, but this redemption also required a human who was willing to act for God. The chosen person was Moses. Moses was not passive or simply acquiescent to the call of God. *He heard but refused to go five times!* Another aspect of the character of God is shown in the willingness of Yahweh to continue working with chosen messengers even through their initial refusal to act.

> It is with Moses that Yahweh has the most direct and significant contact....the upshot of the encounter is that a vocation is assigned to Moses for the sake of Israel...the personal encounter is not for its own sake – it is for the sake of the community, as was the case with Abraham.[47]

The experience of deliverance began with someone who had no history with this God in a dramatic appearance of God, a theophany, at the burning bush. God was not an impassive deity, but someone in relationship who *saw* the suffering, *heard* their cries of anguish and *deeply knew and suffered* with his people. When Yahweh revealed his name to Moses, it was an act of intimacy for which his response was deep reverence and awe.[48] In the ancient world, knowing the name of a person was to deeply know their inner essence, making them vulnerable in relationship with the other. At this point in the life of Moses, he was the fugitive son of Egyptian royalty wanted for the killing of an Egyptian taskmaster and the son-in-law of Jethro, the

---

[46] Ibid., 104.
[47] Brueggemann, Theology, Testimony, 571.
[48] Birch, 116-126.

priest of Midian, a man without a clear place in a family. Yahweh's first self-identification was as the God of your ancestors, Abraham, Isaac and Jacob. Yahweh God first affirmed Moses' clear place in the chosen family of blessing to the world.

The God of the Judeo-Christian family is a one whose existence does not have to be proven but is part of the family story.[49] The name also indicated a Hebraic sense of time where the past, present and future all exist together. The name of Yahweh is sometimes "I am that I am" or "I will be as I will be," but always the assurance is "I am the Creator; I will be there with you."[50]

Encounter with Yahweh forever changed Moses to become one of the most powerful spiritual leaders that has ever lived. This empowering authority enabled him to take a band of slaves whose memory of Yahweh had been dulled in their years of brutal oppression. They were transformed in their forty-year sojourn in the wilderness into readiness to enter the Promised Land as a people, a community. Moses became a powerful leader, a new unprecedented social reality and the prophet of the powerful radical freedom of God.[51] Moses did away with the politics of oppressive exploitation, replacing slavery with the politics of justice and compassion.[52]

The people also had a role to play. The long years of slavery were palpably brutal and crushing to the human spirit, but hope was kept alive through the worship of Yahweh, the rehearsal of their story in ages past particularly in worship that brought a sense of hope and

---

[49] Exo 3:6. Frymer-Kensky, Novak, Ochs, Sandmel, Signer, 52.

[50] Cahill, 109.

[51] Walter Brueggemann, *The Prophetic Imagination*. (Minneapolis: Fortress, 1978), 16.

[52] Ibid., 16.

joy to them. Even in the midst of slavery, there were acts of bravery to be celebrated by the community. Women and children could stand courageously. There were five women who were especially remembered: the mother and sister of baby Moses who risked their lives to save him, Pharaoh's daughter who rescued and raised Moses, and the two midwives who found ways to preserve the lives of Hebrew children. When given the orders to kill Hebrew babies, they refused and told their task masters that Hebrew women, unlike their Egyptian counterparts, were so strong that they delivered their babies by themselves so the midwives could not take the babies from them and kill them.[53] But these acts were heroic exceptions to their years of being beaten down at every turn. However weak it would appear as the saga unfolded, there was a base of remembrance of Yahweh God who was not only with them but also for them. Their story in the past and also their experience together as slaves fused together in becoming a free covenant people. Ultimately the freedom of God to act for his people became their celebrated song and dance of joy.[54]

"Once you were slaves" began the observances of ritual memory. The exodus was so powerful, compelling and dramatic that their entire lives were forever altered by this experience. This event became the lens through which the rest of their life experience would be viewed. This recollection was indelibly etched in the totality of their being not only individually but also collectively as community. Because deliverance was a gracious gift of Yahweh, it was to be a corrective to pride, riches and self-sufficiency that would mark later accomplishments. They would always know that once they were slaves completely dependent on the mercy of not only their task masters, but also Yahweh God.

---

[53] Brueggemann, Theology, Testimony, 669.
[54] Brueggemann, 23-25.

As they told the story, considered it and analyzed principles of application to their contemporary lives they saw a pattern. The pattern that emerged in retrospect from the Exodus deliverance would be repeated in the their future experience. First, there would be a situation of *distress* where hope was lost in grief and despair. *Unexpected deliverance* would then come from God. People then responded with praise and thanksgiving and the making of a *covenant* to carry the experience of salvation forward so that they would always remember. Salvation was the activity of God restoring wholeness and promise. Worship was the remembrance of the salvific activity and covenant in doxology and praise. Thus the liberated community is to always be a thankful and joyful worshipping community, knowing that God is Lord of all creation and that our lives are dependent on the grace-filled mercy of Yahweh.[55]

The Mosaic Covenant of Shalom

God's covenant with Abraham was the first covenant considered in this work. The second covenant is the Mosaic Covenant. The beginning of all covenant relationship is the <u>righteousness of God</u> who is known by ultimate holiness, steadfast love, justice and compassion.[56] The Mosaic Covenant outlined the relationship between the sovereignty of God and human agency. God called the people to responsible partnership. The blessings of God would be tied to the behavior of the people; if they were faithful they would be blessed.

---

[55]Birch, Brueggeman, Fretheim, and Petersen, 107.
[56]   Ibid., 147.

The people were to imitate what they experienced in God – "be holy for I am holy, be merciful, bless others, visit the sick, be forgiving". [57] These texts are sometimes called the reciprocal texts where God enjoins the human family to practice the positive attributes of God in their conduct with each other. Like creation in the image of God, humans were to model their conduct on what they knew to be true of God. There would always be a gulf between the Creator and the creature, but the human family was to re-present God as steward of other persons and the created world. They were to understand that their response to the love of God manifest in daily miracles and also in mighty deliverance was to be in the context of covenant with all-embracing love of God and one's neighbor.

The miracle of deliverance did not mean that life would be without struggle. Their liberation was not to the Promised Land, but to an inhospitable dessert wilderness without life-sustaining water, food, or protection from harsh elements or enemies. They had no knowledge of this environment, systems of governance or any skills that would enable them to survive in this harsh, inhospitable environment. They were completely dependent upon the God who had rescued them. This was to be their means of being blessed in learning a new way of life – complete with successes and failures.

Any understanding of this miracle of deliverance is incomplete without an examination of the years in the wilderness of developing community and being nurtured by the bread of God, manna. Manna was a symbol of the abundance of God that transformed a desert of hopelessness into life and promise.[58] The dessert experience was a laboratory of both successes and failures in moving

---

[57] Lev. 19:2, Joel 3:5, Is 43:7, Gen 1:28, 2:22, 18:1, 35:9, Deut 32:6.
[58]Brueggemann, *Theology, Testsimony,* 204-205.[58]

from building Pharaoh's cities as slaves to building community based on the freedom and holiness of God.

The role of Jethro, the father-in-law of Moses, was critical. He gave "counsel that began the *institutionalization of liberation in judicial and social structures* and provided an occasion for non-Israelite recognition of God's deliverance from the hand of Egypt."[59] The initiating grace of God in the miracle of exodus required the faithful, committed response of both the leaders and people in the difficult work of building the community of shalom.[60] *This community that began with a group of Egyptian slaves completely dependent on God in a hostile desert whose daily life exhibited both selfishness and shalom lasted two hundred and fifty years.*[61]

> At Sinai, Israel was called upon to embody the experience of God's deliverance in a community for whom love of God was intimately bound with love of neighbor. (Lev. 19:18) Israel was liberated from oppression and suffering but she was liberated for community and mutual responsibility.[62]

Communal life needs not only organization but also essential foundational principles or values. The most basic foundational understanding was the *Sh'ma,* the love of God that summarized the law for the community.[63]

> Hear, O Israel: the Lord is our God, the Lord alone. You shall love the Lord your God with all your heart, and with all your soul, and with all your might.[64]

---

[59] Ibid., 106.
[60] Birch, 157.

[61] Brueggemann, *Prophetic Imagination,* 17.
[62] Birch and Rasmussen, 85.
[63] Birch, 164.
[64] Deut. 6:4

These words were to be written in their heart. They were to be taught to their children, remembered when they were sitting or walking, the first words of the new day and the last words before sleep and written upon the entrance of their homes. In a land where all the other nations had multiple gods, they were never to forget that their God was one and they were to love God with the totality of their being.

The function of further laws was to ensure their memory of God, the holy liberator and themselves as delivered slaves or sojourners. The law was also an expression of the will of God "initiated by the revelatory activity of God".[65] The purpose of the law was shalom – being in right relationship with God, with the human family and the created world, the blessed way of God's good creation that could be summarized as - happiness, joy or being blessed. Obedience to the commandments was not in order to *establish* a relationship with God, but described the relationship that already existed.[66] This association was the key to all other relationships with the benefit and responsibility of holiness for the sake of the community and world.[67]

The Law

Torah composed of Genesis, Exodus, Leviticus, Numbers and Deuteronomy and the Ten Commandments, sometimes called the Decalogue, was to always occupy the preeminent place as foundational authority, power and presence of Yahweh God within the community. Torah was also dependent on a human person, Moses the mediator of the covenant that was received on Mount Sinai.

---

[65]Birch 166-167.
[66] Ibid., 168-169.
[67] Birch, Brueggemann, Fretheim and Petersen, 138-139.

Moses was the living presence and reminder of the whole drama of both the exodus from Egypt and the Sinai Covenant, or the Ten Commandments. Moses not only received Torah but also made it possible for the continual interpretation of the Torah. From the beginning, Torah was not to be understood as a closed revelation. *The revelation of God was to be dynamic calling the people to move ahead*, not static allowing them to be securely planted in one time and place.[68] They were to be called as a community, not just the prophet, but the prophetic community for all time to question, struggle with and perhaps even doubt in seeking for greater truth and understanding of the will of God.

The covenant was both the commandments and also the means of entering into the presence of the holy, establishing communion with Yahweh. First, the covenant itself was a summons to obedience with conditional terms. These promises were to be the result of a singular covenantal commitment on both the part of Yahweh and Israel. Second, the Torah was to provide loving guidance, instruction and nurture that would make it possible to live in a difficult world.[69]

> Whereas Torah as command is focused on the ethical dimension of existence, Torah as instruction, guidance, and nurture is preoccupied with the aesthetic and artistic, a realm that comes to be expressed as the mystical and sacramental...Torah is as much concerned with the inscrutable mystery of presence as it is with the nonnegotiability of neighborly obedience.[70]

---

[68]Reed M. Holmes, *Dreamers of Zion – Joseph Smith and George J. Adams – Conviction, Leadership and Israel's Renewal* (Portland, OR: Sussex Academic Press, 2003), xiv.

[69] Brueggemann, Theology, Testimony 578-583. Brueggemann, Theology, Essay, 10-11. The Sinai Covenant clearly outlined a system of divine blessing, justice and love or curses, punishment and death.

[70] Ibid., 582.

The Decalogue was addressed directly to the people and became foundational for their life in community. As they struggled with the meaning of revelation and their relationship with God, they realized that not all commandments were of the same moral, ethical and spiritual weight. It was determined that even the place where revelation was experienced was critical to the importance of that which was received. *These commandments had the greatest authority because they were given by God on Mt. Sinai,* the holy mountain. This was interpreted to mean that they were not only binding upon the community at that time but these commandments were also for the future generations.

The structure of covenant life was the law that had been given to enable life, "that things would go well with them".[71] Both the initial language of creation, promise and deliverance and the judicial language of covenant is necessary in understanding the commandments.[72] The stipulation of their covenant is that blessings would be tied to their obedience. "Israel's sense of obedience is always more than the commandments, but never less than the fulfillment of commands."[73] Four commandments dealt with their relationship to God and the remaining six addressed communal issues. Those six laws were binding upon persons irrespective of status, economic privilege or lack thereof, including slaves, or aliens.[74] Although there is similarity to some laws in existence at this time, their laws were unique in several ways. A uniform law stipulating the same justice for the rich and poor was unknown in the religions of their neighbors as was the whole concept of the

---

[71] Deut. 5:33.
[72] .Birch, 126.
[73] Birch, Brueggemann, Fretheim and Petersen, 187.
[74] Aliens sojourners among them were to respect all the commandments but were not required to obey those dealing with Yahweh. Their community was patriarchal.

Egalitarian ideals did not normally extend to females.

righteousness and holiness of God. The gods of other lands were capricious and certainly did not manifest steadfast love for creation. A further departure is that the codes of Yahweh God also extended to animals and the created world.

The Decalogue, with other codes such as the Holiness Code, was a part of the Pentateuch or Torah.[75] God gave the commandments that were "the source of divine teaching and guidance which defined the life of the faithful community".[76] These commandments outlined the relationship between God and humans with norms of justice. The Torah presumes that people, including slaves, are human and human life is sacred. The constant bias is for the poor and powerless. This is unique in ancient law. "However faint our sense of justice may be, insofar as it operates at all it is still a Jewish sense of justice."[77]

The law insured stability in communal life enabling the needs of the disadvantaged to be met. The laws for the protection and nurture of the poor and needy are among the oldest in the Old Testament.[78] They were to remember that once they were slaves and open their hands to the poor. Voluntary charity was a commandment but was never an adequate response to the suffering of others.[79] The community was also to act to care for the poor. By remembering that they were once the poor, they were to treat the poor with respect, including their integration into the full life of the community. They were to make sure that the needy were drawn into the heart of Israel's worship.[80]

---

[75] Ex. 20:2-17, Deut. 5:6-21, Ex. 20:22-23:33, Lev. 17-26.
[76] Birch, 172.
[77] Cahill, 154-155.
[78] Birch, Brueggemann, Fretheim and Petersen.161. Deut. 15:4-5, 7-8, 10-11.
[79] Deut. 15:11, 16:17.
[80] Birch, Brueggemann, Fretheim and Petersen, 161, 162.

They were not just bound in obedience to the Ten Commandments, the Torah contained more than six hundred additional laws, often expanding on aspects of the original ten. The additional six hundred plus laws in the Torah dealt with almost every aspect of their lives. Like the Decalogue, they were considered to be the gift of God to direct the conduct of the community.

> The Torah is intended to guard Israel against idolatry....idolatry (hatred of the true God) comes down to oppression (hatred of neighbor). Thus the Torah binds Israel singularly to Yahweh in the two practices of love of God and love of neighbor. Without Torah, Israel would disappear.[81]

Like others, they sometimes needed something visible to make the presence of God among them seem real. The presence of God symbolized in the desert tabernacle was their assurance that God had chosen to be with them. The tabernacle or tent of meeting was the place where the Ark of the Covenant that contained the Ten Commandments was kept. Everyone who sought the Lord could go to the tent. Like their dwellings, the tabernacle would be moved as they journeyed in the wilderness. While the Sabbath sanctified time, the tabernacle sanctified space where God could be among them.[82] This meant that the presence of God was accessible to them, always ahead, just out of, but within their reach.[83]

The experience of Exodus gave birth to a unique spirituality that retained the memory of liberation with each new generation looking at their world. They understood that their liberation must lead to justice not only in terms of their relationship with God in liturgy but also in every aspect of

---

[81] Brueggemann, *Theology, Testimony*, 697.
[82] Bernhard W. Anderson, *Contours of Old Testament Theology*, (Minneapolis: Fortress Press, 1999), 111.
[83] Hamma, 65.

daily life in their families and the larger community. The deliverance provided by God, both from slavery and to community in the dessert, gave birth to the vision of Jubilee.

Jubilee – God's Corrective to Injustice

Jubilee has been a subject for controversy. Earlier it was thought that it had never happened or had any real influence on the people. Now scholars are discovering more about the role of Jubilee in the ongoing story of the people of Moses. "The original Jubilee mandate was announced on the Day of Atonement, the holiest day of the year. It was accompanied by the sound of trumpets."[84] The trumpet proclaimed hope and liberation from the injustice of the world, a time of celebrating the covenant of God's Shalom.[85] Jubilee was God's system for protecting the ideals of the Mosaic Covenant.[86] "Jubilee in its most simplistic definition was about bringing peace and justice to the Israelites and to the whole of creation."[87]

Their own story with its failures and successes was evidence that would prevent them from being idealistic. The people knew that the Mosaic covenant would be broken. Over and over again, it would be clear that selfishness would result in injustice and even violence. There would be abuse of the laws and systems given to ensure community and care for the poor and vulnerable. Correction was built into the system with Sabbath, the Sabbatical year and most of all, Jubilee. *Given on Mt. Sinai and therefore binding upon the generations, Jubilee was given to correct economic and social inequity that inevitably occurs in community.*

---

[84] Ross Kinsler and Gloria Kinsler, *The Biblical Jubilee and the Struggle for Life.* (Maryknoll, NY: Orbis Books, 1999), xv.
[85] Lisa Mackender and Brad Martell, *Jubilee – A Cycle of Justice.* (Independence, MO: Herald Publishing House, 2000), 7.
[86] Lev. 25, Deut 15, Exo. 21:1-6, 23:10-11, Isa. 61:1-2, Luke 4:16-19.
[87] Mackender and Martell, 6.

The tenth commandment against coveting is thought to be the foundation of Jubilee's egalitarian social practice. In the conduct of their communal life, they were to have the things needed for life. There was never any assertion that the people were to be exactly equal in terms of property, but they were to have opportunities to make a living and be helped in order to make this possible. Jubilee makes two basic assertions. The first concerns the ownership of the land. It is clear that the land belongs to Yahweh (Lev. 25:23) therefore it is not to be owned or managed in the ways of other nations. This would mean that any ownership of the land was conditional. The second fundamental element concerns the people. Yahweh has redeemed his people, nurturing them with manna in the desert. They are *his* servants and thus cannot to be sold as slaves to others (Lev. 25:42).[88]

Jubilee was based on a system of sevens. The Sabbath was the seventh day in which rest and remembering God was the activity of the day. Every seventh year was the Sabbatical year and then after seven complete cycles, the following year – the fiftieth – was hallowed as Jubilee, the year of God's favor, the acceptable year of the Lord.

The law of Sabbatical year or the year of release (Deut.15:1-18) had three dramatic parts. The first was cancellation of debt owed to any community member. Debt was the primary cause of imprisonment. For the people of God, debt was forgiven in the seventh year. Second, *the community is strongly encouraged to care for the poor, heeding their cries. If the community does not, it is sin unto them.* The third aspect of this law stated that not only are servants or slaves to be set free in the seventh year, they are to receive liberal provisions enabling them to begin their new

---

[88] Walter Brueggemann, *Old Testament Theology – Essays on Structure, Theme, and Text.* (Minneapolis: Fortress, 1992), 128.

lives with dignity. The use of language is intense and intentional. If Israel does not obey these laws, their community will fall into the familiar patterns of their neighbors and not receive the blessings of God.[89]

Jubilee is based on rest, repentance, restitution, redemption and release. In Jubilee, the land was to lie fallow. Everything was rested in Jubilee. Any crops that grew in Jubilee year belonged to the poor. For the landowner, Jubilee was a time to live in holiness before God and in simplicity, trust and true solidarity with the poor since at this time the landowners also lived in dependence upon God for their sustenance. God was celebrated as the real owner of all. The "nahala" (original land inheritance in the Promised Land) was to be returned to the original possessors, land or tribe.[90] Anyone who sold himself into slavery was released with provisions to begin a new life.

> No doubt the jubilee represented an ideal standard of radical societal renewal to restore wholeness and equity. But even if utopian, jubilee has come to represent the kind of daring vision called for on the part of God's people. There is considerable evidence that many of the faithful figures of the Old and New Testament, such as Jeremiah and Jesus himself, took this ideal standard of jubilee seriously as the just society for which God calls us to work even if society at large refuses the vision.[91]

Jubilee called for an ethic of "Sabbath economics," social and economic justice in three axioms. (1) God created a world of abundance. (2) Disparities in resources needed for life or power were not the intention of God and must be mitigated through practices of redistribution to the poor. (3)

---

[89] Ibid., 56-57.

[90] Num. 26:52-56, 27, 36:6, Lev. 25:23-24, 25-27, I Kings 21:3, Micah 2:1-2, Ezek. 47:2.
[91] Birch and Rasmussen, 87-88.

The prophetic message that calls the people of God to this task was and is the gospel, the "good news" to the poor.[92]

> ...the Sabbath Day, the Sabbath Year and Jubilee were institutional ways of continuing the spirit and practice of Exodus. Freedom from slavery was not a one-time act for the Hebrew people. It was to be ongoing in the life, culture, and traditions of the people of Israel. By their covenant with God, they were to restore justice to their social, economic, political and ecological systems.[93]

---

[92] Kinsler and Kinsler, ix.
[93] Mackender and Martell,

Chapter 4

The Constitution of the
Shalom Covenant Community

There was to be *a new social reality in order to embody God's gift of freedom*. The radical freedom and <u>righteousness of God</u> had its counterpart in the way the human family was to conduct itself in relationships of equal access to the goods needed for life, an <u>economics of equality</u> and fairness in the distribution of power, the <u>politics of justice and compassion</u>. Their experience of manna was foundational: everyone had what they needed, it could not be hoarded or stored and access was free and open. Former slaves understood that it was necessary for persons to be given equal consideration and protected from exploitation. Faithfulness to the covenant meant the embodiment of righteousness, justice and steadfast love in systemic structures that ensured equality under law.[94]

> The Mosaic revolution has political, economic, moral and ethical connotations, but its main force is to establish justice as the core focus of Yahweh's life in the world and Israel's life with Yahweh...Yahweh is here known to be a resilient and relentless advocate of and agent for justice, which entails the complete reordering of power and arrangements in the earth...The intention of Mosaic justice is to redistribute social good and social power, thus it is distributive justice.[95]

---

[94] Birch, 174, 178.
[95] Brueggemann, Theology, Testimony, 735-736.

32

Economics of Equality

The covenant community was to seek shalom in all they did.[96] The wilderness experience of manna was to be the model for distribution of goods according to the Mosaic covenant of shalom. Other societies in the known world practiced economics based on scarcity, the idea that no matter how much is produced, there would never be enough to satisfy the insatiable desires of humans. In that economic system, a few people would accumulate great wealth while the majority would live in poverty or even slavery.[97] But they were to remember Yahweh and their deliverance from slavery by practicing justice and care for the needy and vulnerable. The new covenant community of shalom created a decentralized, egalitarian, communal way of life that insured sufficiency for all the tribes, clans and families.

The divine mandate of the Sabbath was key to their communal life. Public worship and the daily honoring of the covenants were essential to this way of life. They did not separate religion from economics or the spirituality from the material. This meant that they did not "spiritualize" economics or justice in ways that undermined the concern of God for the poor.

The covenant required that each extended family have access to the basic resources for survival, particularly through the spirituality and practice of the Sabbath Day, the Sabbath Year and the Jubilee.[98]

---

[96] Lev. 11:45, Exo. 19:6, Micah 6:8, Amos 5:24, Hos. 10:12, Jer. 29:11
[97] Meeks, *God The Economist,* 12
[98] Ibid., 34.

Some persons may have had more wealth or prestige but it was understood that all persons had equal claim on communal resources for their livelihood.[99] They understood genuine need as a fault of social distribution systems or situations of status such as widows or orphans that were clearly not the fault of the person, but the system. "Thus the responsibility for initiative lay with the privileged rather than the dispossessed themselves even as God, from the position of divine power, had taken the initiative to deliver Israel."[100]

The ideal for relationships in the covenant community was equality and compassion. Equality of access and distribution of the resources needed for life was based on the manna principle and built into the structures of society. The basic value was that since God is the owner of everything, the resources of the community are to be shared. Hence, *the importance of persons ranked above rights of individual property.*

The governing principle in these early communities was communal property. Private (the original meaning was to deprive) property was justified as long as it served the interests of the group. When societies moved away from a participatory communal model where everyone was of value, individual property rights became more important than persons or the community as a whole.[101]

One of the basic economic rights observed by the Covenant Community of Shalom included adequate food for everyone in the community without exception. Although there were laws against able-bodied persons not working, they were still to be given food. Subsistence was not based on

[99] Perry B. Yoder, *Shalom: The Bible's Word for Salvation, Justice and Peace,* (Nappannee, IN: Evangel Publishing House, 1987), 88.
[100] Birch and Rasmussen, 86.
[101] Fritjof Capra, *The Turning Point – Science, Society, and the Rising Culture,* (NY: Simon and Schuster, 1982), 194. Meeks, 75-123.

ownership but on membership within the community. People were commanded to give to the poor.[102] Food was to be left in the fields for the poor to glean.

Other measures aiding the poor included the poor receiving daily wages and not charging interest on loans to the poor. If the coat of a poor person was taken in pledge to repay a debt, the coat could not be kept overnight. The poor were to receive the tithe every third year. Every seven years, Hebrew slaves were to be released and debts remitted.[103] Children of slaves were always free. Hospitality and the treatment of sojourners were not just marks of honorable conduct, these were an absolutely essential part of the group ethos.[104] The motivation of conduct toward the poor and vulnerable was to be marked by how God had cared for them. Not only were their dealings to be fair, they were to open their hands to the poor; generosity was the response of the faithful.

> The main concerns of this alternative socioeconomic system were to resist the accumulation of debts, the concentration of land in the hands of a few, and slavery. To ensure the long-term security of the families of Israel, provision was made to rescue or restore...their land and release family members from bond service.[105]

The principles of shalom economics were unique. Because God was owner, people had access to resources with open gleaning and Sabbatical laws. Distribution and consumption were based on need; those who have were to share with those without resources. The basic value was

---

[102] Exo. 16, 23:10-11, Lev.19:9-10, 23:22 25-27, Num. 27, Deut. 14:28-29, 15:4-11, 23:24-25, 24:19, 26:12, Ezek 47:2, Micah 2:1-2, Ruth 2:1-3, Matt. 12:1-8, II Cor. 8:13-15.
[103] Deut. 15:1,2.
[104] Exo. 15:1-11, 16:18-20, 18:21, 22:25-27, 23:8, 24:14, Lev. 19:15, Deut. 15:7-8, 24:10-13, II Chron. 19:7, Jer. 22:15-16.
[105] Kinsler and Kinsler, 35.

trust and reliance in God with the assurance that there was enough for all. Affluence was measured by opportunity for leisure and greater opportunities to share with others. The goal was finite - that there will be enough for all with distribution of surplus given to those in need. The results were a stewardship of resources marked by justice. Minimal force was required to maintain this system.[106]

In contrast, the economics of wealth that would develop later completely changed this system. In this system, people had exclusive rights of ownership to property and capital resulting in a concentration of resources or wealth to individuals. Consumption was based on self-aggrandizement. The central value was scarcity and hoarding. Affluence was measured by the accumulation of possessions. The goal was infinite wealth – there was never enough since someone else always had more. Surplus was distributed as accumulation to support separate classes. The results were the exploitation of resources and separation of the rich and the poor. Class separation was maintained by increasing oppressive force.[107]

The Politics of Justice

In many ways, the ideals of economics and justice merge in compassionate practice since justice is often tied to economics. The politics of justice describe how power is distributed within a society. Their justice was characterized by a legal system that sought redress of grievances by advocacy, someone to plead one's cause. Authority within the covenant community was more "grassroots" than hierarchical where laws were to function as norms for justice. Legality was not the critical test since the laws

---

[106] Yoder, Shalom, 111-112.

[107] Ibid. Scriptures that support this: Lev. 25:14-17, 25-28, 29-31, Deut. 15:1-11, Exo. 23:10-11, Deut. 14:28-29, Isa. 5:8, Amos, 6:1-6, 3:15, 8:4ff, 2:6-8, 3:10, 4:1, Luke 6 27-36, 2 Cor. 8:14, 9:8, 10-11.

themselves could be unjust.[108] The covenantal system of justice sought to honor twin principles of justice and judgment, guarding against the exploitation and marginalization of the poor and vulnerable. In order to do this, persons had to be able to understand the difference between right and wrong and be able to use discernment in the cause of justice.

> To begin life in the Promised Land the moral order that permits justice must first be established, a task that requires the ability to discern and choose between good and evil, to find the path of justice.[109]

There are two basic kinds of justice. *Procedural* justice preserves order and the status quo with laws that insure civil stability. *Substantive* justice addresses concerns that work for the transformation of communities for relationships of equity. Both kinds of justice needed to function within this society, but the justice of God's shalom required that persons were vigilant in their commitment to welfare and justice for others.[110] They struggled with these issues but more than many other societies, their concern was for egalitarian relationships.

Sabbath

One of the oldest parts of Pentateuch law is the commandment to give rest to the land, and those who work the land, including the animals.[111] Because Sabbath rest was given on Mt. Sinai, it continues to be an essential part of the code. Sabbath was a time when every part of life was devoted

---

[108]   Perry B. Yoder, *Shalom: The Bible's Word for Salvation, Justice and Peace,* (Nappannee, IN: Evangel Publishing House, 1987), 83.

[109]   Frymer-Kensky, Novak, Ochs, Sandmel and Signer, 306.

[110]   Yoder, Shalom, 83.

[111]   Exo. 20-23, Deut. 5.

to the praise and worship of Yahweh God. Worship was a means of solidarity with the worshipping community as the people of God and also a time for introspective consideration of one's walk of faith. Not only is the Sabbath a time for contemplation of the divine and worship in the community of faith, it also has economic considerations. Sabbath rest requires that the people of God honor God, remembering creation, and also that they live in trust, not being relentlessly driven by the continual need to accumulate. This was and continues to be exemplified as "the two primary concerns of God and God's people: social justice and ecological integrity".[112]

---

[112] Kinsler and Kinsler, 36. .

Chapter 5

The Covenant Community of Shalom
1300-1000 B.C.E.

After forty years in the wilderness, the people were led to the Promised Land. "Land is a central, if not *the central theme* of Biblical faith."[113] The land was first a gift of God for the establishment of sacred community where they would receive nurture. Each tribe was given an allotment according to their size and needs but it was their understanding that God was the true owner of the land. The people were stewards over this sacred trust or heritage called the *nahala* over which no person or tribe could claim ultimate tribal or private ownership. According to the provisions of the nahala, each family was guaranteed a portion of land that would be sufficient for their survival.[114] The land was a particular stewardship that would always need to be linked to God and to the understandings developed in the Shalom Covenant Community.[115]

> Israel was called to create and maintain an alternate social reality unlike Egypt, unlike Canaan, unlike the other nations. This was the significance of the giving of the Law at Sinai and the giving of the Promised Land.[116]

But the call to create alternate community based on shalom does not reconcile easily with the actual taking or

---

[113] Walter Brueggemann, *The Land: Place as Gift, Promise, Challenge in Biblical Faith* (Philadelphia: Fortress, 1977), 3.

[114] Birch, Justice, 179-180. Hanson, *People Called*, 64.

[115] Deut. 7:11-13.

[116] Kinsler and Kinsler, 33-34.

conquest of the Promised Land. Even with the most partisan biblical defense, the rampant violence and bloodshed outlined in scripture relating this part of the journey seems completely alien to the vision of God and the covenant community in the Promised Land. While newer scholarship mitigates and negates past understandings of a *total* bloody Canaan conquest, nevertheless violence cannot be discounted. The Hebrew Bible reports more than six hundred passages of explicit violence, often *attributed* to Yahweh God, but for the first time in human history, God identified with the victims of the violence rather than exultation of the victors in the strife.[117]

There would also be questions of historical accuracy in writing and interpretation since many of the texts were never finally written in an exact form or codified until their period of Babylonian captivity when they, themselves, were victims of brutality as a conquered people. At this time, it seemed especially important for them to be seen as powerful victors in warfare so this aspect of their story took on tremendous importance. Their redaction and editing of texts would also repeatedly lay claim to the land. For dispossessed slaves, the sense of their power and place was of utmost importance to their survival. All of these aspects were based on the foundation of their call as the people of Yahweh God who had redeemed them. The idea that God would have acted in ways that were violent toward other people would have given them reassurance that God would also act for them.

---

[117] Anthony Ceresko, *Introduction to the Old Testament: A Liberation Perspective.* (Maryknoll, NY: Orbis Books, 1992). This is a theme of the book, citing the work of other contemporary scholars. Walter Wink, *The Powers That Be – Theology for a New Millennium,* (NY: Galilee Doubleday, 1998), 84-86. The above reference does not negate violence in the Old Testament. Wink reports the work of Raymund Schwager. The story of God's intervention in the expulsion of Hagar and Ishmael to certain death in the desert is an example of this principle.(Gen. 21:9-20)

41

But the story of a *total* bloody conquest is not that clear in either scripture or other evidence. Archaeological research and a careful reading of Judges indicate that the process of conquest and settlement extended over a long period of time. Several places such as Shechem were incorporated peacefully.[118]   There were also other considerations.   Factors such as a weakening of Egypt's power and the move from oppressive city-states to more agrarian economies with compatible social ideals and systems had paved the way for their more peaceful entry into the Promised Land.[119]

Joshua

Joshua had been with Moses during most of the period of his leadership and became his successor. He continued Moses' practice of Torah Covenant mediation and designated the place for this, Shechem. Shechem had been the first place that Abraham stopped where he built an altar. The Shechem Convocation was an annual gathering of the full tribal confederacy where they renewed their covenants of devotion to God and to each other in fully accountable relationships. They did this by the recitation of laws, songs and stories. Their covenant ceremony had six elements: "Thus says Yahweh", the historical prologue of Yahweh's gracious deeds toward Israel, the fundamental stipulation that the people are to place complete trust in Yahweh, the writing of covenantal stipulations in their book of law, the witness of the people to each other and the recitation of blessings or curses that follow obedience or disobedience to the covenant.[120] It was their understanding that knowing

---

[118] NRSV Joshua 24:1-8, note, 298.

[119] Kinsler and Kinsler, 33-34.

[120] Joshua 24. Bernard W. Anderson *Understanding the Old Testament,* (Upper Saddle River, NY: Prentice Hall, 1998), 133-134.

and being in relationship with Yahweh would bring welfare and peace whereas disobedience would lead to hardship and defeat.[121] Joshua and leaders like Samuel worked to keep the Mosaic ideal alive and growing by placing Yahweh God above all else and working for freedom and justice.

Entry into the Promised Land became an opportunity to organize new systems of justice. They did not need to have governance systems of exploitation, greed and brutality that were characteristic of other nations. They could devise concrete practical ways of organizing daily life where the grand vision of God could be practiced.[122]

Life in the Promised Land

Communal organization of daily life centered in local networks of mutuality for support and protection. Shalom communities were inclusive with persons of the covenant bound not only to each other but also to God in peace and security.[123] Extended families called father's houses were the units of production and consumption. Villages of father's houses banded together into tribes or clans. The patriarch of the house was responsible for the conduct of the family. The clans engaged in common agricultural activities as well as protecting individuals by such activities as offering loans without interest. The land was the basis of survival and also identity so access to the land was critical. Life was difficult but their mutual alliances insured protection against warfare, loss of crops, disease or drought. Most people lived in unwalled small villages, working in outlying fields during the day. Large flocks and herds were rare. They worked together to provide wells or communal grazing lands in order to protect families, clans and tribes.

---

[121] Judges 2:6-3:6.
[122] Brueggemann, Theology, Essay 55-56.
[123] Brueggemann, *Vision,* 17.

The governing principle was organized around the wisdom of the elders that consisted of the full participation and responsibility of adult males in a loose confederation of tribes. Poverty was always an issue as was conflict with neighboring tribes based on their isolationism and exclusivity.[124] There were no permanent governing institutions. Emergencies such as warfare were considered spiritual in nature with leaders and armies being called as needed. At such times all twelve tribes acted together. They did not differentiate between sacred and secular except in terms of the sanctification required for worship; their understanding of God as creator and sustainer meant that all things were of God.[125]

The history of a people can be seen as the ways they created or adapted to the forces of change around them. For the people of the Mosaic Covenant, change brought massive new challenges. There were natural social developments brought about by progress. The iron plow made large harvests possible with fewer workers. Other technological improvements such as terracing of farmland required more capital investment. There was demand for other goods and services that encouraged specialization of vocation that in turn resulted in a more complex social structure. There was a move toward walled cities with far greater population density. All of these things resulted in greater wealth differentiation with redistribution of the land. The role of the Sabbatical year and Jubilee in ensuring equal access to the land was greatly reduced, deferred, omitted or "spiritualized" without the necessity to act on the provisions for the poor. *Property came to be valued more than persons.*

---

[124] Birch and Rasmussen, 100.
[125] Yoder, *Shalom,* 88.

With increasing social complexity, inner social tensions, and outside military threats, a new form of governance seemed necessary. Real dangers and needs seemed to justify the people's call for a king....regardless of whatever benefits people hoped to reap as a result of kingship. They also received the burdens to be borne.[126]

---

[126] Ibid., 93-94.

Chapter 6

The Movement Toward Monarchy

It was also a time of transition and flux from within and military threat from their neighbors. Unresolved conflicts within and between tribes had weakened their resolve to work or fight together. Because they were perceived as weak, this was a prime opportunity for neighboring rulers to conquer or annex their lands, or in their terms, to take back their land. Continual military threat demanded the unified response of a strong leader. They were the only nation governed by the people. Other nations had kings whose armies protected their citizens. The establishment of a monarchy was thought to be the only remedy.

The military threat was not the critical issue. The most serious change was the breakdown of the moral and spiritual governance. The old model was not working. As time passed and new generations arose, the Mosaic covenants were harder to maintain. There was a lack of committed religious leaders with the result of internal chaos and rule by might that violated social, moral and ethical norms. Judges 18 begins with the statement: "In those days there was no king in Israel" and lists the results of lawlessness. The book ends with the same phrase adding "all the people did what was right in their own eyes".[127]

They knew how to survive by keeping faith with each other and sharing in times of scarcity and danger. The more difficult task was how to maintain that vision in the

---

[127] Judges 18:1, 21:25.

Promised Land where former slaves had become the taskmasters and peasants had become wealthy. They now needed a god that would legitimize their current status that by this time included social, political and economic stratification. "It is difficult to keep a revolution of freedom and justice underway when there is satiation."[128] When they had more than they needed, their viewpoint and concerns were changed. Their prosperity altered the Mosaic vision.

By Judges 8:22, the men ask Gideon to be their king. He refused because kingship was inimical to the rule of Yahweh but the movement toward monarchy was born. It was to grow very strong and finally becoming another factor in overcoming the Mosaic Covenant of Shalom.[129]

"The revolution, both religious and political, of Moses was able to sustain itself until the year 1000 B.C.E. as a viable social reality."[130] Samuel had been a righteous judge and leader, but his sons who were also judges were corrupt and immoral. All the elders came to Samuel and asked him to appoint a king over them. Samuel prayed in this matter, not willing to have a king over Israel. The Lord told him that the people had not rejected his leadership, but they had rejected God as their king.[131] Samuel finally acceded to the wishes of the people and Israel's monarchy was born.

In *theory*, the monarchy was a natural extension of the Mosaic Covenant of Shalom. The king was to be the Regent of God, responsible to see that the righteousness of God is upheld. As guarantor of the rights of the poor and vulnerable, the monarchy was to function to uphold justice through the courts. Kingship was thought to be a means of instituting justice and working for the good of all citizens,

---

[128] Brueggemann, Prophetic, 32.
[129] Brueggemann, Theology Essay, 133-134.
[130] Brueggemann, Prophetic, 31.
[131] I Sam. 8:1-9.

protecting the weak underclasses against the wealthy and strong. The king would make sure that the tithe was collected and distributed to the poor. The king was to publish and enforce just laws such as the Mosaic codes that declared the Sabbatical Year and Jubilee. He would decide individual cases and institute reforms for justice. The king's justice was to be God's justice.[132]

> Thus in the ideology of kingship in Israel as it is related to justice and shalom, the responsibility of the king was to meet the needs of the people by seeing that substantive justice was a reality in the land. By this action, the justice of the state mirrored divine justice.[133]

In *practice*, kingship led to the abandonment of the Mosaic vision of the Covenant Community of Shalom. In the time of Moses, there was scarcity and people were dependent upon God for their basic needs but by the time of Solomon, there was satiation and people thought that they did not need God to be their leader, but to give credence to their wishes.

Solomon and the Changes Brought by the Monarchy

The changes were made concrete by the time of Solomon, 962 B.C.E. Before this time, there was great thanksgiving in the birth of a child that was assurance of a future but with Solomon's vast harem there was self-generated progeny. The harem also extended Solomon's political power and brought the presence of foreign gods with their temples and priestly classes into the holy city of Jerusalem. In the former system, clans and tribes collaborated, governed, sat in judgment and raised funds or

---

[132] Yoder, Shalom, 95, 99. Ps. 72, 89,146.
[133] Ibid., 98. Ps 72, 82, 89, 146.

armies if necessary. Solomon replaced these leaders with impersonal bureaucracies and tax districts responsible only to him. A standing army enforced the will of the king and fought at his command rather than the self-interest of the people or the perceived will of God. The king made temporary slaves of his own people through the use of the corvee, forced citizen labor for his building projects.[134] The state became the oppressor. The only mandate of a biblical state was to carry out justice that was to be judged by the welfare of the poor and vulnerable.[135] This was completely negated as the monarchy developed, particularly after Solomon.

> With Solomon's accession this royal ideal is deeply challenged by a royal reality removed from the influence of the people, seemingly absent of any prophetic influence (in spite of Nathan's role at the accession), and reflective of Canaanite models of kingship and ideology.[136]

The transformation of Israel was complete with the building of the temple. In many ways it was a Canaanite, pagan structure with a cadre of priests who stood between the people and Yahweh. The *righteousness and freedom of God* had been replaced with the permanent accessibility of a domesticated God to the existing power structures. God was confined to the temple, functioning to legitimize the rule of the king and his priests. This God would act on behalf of the king and was absolutely invincible. The *economics of equality* became changed into the rule of privilege and affluence. The king as regent of God who was owner of all could seize lands that ultimately belonged to God, including the "nahala", the original land distribution or inheritance in the Promised Land. The *politics of justice* became a fiat of oppression with

---

[134] Bruegemann, *Prophetic*, 30-31.
[135] Yoder, 99-100.
[136] Birch, *Justice,* 221.

the emergence of a permanent class of poverty from which persons could not extricate themselves.[137]

> We can see...the tremendous shift in the structure and function of Israelite society from the period of the judges to that of the kings. From a ranking society, where everyone had equal access to basic resources, it shifted to a stratified one, where the urban elite in Jerusalem...enjoyed a way of life far beyond that possible for the people working the land in their rural villages. Thus emerged the possibility and actuality of poverty and affluence existing side by side.[138]

The biblical mandate was for the state to be a means of justice. The responsibility was for rulers, whose authority was from God, to be an instrument of justice. Because of this position, they had far greater responsibility and would be judged accordingly. Those in power bore particular responsibility and were to be judged by how the poor and vulnerable fared. [139] Oppression was never to be justified in the name of the state.

---

[137] Ibid., 36-37.
[138] Yoder, 91-92.
[139] Ibid., 100. Wisdom of Solomon 6:1-11.

Chapter 7

Davidic Theology, Creationism and Messianism

The third main covenant or promise of God was made to David from which emerged <u>Davidic theology.</u> This theology took earlier strands of Israel's faith and used them to justify a Davidic dynasty that was to be an eternal, unconditional promise of sovereignty for which David was the model.[140] This was based on the conviction of the abiding presence of Yahweh God especially with the royal house and temple that joined priestly with tabernacle scripture and thought in the creation of a new theology. The Davidic ideal was based on three basic premises: the king was absolutely subordinate and dependent upon Yahweh and the established covenants, the king's responsibility was to be Yahweh's instrument of blessing to the people and the central role of the king was in reading and keeping Torah.[141] An important contribution of Davidic theology was that it extended the rule of God to all nations and was symbolized by the presence of God in Mount Zion, the city of our God.[142]

One of the contributions of Davidic thought is the development of <u>creation theology</u> first told through story. Creation stories had been told for millennia, but in this period, the concern was to understand the meaning of the world, to answer the "why questions". Ideas of creation began with the questions about God and the moral order of

---

[140] Birch, 216-218.

[141] Ibid., 220-221

[142] Anderson, *Contours*, 236.

creation. The people were not concerned with being rescued or their survival as was the case in earlier times, but their concern was with order in a moral universe. Concentration on issues associated with creation generally gives priority of procedural order that explained why things were the way that they were over issues of substantive justice that would have looked at issues of injustice in order to find solutions to inequity. Thus in Davidic thought, the created world was where God was experienced as harmony, balance and order for all the earth.

Another contribution of Royal or Davidic theology and the prophets who spoke this message was <u>Messianism</u>, the belief that one day, in spite of the wickedness and evil of some monarchs, there would finally be a last or eschatological king who would reign in righteousness and justice and establish peace. King David was a person who in spite of grave sin and significant misjudgment was fully committed to Yahweh God. Over time, his faithfulness to God and kingly rule took on a "rosy" glow as people looked at him as the ideal king. The promise of an eternal reign of his royal family created an expectation and hope of another king like David. This gave birth to a hope that even in spite of human weakness, there would emerge a king who would be a righteous servant of Yahweh God who would execute righteousness and blessing according to the provisions of Torah. This servant would be identified as Messiah, the anointed of God. This monarchy would insure stability, order, peace and prosperity.[143] Thus the Messianic hope was born and grew as the ultimate hope of the people.

Messianic hope was the vision of the future of the anointed one, the high priest who would reign in justice and righteousness.[144] The Messianic king was not to be embodied

---

[143] Brueggemann, Theology, Essay 273-274.
[144] Isa. 9:1-6, 11:1-9, 15-17, 32:1ff, Micah 5:2-4, Jer. 33:14-18.

in a peasant revolt or a new system of government. The system was not the issue; the issue was shalom justice for the underclasses.[145] Their concept was that the state would be transformed to practice justice resulting in a community of shalom.[146] "The royal ideal...lived on as God's promise, rooted in the ultimate reign of God."[147] An idealized David was the source of this hope that became extended to become a covenant of peace or true shalom, called the peaceable kingdom. The peaceable kingdom was meant to include all nations and the entire created order.[148]

> King and temple symbolize God's ordering of creation and God's will that the social order reflect the peace and righteousness of the cosmic order. The people learned to "sing a new song" – and the new notes of the kingdom of God that is to come on earth as it is in heaven...in this covenant the primary symbols are throne and temple...the eschatological consummation when all nations will make a pilgrimage to the center, the elevated temple mountain of Zion, in order to hear the word of God that brings order, security and peace.[149]

But Psalm 132 states that the promise of a joyous future where the saints would shout for joy and the habitation of God would be in Zion forever was not without human responsibility. *The priests were to be righteous* with the *poor being cared for* out of the abundance of Zion. The promise of God to David for an eternal dynasty included the

---

[145] Yoder, Shalom, 115.
[146] Ben C. Ollenburger, . *Zion, The City Of The Great King – A Theological Symbol of the Jerusalem Cult,* (Sheffield, England: Sheffield Academic Press, 1987), 115.
[147] Birch, 230.
[148] Isa. 9:6-7, 11:1-2, 4-5, 6-9, 55:12-13, Jer. 23:5, Ezek., 34:23-24, Micah 4:1-5.
[149] Anderson, 236.

word, IF. In order for these blessings to come, his sons were to keep the covenant and be open to the continued guidance of God.

Chapter 8

Zion

Although Zion is a recognized theological symbol, "There is no scholarly consensus regarding the date and origin of the Zion tradition."[150] The first use of the word, Zion, was geographical as the fortress, rock or hill of what came to be called Jerusalem. Sometimes Zion was a synonym for Jerusalem or the beneficiaries of the grace or judgment of God such as the sons or daughters of Zion. Zion was usually a part of eschatological or apocalyptic writings that outlined the last community where Messiah would appear. In Old Testament use it was most often the mountain of the Lord, but it could also refer to God's heavenly city.[151]

The origins of Zion are unclear. Newer research indicates that the psalms called "Songs of Zion" predate the Moses tradition; *this liturgy clearly states that Yahweh, the God of Zion was in residence there as monarch.*[152] Other ideas of Zion included a continuation of the traditions of the Jebusite city that David conquered, an invention of the Davidic court or an older tradition combining Israelite and Canaanite theology.[153]

---

[150] Ollenburger, 17.

[151] Donald K. McKim, *Westminster Dictionary of Theological Terms,* (Louisville, KY: Westminster/ John Knox Press, 1996), 308. In the Christian church, it is also an image for heaven. Isa. 60:14, Heb. 12:22, Rev. 14:1.

[152] Brueggemann, Theology, Testimony, 655. Ps. 46, 47, 48, 76, 84, 87, 93, 96-99, and 122

[153] Ollenburger, 22.

Because Yahweh was king in Zion, creation was assured against chaos, and the people of God were assured of well-being and safety. Although monarchical language was used in Zion symbolism, human imperialism was prohibited, never legitimated. The exaltation of Yahweh defined the boundaries of humanity.[154] Because Yahweh exemplified the ultimate righteous king, Zion was to be a secure haven even as Yahweh was a fortress and refuge for the poor.[155]

> For that reason Yahweh opposes all that perverts this world-order, such as injustice against the poor who have a refuge in Zion, or stands in opposition to his exclusive prerogative, such as dependence upon arms and alliances for security....the world order of God's good and just creation is offered in the traditions of the Jerusalem cult as a statement of the way things really are.[156]

"The central feature of the Jerusalem cult tradition, and that which bestowed upon Zion its sacral character, was the belief that Yahweh dwells among his people in Zion."[157] Because Yahweh, creator of the cosmos dwells there, Zion became an inviolable place of security rooted in that presence as creator and defender. Yahweh was the only source of security and strength.[158]

Over time, this belief became separated from the ideals of the Mosaic Covenant of Shalom where there was the clear call to emulate as humans the character,

---

[154] Ollenburger, 158-161. Brueggemann, Theology, Testimony, 657, Brueggemann differs with Ollenburger in reference to Yahweh's monarchy and the Davidic kingship. He thinks that the Zion functions to legitimate the political claims of the Davidic dynasty while Ollenburger thinks that the Zion tradition is separate.
[155] Ibid., 658. Ps. 2:6-8, 9:11, 40:17, 86:1-2.
[156] Ollenburger, 157.
[157] Ibid., 23.
[158] Ibid., 66, 81.

righteousness and mission of God by caring for each other with the economics of mutuality and the politics of justice. Thus the belief that Yahweh was the source of security and strength of Zion later set the stage for idolatry of the temple and ultimately its destruction.

The mount of Zion, a place of holiness, mystery, sacred encounter and the divine protection of Yahweh, became the location of theological reflection, Torah, covenantal expectations and promises rather than Sinai. This expanded Torah to include the nations of the world that would come to Zion to learn the ways of peace and also to see this vision as "eschatologized" into the future with a new covenant.[159] Zion's symbolism also came to include a theology of creation with a universal vision where possibilities are not limited by history or nature, but by creation itself based on the righteousness, cosmic order, power, moral vision and justice of God who wills shalom.[160]

The Mosaic Covenant of Shalom and Zion

The usual pattern of human thought systems is an evolution or progression rather than abrupt disjuncture, and the changes that result often have clear remnants of former patterns of belief and practice. Thus the ideals of the Mosaic Covenant of Shalom from Torah can be seen in this picture of Zion. The importance of Torah and the traditions that resulted cannot be underestimated in being a concrete witness to the righteousness and justice of Yahweh and the clear desire of Yahweh God for shalom in the earth. Like the tabernacle that symbolized the presence of Yahweh always with them, God is now in the holy temple. God alone is righteous. As God spoke with Moses, so God now speaks with the prophets. The Davidic ideal of Messiah, the

---

[159] Ibid., 593-594. Isaiah 25, Ps. 46, 50.
[160] Ollenburger, 161-162.

righteous ruler whose kingdom would be based on justice, corresponds to the Mosaic ideal of egalitarian human relationships based on equity and justice. Even wisdom's emphasis on human freedom and responsibility for choice can have an important role to play. Creationism picks up earlier strands of thought that recognized the majesty of God and human stewardship for all the earth and her creatures. The wonder of that created universe with its harmony and order anticipate the further magnificent, joyous shalom of the Peaceable Kingdom of prophetic vision.

Chapter 9

The Prophets, Wisdom Theology and Exile
The Prophets

Yahweh, the Creator of all that is or will be, the deliverer and maker of Shalom could not be confined to a temple or summoned to act for the king. Israel's God would have voice and power to BE. The first prophet, who spoke for Yahweh, appeared at the beginning of the monarchy. "Samuel, the first prophet, set the pattern for the prophet's role in the era of kingship."[161] The prophets were to pray unceasingly in support of the kings so that they would be able to instruct them in the right way.[162]

The importance of unceasing prayer and worship in keeping clearly centered on Yahweh were critical to the prophetic task. Many voices were purporting to speak for God. There was the hierarchal system of temple functionaries. Kings had their own prophets and there were even schools of prophets who often denounced each other. In addition to all that were supposed to be the voice of Yahweh, there were also prophets of other gods that demanded attention from time to time.

At the time of Israel's earliest beginnings, when Israel still led a nomadic life, there were no pronounced social differences. The problems arose only after the

---

[161] Vallet, 137.
[162] I Sam. 12:23.

settlement, especially after the economic prosperity of the monarchy. When social distinctions arose, the prophets above all took the side of the poor and inveighed passionately against the rich and powerful, their greed and excesses.[163]

There were four basic messages that prophets of God delivered: judgment, hope, confrontation and repentance.

Judgment

The first was a message of judgment that condemns all that stands against God's desire for shalom – justice, equity and righteousness.[164]   Many prophets arose who spoke the message of a righteous God castigating the excesses of the privileged and the oppression of the poor and vulnerable. The prophets pointed to the righteousness of God that could not even be seen because of the sinfulness of the people. Usually the critique was both economic and political -- improper distribution of the resources needed for life and the lack of justice for the poor and vulnerable. They also criticized the use of militarism since strength does not ultimately preserve a lack of justice.[165]

> ...the prophet's critique and the coming destruction of the state, coupled with their vision of the future when the state would operate as it should, implies that states which operate and promote injustice must be transformed into justly working ones or be destroyed.[166]

---

[163] Wolfgang Schrage, trans. By David E. Green, *The Ethics of the New Testament* (Philadelphia: Fortress Press, 1988), 99.

[164] Birch and Rasmussen, 128ff.

[165] Yoder, *Shalom*, 106

[166] Ibid., 115.

Judgment included a description of the results of continued unrighteousness that was defined not only in terms of straying from the worship of Yahweh but also by their lack of care for the poor and vulnerable. Harsh judgment was reserved for those who oppressed the poor and vulnerable either actively or in passive ways as in choosing not to be involved. Righteousness was always paired with justice as the work of Yahweh and the community.

The prophets would speak and act in terms of divine righteousness. "To proclaim divine righteousness means to proclaim that God sets things right."[167] There could be no righteousness or true shalom that did not find expression in compassionate activity ensuring equitable access to the needed goods for life and justice for those without voice or power. Righteousness must include community-restoring justice in the gate or their law court and also the market place, their economic institutions.[168] For the prophets, sins against the poor were clear disobedience toward God. The prophets exhibited solidarity with the poor, not just a concern for their welfare but also in strong protest against the persons and structures that enabled injustice. [169]

Originally the clear meaning of justice was that God stood with and among the poor and vulnerable and suffered with them. Yahweh was not only righteous, but also had ultimate freedom to be or not to be in any place. Yahweh was present with the slaves who were liberated in mighty

---

[167] Yoder, John Howard. *The Politics Of Jesus – Vicit Agnus Noster* (Grand Rapids, MI: Eerdmans, 1999), 224.
[168] Glen H. Stassen, *Just Peacemaking – Transforming Initiatives for Justice and Peace,* (Louisville, KY: Westminster/John Knox, 1992), 72.
[169] Theodore W. Jennings, *Good News To The Poor – John Wesley's Evangelical Economics,* (Nashville, TN: Abingdon, 1990), 71-72.

miraculous acts to become his people. But as most of the people became prosperous and became residents rather than sojourners, the Mosaic Covenant of Shalom was modified and replaced. The rich and powerful located God with them as part of the hierarchal structure. Yahweh God was placed at the top of the ladder, allied with them and thereby became the judge of the poor rather than their advocate and friend. The ladder also had a full cadre of religious functionaries that protected the presence of God from unworthy lesser beings. The poor and vulnerable could no longer ask God for *justice* but were to beg for *mercy* that would help them endure their lot. Mercy became tenderness and compassion without any power to make changes or liberate the downtrodden. There was no opportunity for relief either in personal circumstances or in systemic change. The meaning of the word for justice had not changed. Originally justice was not about the judgment of the downtrodden, but was found in activity to assist the poor and vulnerable.[170]

Hope

> In scripture judgment never stands alone but is coupled with hope...The greatest statements of hope in the Bible are born out of situations when those without the eyes of faith would see only hopelessness...Hope is not founded in rational assessment of options. It is the confidence that even when all options seem disastrous, the last word has not been said.[171]

The prophets announced hope and deliverance. Things did not need to be as they were. There was a way out

---

[170] Matthew Fox, *A Spirituality Named Compassion.* (NY: Harper Collins, 1990), 203.

[171] Birch and Rasmussen, 140-141.

and promise for the future. They proclaimed peace, justice, salvation, the reign of God with a new creation of shalom where there would be peace among nations and the healing of sickness and disease.[172] The kingdom of God was not a place, it was to be a "process of peace, justice, and the reign of God" which was to be known in God's reigning or God's delivering more than God's kingdom.[173]

Confrontation and Repentance

Hope for the future was based on transformation of the heart and mind. This change was only possible when persons were prophetically confronted in their situation and they not only acknowledged their sin, selfishness, alienation and brokenness but also their earnest desire to turn away from these and return to God. Accepting the grace-filled invitation of God in repentance – turning away from sin and turning toward God – had been the message of scripture from the beginning. Sin had been caused by and also resulted in the brokenness of relationship. God offered healing in forgiveness that enabled persons to become agents of healing for the earth and her creatures, participating in the righteousness of God, the tikkum olam.

One of the Hebrew meanings of the word, righteousness, is "community-restoring justice" or shalom. The righteousness of God that persons were to emulate was not just a matter of personal piety but was full participation in a new shalom community of justice and peace.[174] Some of the aspects of God's shalom included personal peace based on sufficiency and the security of sitting under one's own vine and fig tree with none to make them afraid, the social

---

[172]   Isaiah 9:6-7, 54:9-10, 55:12, 60, 61, Ezek. 34:25-31, 45:9-10 -
prophets' foundation for hope.
[173]   Stassen, 40- 41, 72
[174]   Ibid., 42. Birch, 153-155, 176-177.
[175]   Micah 4:3-5, Isa. 54.

peace between nations, and the deep abiding sense of mercy, love and protection of God for his people.[175]

God had a different vision for the people that they needed to deeply understand. The power of this alternative consciousness announced by the prophet whether in prosperity or defeat and exile was that the people of God needed to not only repent and believe but that belief must be translated into daily activity. Faith would always be the basis of moral, compassionate action but true faith would not exist without activity that made it a reality.

Wisdom Philosophy

The counterpoint to the voice of the prophet, particularly in prosperity, was wisdom the voice of order and reason. Wisdom literature or philosophy had a human or anthropocentric base rather than a foundation that endeavored to discover the will of God, being open to repentance. The questions were not so much an effort to understand the being or will of God, but how to use human reason to have the good life. God in wisdom texts was not the deliverer from oppression but was the God of a good and benevolent created order. Knowledge of God, the source of wisdom, was order and happiness. Shalom was the wholeness that God desires for all persons in the ordinary human experience of community. Wisdom was optimistic in its view of human freedom and responsibility rather than reliance on the dramatic deliverance of God.[176] While the intervention of Yahweh in the avoidance of natural consequences of folly was possible, the normal activity of Yahweh was the rule of law and order. The goal of wisdom's righteousness was the good life based on law and order.

---

[176] Birch and Rasmussen, 101-104.

65

Part of that law and order was an economic stratification based on individual choices and industriousness. Wisdom taught that while it might be regrettable, the poor and vulnerable simply reaped what they did or did not sow. Each person was just responsible for themselves and their fate.

> The rabbis usually consider poverty a disaster, reckoning the poor with the dead but extolling the rich. Of course they inculcate generosity toward the poor, for charity and work of love outweigh all other commandments of Torah.[177]

The book of Deuteronomy stated in the most emphatic terms that the people were *commanded to care for the poor.* "This is a part of what it means to be a people of God, and it is not an optional activity."[178]

Mosaic *distributive* justice that stressed sharing with the poor had been replaced with wisdom's *retributive* justice wherein the righteousness is equivalent with the rewards of health and prosperity while wickedness or folly led to destruction and ruin.[179] God, the source of blessings would reward the righteous with riches, honor and wisdom. Therefore those who did not have these things could not be righteous. Thus they had already judged themselves in their laziness and folly. Originally wealth had been associated with idolatry or seen as the fruit of injustice but in wisdom philosophy, wealth was the blessing upon the righteous and faithful that was the result of their industriousness.[180]

---

[177]   Schrage, 99.
[178]   Birch 181. Deuteronomy 15:4-5, 7-8, 10-11.
[179]   Birch, 338.
[180] Sondra Ely Wheeler, Wealth as Peril and Obligation – The New Testament on Possessions. (Grand Rapids, MI: Eerdmans, 1995), 132.

Unlike the prophets there was no awareness of the wealthy profiting at the expense of the poor, no desire to seek a social ordering that would lift them from poverty, no hope for a divine transformation to redeem them from their fate, no conception of friends and corporate support which transcend economic condition, and no conception that poverty is not brought upon the poor by themselves.[181]

Exile and the Renewal of Hope

Brutal defeat, complete and utter demoralization with exile into Babylon was the result of not listening to the warning voices of the prophets. In its deepest meaning, exile was a spiritual crisis, causing people to examine the foundation of their lives. The love of God had not failed nor had God broken the covenant with them. Israel had been unfaithful to God, not keeping the commandments or listening to the prophets, arrogant and unjust in its treatment of the poor and vulnerable.

God provided redemption and the renewal of hope in the strange and alien land of exile. It was God who would forgive and redeem them and allow them to return to their land even as they suffered for their sins because God suffered with them. Again, God had taken the initiative for their salvation. It was in the midst of their exile that God announced their redemption, plans to give them a future with hope. Away from their false sense of security, they came to understand more of the forgiving grace and

---

[181] Birch, 336-337.

universality of God that offered them a way to become reborn as a people.[182]

The message of the prophets of the exile had two basic parts. It was important for the people to clearly understand their *heritage*. Their past was rooted in powerful images of a strong and resilient people taken from Egyptian slavery who learned as they formed community in the desert. God also called them into a future with hope. The prophetic call was not to memorialize the past, but to *use those strong roots to build a new future, God's vision of an alternate or new community that embodied shalom.* The prophets envisioned a new community with a new covenant of peace where all would live in harmony with God, humankind and the environment.[183]

---

[182] Lam. 5:20-22; Isa. 40:1-2, 12-31; 42:10, 24; 43:25; 44:9-20, 22;46:1-5; 45:1-13, 22; 51:9-11; 54:7-8; 55:6-7; 63:9; Ps. 137:1-4; 139:7-12; Ezek. chapters 1, 8, 10-11, 22; 33:10-11,16; 37:1-14; 48:35; Jer. 9:17-18; 29:11; 31:34; Zech. 12:10.

[183] Isa. 9:6; 54:9-10; Zech 9:10; Jer. 1-16; Ezek. 34:25-31; 45:9-10; 48:35.

Chapter 10

The Suffering Servant and the Kingdom

Isaiah's Servant Songs stand in bold opposition to wisdom's enlightened self-interest.[184] The Servant Songs describe a disturbing new image of the way that God acts in the world that also contrasts with Davidic royal images of Yahweh God.[185] This is the God of the Hebrew slaves, not an impassive deity but one who saw their suffering, heard their cries and suffered with his people.[186] This was the God who declared that although Israel had forsaken him, even more than a mother cared for her child, God would not forget his people. Their names were inscribed on the palms of his hands.[187]

It was in this setting that Isaiah announced Jubilee, the acceptable year of the Lord, to this struggling band of refugees, "The spirit of the Lord is upon me because he has anointed me to preach good news to the oppressed, to bind up the broken hearted, to proclaim liberty to the captives, and release to the prisoners."[188]

They had wanted a powerful, warrior god who would destroy their enemies. For a generation that had suffered greatly in exile and desired bloody retribution and vengeance, Isaiah proclaims a vision of an obedient servant, not a regal king, who willingly renounces power and suffers physical abuse for the sake of righteousness. *The power of undeserved suffering paved the way for deliverance,*

---

[184]   Isaiah 42:1-4, 19:1-6, 50:4-9, 52:13-53:12.
[185]   Isaiah chapters 42-53 and 61.
[186]   Page 19, this work.
[187]   Isaiah 49:13-16.
[188]   Ibid., 61:1-2.

reconciliation and harmony.[189] The Suffering Servant would become a completely new means to understand the mission of the shalom of God in the world.

> The nature of moral community in its covenantal commitment to justice, righteousness, and shalom has not changed but its way of being in the world is changed...Thus, the image of God's Servant who suffers for God's justice is appropriated by succeeding generations who see their story in the Servant's story. Their suffering was not a sign of God's wrath, but the necessary path of their mission as God's people.[190]

For Christians, the Messianic tradition, the oracles of the Suffering Servant and the vision of the New Community of Shalom were seen in the person of Jesus and his teaching and preaching of the kingdom of God. Jesus of Nazareth was God's anointed, the Messiah.

> The presence and the approach of God's kingdom laid a new and urgent moral imperative on Jesus' hearers to live a life of discipleship in keeping with the ethical demands of the kingdom. It is our contention that these are in harmony with the covenant ideal advanced by Moses, defended by the prophets, and anticipated in its fullness by the visionaries. It is none other than the God who reigns as king in the proclamations of the Old Testament, whose kingdom is brought near in the preaching of Jesus.[191]

---

[189] Birch, 297-300.

[190]Ibid., 300.
[191] Op. cit., 231.

Part Two

The New Witness

Chapter 11

Continuity Between the Testaments

The Hebraic Covenant (Old Testament) is critical to our understanding of the New Testament since it was carried forward, enabling continuity between the testaments. The Hebraic Bible was the Bible of Jesus and the early church. This witness was the soil from which the new covenant sprang so concepts about God and the nature of mankind were carried forward into the New Testament. One of the most important connections was in the concept of grace.

> Grace does not wait until the New Testament for its appearance. God's graceful activity is already manifest in full measure in creation, promise, deliverance, steadfast love, forgiveness, redemption and renewal in the pages of the Old Testament witness. It is our knowledge of God's grace from creation onward that allows us to fully understand the divine grace we see in Jesus Christ. The God of Israel is the same God made incarnate in Jesus Christ.[192]

---

[192] Birch 356.

The concept of the kingdom of God or the time of the reign of God on the earth begins in the Old Testament.[193] There is also continuity in the concept of being the people of God. The sacred literature clearly outlined foundational morality, ethics and the religious traditions of Second Temple Judaism and "bridged the gap" between testaments, providing the bedrock for the early church.[194] The early church was also a product of the continuity in liturgy since the church's scripture was the Hebrew Bible. The idea of the active involvement of God and the presence of the Holy Spirit links the Old and New Testaments. "The prophet's hope for a future in which God's justice and shalom would be realized on earth was alive in the New Testament period."[195] The foundational communal covenant of peace, the Shalom of God, where there is unity and sufficiency for all is expressed in both the Old and New Testaments.

Because the Hebraic Testament is the root of the second witness, the New Testament, there is common ground between the basic tenets of Judaism and Christianity. Some of these are:

> ...that the one God of Israel created the universe through His word; makes humans in His image; speaks to humanity through His word, commanding them to imitate Him; speaks to each nation through its own language; sends Israel the Torah and makes a special covenant with Israel to serve as light to the nations; will send His Messiah to redeem Israel and the nations in the end of days.[196]

---

[193] Dorothy Yoder Nyce, *Jesus' Clear Call To Justice,* (Scottdale, PA: Herald Press, 1990), 53.

[194] Birch, 356.

[195] Yoder, Shalom, 120.

[196] Frymer-Kensky et. al., 60.

Some elements of Judaism are especially important in the understanding of Jesus and Christian foundations. Judaism as a defined religion began in the time of Ezra when the actual identity of a unified Jewish people centered in Torah.[197] The foundation of this covenantal relationship had four interacting parts: (1) God, (2) Torah, (3) the people, not as individuals but in community and (4) the land of Israel. Each part was dependent on and supported by the other elements.[198] The importance of the covenant community was critical. Not only was the covenant made with those present, it was also made with future generations.[199] The idea of a covenant community based on the living word of God and the witness of scripture became extended into the Christian faith.

From its earliest beginnings, Torah was not static but was considered a living document that would yield new truths and revelation in its study. For this reason, study and meditation upon the Torah were considered to be the highest form of worship since new truths were revealed by God in this process. When two or three Jews studied Torah together, it was said that one could be certain that God was in their midst.

Rabbinic Jews followed the teaching of the Pharisaic predecessors who propounded the idea of Oral Torah...as a primary framework for expanding the written words of Scripture...They considered their oral traditions to be part of the *continuous revelation* that God had given Moses at Sinai.[200] (italics by author.)

---

[197] Howard Clark Kee, *Understanding The New Testament,* (Englewood Cliffs, NJ: Prentice Hall, 1993, 5th edition), 50-51.

[198] Marvin R. Wilson, *Our Father Abraham – Jewish Roots of the Christian Faith,* (Grand Rapids, MI: Eerdmans, 1989), 32.

[199] Wilson, 187. Deut. 7:6-9.

[200] Frymer-Kensky et. al., 89-90. Kee, 58-59. Kee characterizes this as "religious imagination" based on Torah.

Rabbis also reported hearing voices from heaven called *bat qol* which literally meant "the daughter of the Voice" and was thought to be a form of inspiration that had replaced more direct prophetic revelations.[201] Whatever form it took, those who sought the Lord understood that God would reveal new or greater truths.

These principles enabled the ministry of Jesus to be more broadly understood. They were used to questioning and seeking greater truths in the revealed word of scripture. There was also a tradition of traveling itinerant teachers or rabbis who discipled followers. Although the teachings and ministry of Jesus are not confined to their Judaic roots, the foundations both in terms of underlying principles and also the structure and means of communication of that vision are Hebraic.[202]

Rabbinic Judaism

Yahweh God had always been a transcendent deity – a being wholly other, above and beyond human experience, but the Rabbis made God intimately present and concerned with the details of common life. Not only was Yahweh God the Creator of all, this God was also concerned with every part of life and longed to be present with his people. Thus while not all things were sacred, because God created the world, all things were spiritual.

One of their favorite ways to understand God and the Holy Spirit was the Shekinah, which literally meant the dwelling or tent of God in their midst; their spiritual home that would be with them wherever they were. Whereas God

---

[201] Karen Armstrong, *The History Of God, The 4000-year Quest of Judaism, Christianity and Islam*, (NY Ballentine Books, 1993), 81-82.

[202] Frymer-Kensky et. al., 88-89. Bruce Chilton and Jacob Neusner, *Judaism In The New Testament - Practices and Beliefs*, (NY: Routledge, 1995), 4-10.

had been identified with a rushing wind or blazing fire, the Rabbis said that the presence of God could be sensed in a multitude of other ways. They spoke of the God that could not be contained or defined by any human statement, a God that would be perceived by each individual in a distinct way. The goal of knowing God was in perceiving that mystery and wonder in life, not in finding simple solutions to life's problems. They were called to be a holy nation, a kingdom of priests who were to be defined by their acts of loving-kindness.[203]

Although they separated holiness from spirituality, the Rabbis taught that God was to be seen and known in common, everyday life. They taught a spirituality that was robust and life-affirming, insisting that Jews had a duty to keep well and happy because it was not the will of God that humans suffer.

Sometimes Rabbis were seen as incarnations of Torah because of the depth and power of their understanding. Rabbis taught that loving one's neighbor as oneself was the great principle of Torah. They were to see humanity as sacred because men were made in the image of God so offenses against another person were offenses against God. Because all were created in the image of God, all men were equal before God. Even the High Priest should be beaten if he injured another, because in this, he was denying the existence of God. God had created a single human to illustrate the principle that whenever a single human life was destroyed, it was as if the entire race had been obliterated. The opposite of this was also true, whenever a single human life was saved, it was as if the whole world had been redeemed. This teaching provided the foundation for the belief that a human life could not be taken in murder or honor killing for the sake of the group and to humiliate

---

[203] Armstrong, History, 72-75.

anyone was worse than murder, denigrating all men. This also pertained to the spreading of rumors or scandal that denied the existence of God by the treatment of others. The most important aspect of their relationship with God was the cultivation of the sense of the holy that would enable them to see God within other beings, making each encounter sacred.[204]

---

[204] Ibid., 77-78.

Chapter 12

Jesus and the New Covenant

Introducing Him

"The only shalom is one promised in the midst of historical reality...incarnation. The only God we know entered history, appeared as a person."[205] Ephesians 2:14 states, "He [Jesus] is our shalom." John's gospel states, "The Word became flesh and lived among us" in the person of Jesus of Nazareth (John 1:14) but from the beginning of his life until its end, Jesus was to be an enigma.

Scripture records that the declaration of Jubilee was Jesus' first known public message. Luke records that it happened in this way: according to his custom, Jesus stood in the synagogue to read. The scroll from Isaiah was handed to him.

The spirit of the Lord is upon me, because he has anointed me to bring good news to the poor. He has sent me to proclaim release to the captives and recovery of sight to the blind, to let the oppressed go free, to proclaim the acceptable year of the Lord's favor...Then he began to say to them, "Today this scripture has been fulfilled in your hearing.[206]

---

[205] Brueggemann, Vision, 24.
[206] Luke 4:18-21; Isa. 61:1-2a. One statement is different between these passages: Isaiah states that the brokenhearted would be healed while Luke states that the oppressed are to be set free.

Jubilee could only be declared by religious authorities so in their eyes, Jesus did not have the right to declare or identify himself with Jubilee – a time requiring great social upheaval and change involving the cancellation of all debt, the release of the captives, restoration of all property back to original tribal allotments and finally the proclamation of liberty and celebration.[207] At least some present would have known of the efforts to enforce Jubilee during the Maccabean Period (I Macc 6:49, 53) in addition to Jubilee as the basis of several important reform movements in their history.

Jesus followed the reading by saying that the scripture had been fulfilled on that day. His sermon that followed was a criticism of their doubt in him as a healer and a castigation of their ideas of divine election. The sermon ended abruptly as they angrily arose and drove him out of the synagogue and attempted to throw him from a high cliff.[208]

The dramatic mob response occurred because in those few short sentences Jesus confronted and challenged the whole fabric of their lives. Jesus had proclaimed the reign of God in Jubilee, the acceptable year of the Lord. They knew the requirements of Jubilee and they also knew Moses and the prophets who had condemned injustice. Many even prayed daily for the fulfillment of this prophetic promise to become reality in their lifetime.

"The prophet's hope for a future in which God's justice and shalom would be realized on earth was alive in the New Testament period."[209] For some Jubilee and the time of God's shalom was a source of hope in their present suffering, but for many others it was the ultimate threat to their security and stability. "The Sabbath-Jubilee mandates

---

[207] Lev. 25; Exo. 21:2, 23:9-12, 25:1-7; Deut. 15:1-11, 12-18.
[208] Luke 4:20-30.
[209] Yoder, *Politics,* 120.

were a direct challenge to the way power and wealth and even religion were organized."[210]

Jubilee was Jesus' mission statement and the tenets of Jubilee were to be a persistent theme throughout his ministry. Later when John the Baptist's disciples asked Jesus if he were the one they were waiting for, Jesus answered that the blind receive sight, the lame are made to walk, the deaf are made to hear, lepers are healed and cleansed, the dead are raised and the poor have the good news preached to them.[211] Justice is proclaimed. These were the tenets of Jubilee that he had proclaimed in his first sermon and were indications of his role as Messiah.[212]   These scriptures were being fulfilled in the ministry of Jesus.[213]

Knowing Him

It has been said that Jesus was the personification of Mosaic Jubilee and Shalom, the kingdom in miniature. But who is this Jesus whose first public proclamation almost resulted in his death? How can he be known two thousand years later?

Jesus was an observant Jew, taught by Pharisee rabbis, who traveled to the temple for holy days and festivals and was attentive to normal worship in the synagogue and home. His life was spent mostly among poor people in Galilee. He was well-versed in the Hebraic scriptures and seemed to possess an extra depth of understanding that enabled him to question current practices and teachings of Judaism.   He was an especially charismatic person whose very being seemed to attract people, some of whom he simply "called" and they left everything to follow him.   Jesus'

---

[210]   Kinsler and Kinsler, 125.
[211]   Luke 7:19-22.
[212]   Yoder, Shalom, 125.
[213]   Yoder, *Politics,* 21-24.

disciples were all Jewish from a variety of walks of life; the common factor was that almost none of them would have been considered "religious" by people of that day. The vast majority of his ministry occurred on Jewish soil within a Jewish social and religious context.

Jesus has been described as a Spirit person, healer, wisdom teacher, social prophet and the founder of a movement.[214] He was called the Son of God, perhaps as a means of speaking about the intimate relationship that he evidenced with God. Jesus was considered by some to be divine wisdom or the personification of Sophia. Sophia, the Greek word for wisdom, was a personification of God that acted as the agent of creation and a guide for the world that was referenced in both the Old and New Testaments.[215] Jesus was also considered the victor over death, a divine teacher, the personification of cosmic reason – logos and the ruler of the world – the shepherd and savior grew to heavenly empowerment.[216]

Jesus was also Messiah, the anointed one.

Just as modern scholarship of Jesus has missed the point by marginalizing Jesus from his own Judaism, it has also missed the point by claiming that Jesus claimed no messianic status. It is perfectly true that he was suitably cautious about the *language* he used...After all, he was one humble member of a subject people whose political aspirations were of concern to Rome. But there can be no doubt about his *implicit* claim to the messianic authority to explain what

---

[214] Marcus J. Borg, ed. *Jesus At 2000,* (Boulder, CO: Westview Press, 1997), 11.
[215] Job 28:20-28; Prov. 8:22-32; I Cor. 1:24; Col. 1:15-20, McKim, 264.
[216] Borg, 80-83.

Scripture did not: how God was gathering his own people into his kingdom.[217]

These things and many more could be said of him, but this does not explain the fact that his power and presence were conveyed to very ordinary people after his death and resurrection, completely transforming them to give powerful witness of him that resulted in their martyrdom. Not does it explain how the power of the Holy Spirit testifying of Jesus has been passed down through twenty centuries, in the midst of human error and sin, for people to experience the presence of deity in victory and life-changing empowerment through the centuries. The appeal of Jesus has crossed the boundaries of time, nationality, culture, gender, age, social location and intelligence.

The key to any understanding of Jesus both as the historical person and also as Christ or incarnate deity is not simply to have correct understandings of facts or even scriptures that speak of him, although these can be of critical importance in the quest. The way to know him is by being open to the revelation of God in Christ within one's very being. This is the essence of the fullness of life, to truly KNOW him.

> To know Jesus as the Christ is to receive through him what only God can give – a power so creative that it brings creatures in all of their complexity and conflict to completion.... In the midst of such complexity, millions of human beings have experienced Jesus as mediating the power of God, a power so ultimate that it can bring to completion not only our finite creatureliness but that of all creation. It is inevitable that such ultimate power will be comprehended under

---

[217] Jacob Neusner and Bruce D. Chilton, *God In The World – Judaism and Christianity – the Formative Categories,* (Harrisburg, PA: Trinity Press International, 1997), 100.

many metaphors: to the hungry, Christ shall be bread; to the homeless, refuge; to the oppressed, liberation; to the culturally privileged, truth, beauty and community; to the sick, healing; and to the dying, resurrection.[218]

To know someone implies a relationship with openness for both parties. Knowing in the biblical sense takes the concept deeper to an understanding of the very essence of the inner person, including that which is of greatest importance to them. Jesus illustrated this principle by saying that not everyone who calls his name or even serves in his name would enter the kingdom of heaven. Only those that he also knows – those who have come to truly know him – will enter into his joy (Matt. 7:21).

The good news is that Jesus the Christ wants to know his people. All that is required to come into relationship with him is for his people to be open to the indwelling presence of Jesus the Christ.

---

[218] James E. Will, *A Christology of Peace*, (Louisville, KY: Westminster/JohnKnox Press, 1989), 13-15.

Chapter 13

The World of Jesus

In spite of the fact that for two millennia, persons have come into relationship with Jesus from almost every circumstance, the man Jesus lived in a particular time, place and culture. Although his ministry has been *universalized* and has spoken to people for two millennia, in order to come to a greater understanding of him, it is important to *particularize* him – to understand him and the world he knew.

> The life and teachings of Jesus reveal a deep commitment to the Jewish beliefs and practices of his day. He was born of Jewish parents...circumcised on the eighth day in accord with Jewish Law. As a boy he celebrated Passover...and as a youth he learned by interacting with various Jewish teachers, all of whom were amazed at his understanding. Frequenting the synagogue from Sabbath to Sabbath as was his custom at the start of his adult ministry....Jesus was exposed to a wide range of Jewish thought.[219]

In spite of the great variety of theologies or philosophies of his day, there were many factors that promoted unity among the Jewish people. Their lives were centered in Torah and the idea that somehow God had a role for them to play as his people. The covenant made with Israel was based on the faithfulness and loving kindness of Yahweh God. They were to love God with all their hearts

---

[219] Wilson, 40.

and also to manifest this love to others in their conduct. The commandments outlined the responses of covenant fidelity and love. In their observance, Israel would proclaim that Yahweh God is holy and wholly unique among the gods of the other nations. They were to be a holy people among whom the rule of God would be in evidence. Their understanding of all these things was based on their continuing experience of the living Torah, which in turn was the basis of both unity and diversity among Jews in the New Testament period.[220]

One of the aspects of their unity was monotheism, a passionate belief in ONE God. There was general consensus in their hope for the coming Messiah. He would be a descendant of King David, their king and spiritual leader who founded the first independent Jewish kingdom. He would exercise justice and divine wisdom - but as a human being. Although the Psalms sometimes called King David Messiah or the Son of God, it was simply their way to describe his closeness with Yahweh God. Their passionate affirmation of belief in one God had been intensified during Babylonian captivity where not only was there a multiplicity of gods, but these *gods actually had a sons* born of indiscriminate or capricious alliances. For Jews, this was complete anathema; nothing could have been more totally wrong.[221] Their first principle of belief recited all through the day was that God was one.

Jesus used his knowledge of Torah and fundamental principles of Judaism in his life and ministry. He was not only knowledgeable in Hebraic scriptures and principles, he was also warm and loving toward people and articulate in word and deed in communicating his message. He had a

---

[220] Luke T. Johnson, *The Writing Of The New Testament – An Interpretation,* (Phidelphia, PA: Fortress Press, 1986), 42. Exo. 19:6, 34:6; Lev. 11:14, 19:18; Deut. 6:1-4.
[221] Armstrong, History, 80.

mission and was initially seen like other teachers in his day, discipling followers much as other itinerant teachers did, teaching in the synagogues and working with people whenever there was opportunity. Jesus had been taught and lived in the world of Pharisee Judaism so his teachings reflected its major beliefs. They taught that charity or lovingkindness was the most important commandment or value and must be practiced in all that people did.

Rome and the Temple System

Jesus lived in a conquered nation under the domination of Rome; that meant that economic hardship was the lot of most people, including the devastating loss of ancestral lands (the nahala) that resulted in dissolution of social place and desperate poverty. In addition to the purity system that had become highly politicized, there was also the messianic dream of the restoration of the Davidic kingdom that inspired groups like the Zealots to plot revolt against Rome. At least part of involvement in groups such as the Zealots was for religious reasons, but for the majority, devastating, hopeless poverty was the key factor. People considered that they had nothing further to lose. It is not insignificant that the first act of the Zealots in the time of the uprising against Rome was to set fire to the places where the records of indebtedness were kept in Jerusalem.[222]

The temple was the center of worship and devotion and also a unifying force both for Jews within Israel and also those of the Diaspora who made pilgrimages there.[223] The Diaspora were those who had been Jewish by lineage. The Diaspora lived far away from their homeland, perhaps for business purposes and also were those who were descendents of people converted to Judaism during an

---

[222] Schrage, 100.
[223] Kee, 51-55.

earlier brief period of missionary activity, particularly around the Mediterranean basin. After their Babylonian exile, Jews established scattered colonies outside Israel with the synagogue as the heart of their spiritual, economic and social lives. Synagogues thus established enabled Paul and other missionaries to the Gentiles to have a place from which to spread the gospel. It was the common thought that at least once in one's lifetime, a faithful Jew would make pilgrimage to the temple for Passover where the blessings of being a diverse people gathered in worship was a powerful experience of unity. For Jews living in the areas around Jerusalem, the faithful such as the family of Jesus, would have regularly gone to the temple in Jerusalem for religious festivals.

But the temple was also a center of corruption and evil. The temple was one of the richest, most powerful institutions in the world of that time. The alliance between Rome and Israel was based on the religious authority of high priests chosen by Rome from an elite group of men that controlled not only religious life, but also business and trade, called the Sanhedrin. The Sanhedrin was the highest council and tribunal whose scope of duties included the exercise of jurisdiction over religious, civil and criminal matters with the approval of Rome. This council was composed of seventy-one members, the number being traced back to the time of Moses who was counseled to find seventy men to assist him in establishing government. These high priests functioned as Roman administrators in the collection of taxes, tribute, temple tax, the regulation and control of trade and the administration of the debt code. The Sanhedrin had some freedom but essentially functioned to legitimize the rule of Rome.[224]

---

[224] Kinsler and Kinsler, 125. Wink, 80.

The temple in Jerusalem was not just for religious purposes but was also a very large business that made its administrators wealthy and powerful. It was a monopoly that controlled the appropriation of sacrifices and also the issuance of ritually pure temple coinage necessary to pay taxes or fees. During this period of financing such a large operation, in addition to various temple taxes, people were called to consecrate their property *to the temple* rather than support elderly parents or children in a religious vow called "corban" although the clear scriptural teaching had been the primary obligation of support of one's family. (The teaching of the Old Testament was that persons needed to provide for themselves. If for some reason, that was not possible, families were responsible for each other. But if that could not be done, the support of the poor was the responsibility of the community.)[225] The temple employed 18,000 minor functionaries, and the Roman army garrisoned at the adjoining Antonia Fortress had 500 soldiers that constantly monitored activity within the temple.[226]

The Class System

Israel was a highly stratified society under Roman rule. Priesthood, with high priests as the apogees of cultic purity, was the basis of social place. The higher classes functioned to support and stabilize both the national and religious structures. There were various groups based both on religious belief and also economic privilege.

---

[225] Donald B. Kraybill, *The Upside-down Kingdom,* (Scottdale, PA: Herald Press, 1990), 159. Mark 7:10-13. Ronald J. Sider, *Just Generosity – A Vision for Overcoming Poverty in America,* (Grand Rapids, MI: Baker Books, 1999), 71. Lev. 25:25, 28, 35. I Tim. 5:6.
[226] Kinsler and Kinsler, 125-126. J. Milburn Thompson, *Justice And Peace, A Christian Primer,* (Maryknoll, NY: Orbis, 1998), 184. Kraybill, 159-161.

The social pyramid that functioned in Israel was clear and fixed. One's status was not subject to change except perhaps downward. Herodians, the supporters of Herod, and <u>Sadducees</u> were the wealthy aristocratic elite who blended aspects of Greek philosophy and culture with strict Torah observance in temple rites. Their influence was pervasive since they cooperated with Rome in the control of the temple. Membership in this highly selective small group was based on aristocracy and also the power base of their residence in Jerusalem. Little else can be known about them since they left no literature; when the temple was destroyed in 69 C.E. this movement also died. <u>Scribes</u> also played a prominent role. They were the well-educated interpreters of the law and functioned in Jerusalem as well as the outlying areas. Their interpretation of the law functioned primarily to legitimate the socio-economic pyramid: high priests, Sadducees, Scribes, Pharisees, lesser Jews and people of the land. The <u>Pharisees</u> were the largest group and were generally the leaders of local synagogues. Begun as a reform movement within Judaism, their emphasis was on the strict observance of the religious purity codes. After Jerusalem fell, this is the only branch of Judaism that survived. There were many schools within this group with the attendant diversity of thought, but generally this group looked to the strict enforcement of Torah with its more than six hundred laws and purity codes. Generally the Pharisees were sincere, good and devout people but like other groups, they were also threatened by the teachings and ministry of Jesus. No doubt some who called for the crucifixion of Jesus would have called themselves Pharisees.[227] Far below, or perhaps not even on the socio-economic pyramid – certainly not in their thought – were the <u>Essenes</u>. They were a strict separatist group with their own priesthood who rejected all things foreign and withdrew from society to maintain purity according to strict observance of the law. The Qumran

---

[227] Ibid., 126. Kee 52-62. Johnson *Writings,* 5,53.

colony was an example of this movement where initiates sold all their possessions to be shared with the community that lived by a vow of poverty and abstinence.[228] John, called the Baptizer, was probably once an Essene who urged Jews to repent and accept the Essene rite of purification, baptism or immersion, in the River Jordan.[229]

Persons below the Pharisees or Essenes on the socio-economic pyramid were the lesser Jews or the people of the land. They had need of the governance and religious systems, particularly the instituted means for administering relief to the poor, but had no viable means of influence upon the upper levels. They were a part of the subsistence economy. Small farmers had the best circumstances – if they could somehow keep their land. Below them were "the impure" that included shepherds, prostitutes and Samaritans.[230] A large group of persons in various degrees of distress, poverty and impurity were called "people of the land". These people were despised and looked upon with disdain by the Pharisees because they could not pay tithing and did not observe purity regulations (certainly in part because they did not have a mikvah or facilities for cleansing or access to ritually pure food). Being unclean, they could not attend synagogue and were therefore thought to be ignorant and hence, *not really part of the Jewish people.* There is no record of their beliefs, but some authors believe that at least part of this group were pious and devoted Jews who had fallen on hard economic times with the loss of ancestral lands.[231] This was especially difficult because by the time of Jesus, both for the Jews in the Holy Land and also for those of the Diaspora, the Rabbi and his leadership of the synagogue was the center of their spirituality and fellowship within the community.

---

[228] Kee, 62-67.
[229] Armstrong, *History,* 80.
[230] Kinsler and Kinsler, 126.
[231] Johnson, *Writings,* 5, 53.

The world of ancient Israel was patriarchal. Jewish spirituality, fellowship within the community and the emphasis on the leadership of the Rabbi were for males only. Women were not required or permitted to become Rabbis; therefore they could not study Torah or pray in the synagogue. It was unthinkable that women would be able to understand the concepts of Torah or that they could have meaningful relationship and experience with God, especially without a male intermediary. Therefore, women were excluded from the spiritual community. Only men counted and were counted, while women by definition were impure and a source of pollution who had a completely different set of norms or rules for their conduct. The role of women was relegated to maintain the ritual purity of the home, a role greatly inferior to that of men. While Rabbis taught that women were especially "blessed by God," men were commanded to thank God daily that they were not Gentiles, slaves or women.[232]

The clear teaching of the Old Testament was that the people of God were a community and bound to care for each other. Everyone (all males) was a part of the covenant community. Although the prophet, Ezekiel, linked individual Jewish identity with righteousness, for the most part the idea of individual judgment where God would judge individuals and not the community came with the advent of Roman persecution.[233] Many people believed that the time of the prophets had come to an end and would not be restored

---

[232] Armstrong, History of God, 76-77. Carol Cease Campbell, "Women in the Apostolic Church and Their Demise", *Restoration Studies VIII: A Collection of Essays About the History, Beliefs, and Practices of the Reorganized Church of Jesus Christ of Latter Day Saints,* edited by Joni Wilson, (Independence, MO: Herald Publishing House, 2000), 141-142.
[233] Johnson, *Writings,* 47. Ezek. 18:1-32, II Macc. 7:23.
[234] I Macc. 9:27.

until the messianic age.[234] Therefore the idea arose that not all those born of Jewish lineage were really Jews; belonging to the people of God was a choice. The criteria beyond circumcision was complete allegiance to Torah and hence, those who kept Torah most perfectly were the righteous people of God. Thus the poor who did not have access to fellowship, worship and education in the synagogue or means of purification like the mikvah were considered not religious: impure, sinful and thereby excluded from the people of God.

Worship was the lifeblood of the Jewish people and was highly ritualized in the temple, synagogue or home. It consisted of hearing the words of Torah or the prophets, perhaps a contemporary homily or sermon or even midrash on verses or prayers (a written historic interpretation of sacred texts). By the time of Jesus, worship had a variety of forms, but always consisted of the confession of faith called the S'hma – "Hear O Israel; The Lord our God is one God, the Lord alone; You shall love the Lord your God with all your heart, and with all your soul, and with all your might."[235] There were also prayers and songs of blessing and praise.

Sabbath observance was the most important experience of the week and was governed by strict purity rituals. Although their entire lives were grounded in commandments and purity rituals, the most important times were Sabbath and Holy Days. The worship in the home was centered in sacred meal liturgy. "They insisted on eating their meals in a state of ritual purity because they believed that the table of every single Jew was like God's altar in the temple."[236] This meant that everyone needed to be cleansed before going to family meals, synagogue or temple. A non-Jew would not observe these commandments and would be

---

[235] Deut. 6:4-5.
[236] Armstrong, History – God, 72.

92

considered unclean hence Jews would not share a meal with non-Jews or those considered to be unclean. This is why meals were a microcosm, an example, of the essentials of Jewish life where fellowship, intimacy and accord were all based on the class system.[237] Thus all of Jewish life and worship was governed by an elaborate system of ritual and purity codes that strictly enforced their tradition and heritage.[238]

---

[237] Luke Timothy Johnson, *Religious Experience In Earliest Christianity – A Missing Dimension in New Testament Studies,* (Minneapolis, MN: Fortress, 1998), 138.
[238] Kraybill, 157-161. Wink, 73-75.

Chapter 14

The Ministry of Jesus and

The Mosaic Covenant of Shalom

There are many ways that the ministry of Jesus within a brief three-year period might be analyzed. One of those ways is using the principles of the Mosaic covenant that included Jubilee. From his first sermon throughout his ministry, Jesus lived shalom.

Jubilee principles motivated by deep compassion were at the heart of all that he did. Jesus upheld the highest principles of Judaism, the Mosaic Covenant of Shalom, while also deeply criticizing its contemporary practice. He embodied the mercy of God in the power to heal, forgive, overcome hatred with love and restore the lost and excluded. The life of Jesus could be seen as the restoring power of God resident within a human person, upholding the highest ideals of the Jewish religion while pointing to greater, deeper and sometimes, hidden truths. The ministry of Jesus evidenced the belief that the image of God was in everyone, therefore, there was hope and power for persons to be transformed to more perfectly reflect that image.

Jesus' life could be said to be a challenge to contemporary ways of conceiving the world, pointing to an alternate consciousness called the kingdom of God or the kingdom of heaven. Whether the subject is prayer, fasting, almsgiving, the Sabbath, circumcision, prophecy or purification, Jesus offered a critique to the usual practices and ways of thinking. He took symbols like the yoke of Torah, the temple, the atoning sacrifice or bread of Passover unto himself, saying that these were fulfilled in him. The yoke of Torah was a way to refer to the difference that Torah made in one's life. Instead of being unyoked or wildly undirected, Torah gave focus, purpose and direction to life. The yoke of Torah also was the recognition that one walked with all the faithful ancients of Torah, not alone. In all of these ways, Jesus points to their "surface" obedience, their preoccupation with details and minutia while missing the essence of the law or teaching and most of all, to the blatant hypocrisy that existed in the world around him. He did most of this while traveling and teaching in the obscurity of the small, unimportant province of Galilee. Galilee provided protection since the scope of his critique, particularly against the purity practices, Sabbath and temple, would have resulted in his death much earlier.

One of the most powerful ways to consider the life and ministry of Jesus is as an integrated act of worship that proclaimed the righteousness of God as compassionate communal justice and responsibility by those who have come to know and serve that God.[240] The ministry of Jesus will be considered particularly in terms of the ideal of the Mosaic covenant of shalom with the *compassionate righteousness of God* as the focal point of all origin. This compassion is demonstrated by those who have come to know the loving grace of God in relationships within the human family where there is *access to the goods necessary to sustain economic life* and *power is exercised with egalitarian justice.*

---

[239] Dominic Crossan, *Who Killed Jesus? Exposing the Roots of Anti-Semitism in the Gospel Story of the Death of Jesus,* (NY: HarperSanFrancisco, 1995), 46-47.
[240] Letty M. Russell, *Church In The Round – Feminist Interpretation of the Church,* (Louisville, KY: Westminster/John Knox, 1993), 166.

God

The purity system had been designed many centuries ago to separate and protect the righteousness of God from unworthy human approach. God was wholly other, a being of complete righteousness not like or subject to manipulation by humans. But as the purity system and temple worship developed, these functioned to isolate God and deny the radical freedom of God to speak or act. The standard for goodness or Godliness was carefully outlined in more than six hundred Torah laws. God was to be located within the temple where access to God was controlled by the temple priests. For Jesus, holiness was the power of God to cleanse, transform and renew all of creation, not rigid rules to "protect" God from his people, those he longed to bless, forgive and restore.[241] But God could never be contained by human thought or practice and was by definition always free.

One of the most vigorous elements of Jesus' ministry was his attack on the purity system that had become highly politicized and exclusionary in his day. The core value of Jesus' message was not external purity that was required to be in the presence of God, but the love and compassion of God that sought the excluded, lost and forsaken.[242] Unlike those who politicized purity, Jesus deliberately politicized compassion in reaching out to the untouchables.[243] Jesus taught that righteousness was determined by compassion, defined as the purity of heart, not obedience to outward symbols of purity. For the poor and downtrodden, this was good news, liberating to all those who had been excluded.

---

[241] Walter Wink, *Powers,* 73-75.

[242] I John 4:8.

[243] Thompson, 181.

Jesus spoke with powerful authority on the basis of his intimacy with God and also invited others to come into deeper relationship with their Creator. This relationship set Jesus apart from other leaders. The title most often used by Matthew's gospel is "rabbi" or teacher, although there is no record of any formal training or ordination. Luke identifies Jesus as a prophet of social righteousness in the tradition of Old Testament prophets.

Baptism was a powerful symbol of these new understandings. John the Baptizer preached repentance leading to baptism. He announced the coming judgment of God, offering an alternative that circumvented the Jewish ritual of purification. The message of Jesus, although apocalyptic in nature in terms of revealing divine mysteries, particularly in regard to the future, strongly proclaimed the mercy and forgiveness of a loving God. Jesus and his disciples also practiced baptism. Everyone was invited to be baptized as a symbol of initiation into the kingdom. Before, male circumcision had been the sign of being a part of the family of God thereby excluding all women. Now baptism, not circumcision, was the sign of the covenant in which one was joined to Christ becoming part of the family of faith.[244]

> ...the substance of Jesus' message of repentance derives from Old Testament prophecy rather than from Judaism...In addition, penance is not prerequisite for salvation; salvation is prerequisite for penance. Repentance, then, means total devotion to God, not legalistic penitential zeal. God's love means that everything can be expected from God...The message of the kingdom of God goes forth unconditionally, without prerequisites, as God runs to us in love; we must repent

---

[244] Johnson, *Religious Experience,* 74-78. Wayne A. Meeks, *The Moral World of the First Christians,* (Philadelphia: Westminster, 1986), 99.

and turn to him with equal openness and confidence. God does not want a share...he wants us wholly.[245]

Just as Jesus pointed to the compassionate righteousness of God, shown in egalitarian economics and justice for all, so Jesus continually extends invitation for people to be involved in this work of God. Divine and human mercy must come together. The experience of the mercy of God enables, but also requires, that this mercy and kindness be extended to others.[246] "Thus the teachings of Jesus need to be understood as calling for economic and social/political structures within which they make sense, or we are doomed to saying that Jesus' messianic mission is impractical and thus irrelevant."[247]

Economics and Stewardship

The gospels indicate that Jesus spoke about economic issues far more than any other single topic. "The gospel of Jesus is founded on economic equity, because economic inequities are the basis of domination."[248] The teachings of Jesus echo the Hebraic Testament's teaching that the community was obligated to help those who could not help themselves. Adequate food was the inherent right of all so the poor were allowed to glean after a crop was harvested. The owner was to purposely leave food for the poor. Anything grown in a fallow field from the Sabbatical year of rest or any other reason belonged to the poor, not the person who owned the field. The poor were to receive the tithe every third year. A zero interest loan was to be made available to the poor and if not paid by the Sabbatical year, the loan was to be forgiven. Debt slaves were to be set free with adequate provisions in the seventh year. The

---

[245] Schrage, 42-43.
[246] Ibid., 38.
[247] Yoder, Shalom, 126.
[248] Wink, 66.

community was commanded to give to the poor and also pay fair wages to workers, making sure that the poor were paid on a daily basis. The scriptural standard was that the community was to be responsible for those who could not provide for their economic needs.[249]

Jesus taught the familiar principles of care for the poor that were mandated by scripture. The gospels and letters of the New Testament stand both in similarity and contrast to Old Testament teachings on wealth. Wealth in the Hebraic witness was (1) an occasion for idolatry, associated with unfaithfulness to God, (2) a fruit of injustice or unlawful accumulation, neglect of laws that prevent wealth, robbing the poor, (3) a great blessing to the faithful, prevalent in the wisdom tradition, and (4) the reward of labor while the poor were denigrated for being idle. New Testament teachings were that (1) wealth was a stumbling block, preventing one from full participation in the kingdom, (2) an object of devotion that not only replaced God but led to greed, the desire to have more that was always associated with idolatry, (3) a symptom of the failure of the economic system or a testimony against those who were able to help but did not and (4) wealth was also a resource for the community to be shared.[250]

The dichotomy between the rich and poor was addressed in many ways. Sometimes "the poor" did not denote an economic category but were those without power or dignity, having greater dependence upon God. But these were mostly the exceptions. In the vast majority of instances Jesus, like the prophets of the past, spoke of God's preferential option for those who experienced material poverty. Jesus criticized the accumulation of wealth since it led to great disparity between the rich and the poor. If

---

[249] Sider, *Just Generosity,* 68-70. Exo. 23:10-11; Deut. 14:28-29, 15:4, 23:24-25, 24:10; Ruth 2:1-3; Matt. 12:1-8.

[250] Wheeler, 123-132. Kinsler and Kinsler, 96.

people had obeyed the commandments to give liberally to the poor, there would have been far less difference between the rich and the poor.

In a comparison between the beatitudes of Matthew 5:3ff and Luke 6:20, Matthew speaks of those who are poor in spirit while Luke addresses those without social or religious status who are suffering material poverty. Those who are suffering in this way are called blessed because they are open to the kingdom; they have no worldly distractions or other promises and can heed the call to repent and receive the goodness of God.

> Because possessions can only alienate people from God, they cease to be a sign and guarantee of God's blessing. Salvation is promised instead to the poor. Because God is on their side, Jesus declared his solidarity with them in word and deed. On the other hand, Matthew's addition ("poor in spirit"; Matt. 5:3) maintains the truth that the poor are not blessed simply because they are poor: poverty implies dependence on God. Jesus was sober and realistic enough to realize that need can teach people to curse as well as to pray and that poverty is not simply identical with submission to God.[251]

Jesus' teaching on material possessions seemed to differ as to the occasion and person involved. When the rich young ruler came to Jesus seeking eternal life, he was told to sell all that he had and give to the poor. Another way to understand this is that Jesus offered him Jubilee. The rich man went away sorrowfully because he had great wealth.[252]

---

[251] Schrage, 101
[252] Mark 10:17-22.

The rich man stands as a kind of antitype of discipleship because he is unable either to leave or to follow...He cannot leave behind the power conferred by his possessions to become one who receives (which means paradoxically that he is in the power of his possessions); and he cannot travel on the road to Jerusalem because he cannot give up the life he has even for the life he searches for.[253]

In the Lukan account, the rich man is not young but is a ruler who considers himself just and pious. "Luke uses possessions to express the dynamic of acceptance and rejection, and how the language of possessions expresses the interior disposition of the one who responds either positively or negatively."[254]

Another Jubilee story is that of the wealthy tax collector, Zacchaeus, who because of his occupation would never have been considered religious. Jesus was compassionate when he spoke with him, looking deeply into his heart. That encounter with Jesus altered Zacchaeus' life in powerful ways. He was moved to change his life, giving half of everything he owned to the poor and vowing to restore fourfold that which he had gained by defraud. Salvation came to him, because his heart was open and he received the gift and grace of God.[255]

The Jews would have understood the idea of giving away one's possessions. It was done before a holy war or as

---

[253] Wheeler, 51.

[254] Luke T. Johnson, *The Function Of Possessions in Luke-Acts,* (Published by Scholars Press for the Soceity of Biblical Literature, Number 39, 1977), 144. *Interpreters Dictionary of the Bible, An Illustrated Encyclopedia, vol. 2,* (Nashville, TN: Abingdon Press, 1962), 146-147. Joseph A. Fitzmayer, *The Semitic Background of the New Testament,* (Grand Rapids, Eerdmans, 1997), 283, 285.

[255] Luke 19:1-10.

an entrance requirement to Essene communities.[256] But renunciation of material goods was not the universal teaching of Jesus. The apostles still had their businesses and homes where their families lived. The ministry of Jesus was financed to some extent at least by the contributions of wealthy women. Jesus was buried in the tomb of a rich man. The story of the Good Samaritan illustrates the right use of wealth; money certainly was not universally condemned. If it were, to redistribute wealth would only change the location of evil. *Wealth needed to be used to serve others.*

The poor were not necessarily more righteous; they could also be greedy and covetous. But poverty was an indication that Jubilee and Sabbath principles were not being practiced. The poor also needed to make their offering to God. All gifts were to be from the heart. The dignity of the poor was preserved in the teaching that the size of the gift was not the issue but the important thing was the loving willingness to share. Everyone's gifts were needed. All people were to enjoy the blessings of making an offering. Jesus illustrated this principle in his appreciation of the offering of the poor widow as opposed to the rich man who called attention to himself in making his offering.[257] It was a matter of who or what was God. The danger was that wealth could become an idol, usurping the role of God. Jesus offered an alternate view.

> The ordinary functions of possessions – to ensure status and power and invulnerability over against others – are all excluded. Possessions become useful and acceptable within the Christian community exactly insofar as they become dispensable to their possessors, and thus available for dispersal as the material needs of others,

---

[256] I Macc. 2:28; II Macc. 8:14.
[257] Mark 12:41-44; Luke 21:1-4.

or the spiritual needs of their erstwhile owners, make it expedient.[258]

The teaching of the gospels is that wealth and possessions were clearly a danger or an impediment to spirituality. It was so easy to get caught up with "serving mammon" and thinking that ultimate security was of one's own making and that somehow the blessings of the world were deserved by the wealthy. What mattered was not so much the wealth itself, but the location of one's heart. The danger was that wealth could become that person's god, breaking the first commandment. The rich ruler's focus was on himself and his wealth and only on the performance of the commandments, not on his relationship with God. The greatest commandments of loving God with the totality of one's being and the neighbor as oneself had been broken. Giving away possessions would have enabled him to see the needs of others.

There was also the question of how wealth was obtained and the injustice and oppression of economic systems and governance. The power of wealth could lure persons into selfishness and greed, not using the wealth to help others and perhaps not even seeing the plight of those who suffer. One of the clearest stories of Jesus was the powerful Lukan parable of the poor man, Lazarus, who is never helped or even acknowledged by the rich man who passes by him as he begs for help and daily bread.[259]

Jesus does not say how much wealth it takes to turn possessions into "love" of possessions or when possessions take control. But he does state clearly that property must not become an idol, and that even someone who gains the whole world can lose or forfeit

---

[258] Wheeler, 72.
[259] Luke 16:19-31.

his very self....wealth normally so takes possessions of people's hearts that it becomes their real treasure. This does not mean that Jesus demanded universal renunciation of possessions, but neither does it imply indifference toward wealth and possessions.[260]

The issue of covetousness is at the heart of a parable Jesus told of a rich farmer who was blessed with such an abundance of crops that he needed to build more barns to store his wealth. It was not the sixth year when this would have been important for the observance of the Sabbatical year when the land was to lie fallow, not being planted in crops. He had barns full of grain when there were many people who went hungry. The rich man's love of wealth and security was more important to him than his soul.[261]

The crucial point is to use earthly possessions in the service of love. For Jesus, therefore, the problem of property is primarily a problem of social rather than individual ethics...There is no hint that such charity might degrade those who receive alms. The concern is rather that enough might not be offered. It is not just what one gives that matters, but what one keeps. Here as elsewhere the law of love is the absolute norm, to which all other considerations are secondary. This love knows nothing of inviolable property rights and distribution of wealth but controls and restricts the use of possessions lest they become a source of idolatrous dependence.[262]

Jesus honored the Hebraic understandings of stewardship: the earth is the Lord's and everything therein. Persons are accountable as stewards of the manifold blessings and grace of God. When persons honor God first

---

[260] Schrage, 102-103.
[261] Luke 12:13-21.
[262] Schrage, 106-107.

104

with all of their being, then they understand the need to live in harmony with those around them, being attentive to their need for the necessities of life and to be treated fairly. Stewards would want to be reconciled when differences occur because they would not want to rupture the shalom of their lives in community. This is the essence of "seeking the kingdom first" where the children of God adjust their ideas of their own needs so that the resources of the earth may be shared to benefit all.

Justice

Justice often is an economic issue but not always. Jesus did not hesitate to confront these issues either as he acted with power and passion in the cause of justice. Throughout the ministry of Jesus, he not only was the presence of God in deeply spiritual ways, he also acted politically in the cause of justice for those who had been marginalized or left out of the religious and political systems of that day.

> While some Christians have attempted to de-politicize the New Testament, the gospel Jesus preached called for national transformation, not just individual conversion. That gospel led Jesus to confront public issues at the power center of his nation, as well as Roman imperialism – and that gospel cost him his life. The Crucifixion was a political event before it became the transcendent symbol of Christian faith. And the Resurrection proved that such faith could convert governments and outlast empires.[263]

All of Jesus' life and ministry was in harmony with his mission of Jubilee-Shalom justice that would usher in the

---

[263] Alan Geyer, *Ideology in America – Challenges to Faith,* (Louisville, KY: Westminster John Knox, 1997), 115.

kingdom. Every act of healing affirmed the abundant life and was an act of justice since it was believed by people of that day that illness came from their sin, hence sickness the punishment of a just God for sin. Every encounter with persons outside the power structure – tax collectors, the sick, children, women, and the poor – was a violation of social custom that had functioned for so long to deny full personhood, the abundant life to them.

One of the most controversial aspects of Jesus' life was his attack on the dominant patriarchal social system of his day both in terms of women and also the structure of the family. Jesus violated social convention in every encounter with women outside his immediate family by simple acts of consideration – speaking and touching that were restorative of women to creation in the image of God.[264] The Ten Commandments had mandated honoring one's *parents;* now, it was only the rule of the father that was unquestioned. His attacks on the patriarchal family system struck at the heart of identity, security, nurture, enculturation of values and training.[265] It was the desire of Jesus for the family to be transformed to a place of mutuality, love and greater freedom for its members.[266] The family was not to be a place where men ruled over women and children with impunity or violence.

Jesus seemed to feel free to break common rules and stereotypes. The place and dignity of a man was not to be compromised by association with males beneath him in status or class and especially not by any association with women and children. Even male children were for the most part raised by their mothers until they were old enough to learn their religious obligations and vocation. But Jesus

---

[264] Wink, 69-75.
[265] Kee, 91-92. Matt. 10:37. Mark 3:21, 31, Luke 9:58-62, 12:51-53, 14:26.
[266] Wink, 75-78.

openly loved and enjoyed children and spent time blessing and healing them. His very presence stopped a woman from being stoned to death when he asked the person without sin to cast the first stone. Jesus did not consider himself defiled by touching the sick, dead or even lepers as he engaged in his healing ministries. When touched by a woman in the midst of her menstrual impurity thereby making himself impure, Jesus lovingly healed her and commended her for her faith and courage. (Her punishment for doing this could have been severe.)

On many occasions, he publicly denounced religious authorities for their treatment of the poor and disadvantaged. Jesus often confronted unjust economic systems and finally drove the moneychangers, who had a lucrative business at the expense of those who came to the temple on pilgrimage, out of the temple.

His concern seemed to be to empower individuals by allowing them to develop without regard to the ways this might be impeded by unjust cultural rules or stereotypes. This was particularly true in regard to his treatment of women. Not only did he teach women, it is clear that women exercised leadership within the larger circle of his disciples during his life and in the apostolic church after his resurrection.[267]

Jesus challenged the social conventions of his day: He addressed women as equals, gave honor and

---

[267] Karen Jo Torjesen, *When Women Were Priests – Women's Leadership in the Early Church and the Scandal of Their Subordination,* (NY: HarperSanFrancisco, 1995), This is the focus of the entire book. Carol Cease Campbell, "Women in the Apostolic Church and Their Demise," *Restoration Studies VIII: A Collection of Essays about the History, Beliefs, and Practices of Community the Reorganized Church of Jesus Christ of Latter Day Saints,* edited by Joni Wilson (Independence, MO: Herald House 2000) 141-151.

recognition to children, championed the poor and outcast, ate and mingled with people across all class and gender lines, and with bold rhetoric attacked the social bonds that held together the patriarchal family.[268]

His parables and teachings were constantly addressing the issues of justice in the understanding that until there is justice, there can be no true shalom. He promoted the freedom that was in shalom – compassion, health, harmony, balance, reconciliation, freedom from want or injustice, peace within and around the person that extended to families and nations. This peace was seen as wholeness and integrity in every aspect of life. Jesus acted as prophet "...while the Pharisees are probing and testing and rejecting the prophet, there are those, the 'outcasts,' who are heeding him, and the Kingdom is in the process of being formed."[269]

---

[268] Ibid., 4
[269] Johnson, *The Function of Possessions,* 111.

Chapter 15

The Kingdom of God is Like...

Jesus *lived*, against the systemic injustice and structural evil of that situation, an alternative open to all who would accept it: a life of open healing and shared eating, of radical itinerancy and fundamental egalitarianism, of human contact without discrimination and divine contact without hierarchy. That, he said, shows how God would run the world if God, not Caesar, sat on its imperial throne. That was how God's will was to be done on earth – as in heaven...the kingdom *of God* meant just what it said, a religious vision and a religious program but incarnated in rather than separated from the social, political and economic realities of everyday life.[270]

A goal of the life and ministry of Jesus seemed to have been to bring them back to central covenantal concepts – an understanding of how to live together as a people in covenant with God and each other. This had been a part of their heritage, but in their life as a conquered people, the ideal of shalom seemed very far away. It could not be retrieved in their present circumstances. The world of shared manna in the desert was a distant dream in a remote past so Jesus used stories and examples from their world to explain the Mosaic principles of life of shalom to them. It has been said that the whole of Jesus' life was a parable. He walked on water, cursed a fig tree, rode on an unbroken colt, was a part of a vision of heavenly beings, had a special star and magi attend

---

[270] Crossan, 211-212.

his birth, was crucified, resurrected and ascended into heaven.

Frequently his parables spoke of "the kingdom of heaven" or "the kingdom of God" which was described in metaphors – the kingdom of heaven or God is like… An important early parable was the story of the sower. This illustrated what happened to the good news of the gospel that persons had heard. Many parables spoke of the idea that something normally seen as very small, without significant influence can often grow and come to have great importance. These parables always spoke of the total dedication and focus that would be needed to work with God in this goal.

Because the kingdom of God defied exact description, parables were often used to describe an egalitarian society without discrimination or hierarchy, where people had what they needed to live and did not have to fear oppression, where there was access to both material and spiritual goods, and most importantly, where the radical freedom, righteousness and compassion of God was mirrored in the conduct of persons. One author has described this in the work of Martin Luther as "left-handed power."

> Unlike the power of the right …left-handed power is guided by the more intuitive, open, and imaginative right side of the brain. Left-handed power…is precisely paradoxical power; power that looks for all the world like weakness…it is power…it is the only thing in the world that evil can't touch.[271]

The kingdom of God was sometimes described as the reign or the rule of God where God would be fully sovereign in all aspects of life.

---

[271] Robert Frarrar Capon, *The Parables Of The Kingdom,* (Grand Rapids, MI: Eerdmans, 1985), 19-20.

To recognize the reality of God's rule is also to receive an urgent summons to decision, to repentance, and to a full reorientation of life through Jesus. As Jesus' parables illustrate, to live in the kingdom is to replace trust in power and wealth with an attitude of dependence on God, and to break religious and social boundaries by including the poor, the outcast, the sinner, and even the enemy within the community's fellowship.[272]

The actions, teachings and parables of Jesus describe a lifestyle of persons within the community who did not subscribe to prevalent values, but were guided by the higher norms. Old rules of separation and ritual defilement had no place within the new covenant.

The Sermon on the Mount

The Sermon on the Mount portrays a new relationship to God as Father, a relationship that is epitomized in and somehow made possible for others by Jesus. Individuals actually and presently experience this relationship in their own lives and communities: it transforms their relationships so that, like God, they can look selflessly even on their enemies. It makes them doers of concrete actions concerned foremost with grasping the situation and meeting the needs of others they affect. It is a relationship that would be so radical in its fulfillment that fullness never has been experienced.[273]

---

[272] Lisa Sowle Cahill, *Love Your Enemies – Discipleship, Pacifism, and Just War Theory,* (Minneapolis: Fortress Press, 1994), 15.
[273] Lisa Cahill, 29.

The Sermon on the Mount provided the constitution for Jesus' kingdom. One of the most important parts of that discourse was the prayer called the Lord's Prayer. In many ways it is the touchstone of worship and the entire Christian life. One of the important parts of the prayer is that it relates everything to the kingdom of God *on earth as in heaven.* This prayer stands as an embodiment of the Mosaic Covenant of Shalom. There is no question that the righteousness and freedom of God are honored and presented as the pattern for the lives of the disciples. The underlying principle, whether it be receiving daily bread as a direct reference to the gracious gift of God in giving manna in the desert or the forgiveness of trespasses or sins, is directly related to egalitarian principles – sharing with others and justice for others.

> The Lord's Prayer...falls into two parts: after the opening invocation, there are three petitions concerning God's glory, followed by those concerning our needs. The phrase on earth as it is in heaven (v. 10), belongs to each of the first three petitions.[274]

The Sermon on the Mount was in many ways a restatement of Jubilee principles, the way of shalom. Jesus' Sermon on the Plain recorded in Luke was an even stronger statement of these values.[275] Jesus took the difficulties of life and pronounced a benediction or blessing upon them as being the way in difficult circumstances of life in which the healing and redeeming love of God can be received.

> The phrases of the Beatitudes may well have reference to minority social position as well as to discipleship attitudes and thus fit well with the many sayings of Jesus (in the Sermon 6:19-21) about the dangers that

---

[274] The New Oxford Annotated Bible NRSV (NY: Oxford University Press, 1991), note 6:9-13, 8

[275] Matt. 5:1-7:27; Luke 6:17-49.

wealth and power present to the greater righteousness expected of the disciple.[276]

In Matthew's sermon, hierarchy, violence, and the lack of commitment to the ways of God are all absolutely rejected.

The Sermon on the Mount also affirmed the highest principles of their faith, embodying justice and shalom for their world. Jesus proclaimed that the reign of God was present now in righteousness that restores just relationships. The sermon paired principles of righteous conduct with concrete ways to practice those values. The necessity of a life of worship and prayer was upheld as the motivation for all activity. The sermon, like the rest of Jesus message, even contained some things that were difficult to comprehend, let alone practice, often called the "hard sayings".

The ideals of the kingdom do not demand or compel as rules from without. The joy and mercy of God's reign become present within the person and community, through the presence of Christ's Spirit. That which the "hard sayings" depict, then, is not only commended or possible, but real and inevitable.[277]

A significant part of the sermon was concrete instructions for life in a world of oppression that was neither passive acquiescence nor rebellious confrontation, but a third way of transformational initiative that affirmed human dignity. Peacemaking was the third way, the way of shalom, the way of the kingdom, the reign of God.[278]

---

[276] Lisa Cahill, Op. cit., 32.

[277] Ibid., 177.

[278] Matt. 5:21-48. Carol Cease Campbell, "Jesus' Third Way," *Herald,* vol. 149,7:12-15. Glen H. Stassen, *Just Peacemaking – Ten Practices For Abolishing War,* (Cleveland, OH: The Pilgrim Press, 1998), 42-46. Wink, 98-111. Kraybill, 194-196.

...if the ethics of the Sermon is an ethics of discipleship and forgiving love, then (1) the social dimensions of Christian action are integral but presuppose personal transformation; (2) there exists a profoundly serious bias against any act that violates a basic condition...of the well-being of one toward whom the Christian acts....These concerns converge in three claims: (1) God's reign is present in and only in those who, with Jesus, share God's special righteousness (5:45,48; 6:15); (2) the kingdom righteousness of forgiving love is given to those who wholeheartedly seek it, that is, who pray for it (6:33, 7:7-11); and (3) converted active discipleship presents itself to hearers of Jesus' words as a gift but also as entailing obligations for which each will be held responsible (5:22,29).[279]

The reign of God that Jesus proclaimed throughout the Gospels was precisely that alternative socioeconomic-spiritual order inculcated in the Law and the Prophets, epitomized in the Sabbath-Jubilee vision.[280]

On Earth as it is in Heaven

Jesus' preaching centered in the kingdom that while it was present in some ways among them, would await the fuller manifestation of the presence of God – "the not-having come and the having-come of the Rule of God".[281] "Jesus both proclaims that the kingdom is beginning and holds out the prospect of future judgment and completion of the kingdom by a decisive act of God."[282] The completion or perfection of the kingdom was to be by the grace of God

---

[279] Lisa Cahill, Op. cit., 37.
[280] Kinsler and Kinsler, 127.
[281] Yoder, Political, 109.
[282] Lisa Cahill, 17.

whose presence would be there as in the Hebraic teachings of Zion, the city of God.[283]

Jesus passionately wanted his followers to be engaged in living the kingdom in the present. For Jesus, the kingdom had a location – here on earth – and a time – now. The kingdom was not described as coming down from heaven, but rising from God's empowerment of the people.[284] The problem with Jesus' kingdom was not that it was too idealistic; it was just the opposite. It was present in Jesus calling for their openness to experience a new reality and then to take action.[285] "If the kingdom of God is read merely as a symbol, or a possibility of seeing things, the transforming power which Jesus claimed as of its very nature is overlooked."[286] The kingdom would not be perfect. The clear teaching of scripture is that God's kingdom would come by the will and power of God. The eternal call to the people of God was that they were to become co-workers with God for the sake of the kingdom.[287]

Like all those who had gone before, they were called to form community based on the compassion of a righteous God who wills that all his children have access to the things needed for life and opportunities to experience not only justice but also the possibility of an open future as the family of God.

---

[283] See chapter 8, "Zion" this work.
[284] Wink, 66-67.
[285] Stanley Hauerwas, *The Peaceable Kingdom – A Primer in Christian Ethics,* (Notre Dame, IN: University of Notre Dame Press, 1986), 113.
[286] Neusner and Chilton, 105.
[272] Perry B. Yoder, 131.

Chapter 16

The Jerusalem Christian Community

After Jesus

The early apostolic church, indeed the whole Christian movement, could be said to have been born at Pentecost. Pentecost, or the Feast of Weeks, was a Jewish celebration in thanksgiving for the early harvest. It was a time of exuberant, joyous praise to God.

The disciples were empowered while Jesus lived, but mostly because they were close to him. After his death, resurrection and ascension, they were bereft of all that they had known in close association with Jesus. Something dramatic was needed to transform them so that Jesus would continue to live within and among them – and it happened! The Holy Spirit came both as a mighty rushing wind with tongues of flame over the heads of people and also in the ability to speak languages previously unknown in order to share the good news of Christ with people who spoke those languages. Although its most powerful manifestation was on the day of the celebration, Pentecost was not only a one-time event, but was the continual presence of the Holy Spirit among them in ever-increasing ways that empowered and transformed them.

The Pentecost story describes by means of external symbolization the witnesses' internal transformation (Acts 2:1-4). The mighty wind and fire signal the presence of God (Exo. 19:18, 24:17; I Kings 18:38, 19:11-13). The essential work of this Spirit was in transforming eyewitnesses into "ministers of the word".[288]

The earliest church, called the sect of the Nazarenes, began in Jerusalem where the followers of Jesus gathered. They went to the temple daily to praise God, and the apostles also taught there (Acts 24:5). The church grew by establishing groups that began by meeting in the homes of the believers. These communities of faith, where the experience of the Holy Spirit was real, were essential to the spread of the gospel. The good news was available to transform everyone into witnesses for Jesus the Christ.

Hellenistic [Greek] moralists taught an ethics just as pure and far more coherent. Judaism was just as profound and far more ancient. The mystery religions offered a revelation just as transcendent and far more esoteric. The key to Christianity's success lies not in its teaching but in its experience of power. What distinguishes the movement is its claim to have actualized the "good news of God" to humans. What accounts for its spread is its ability to make the claim plausible, persuasive, and even present for others.[289]

Worship was the vehicle for this presence and power to be realized. This was where the memory of Jesus came alive, not only in the remembrance of his life but also in the very real way that he lived within them in their daily lives. The Hebraic Bible was always a part of worship as it was read and interpreted in the light of the teachings and ministry of Jesus. The important sacraments were baptism by immersion, the initiation of believers into the community,

---

[288] Luke T. Johnson, *The Writings Of The New Testament – In Interpretation,* (Philadelphia, PA: Fortress Press, 1986), 224.
[289] Ibid., 87.

and the Lord's Supper. In addition to their worship at the temple, they gathered as family for a common meal on the Lord's Day. Their meetings were marked by spiritual utterances in the form of prophecy or speaking in tongues. Prophecy was the word of the Lord to them, giving the community guidance and direction for their present life.

> The Christians...claimed a superior wisdom that came by way of revelation in the present from God and that was available by gift, not by study...The authority of Christian leaders and teachers did not rest, as with the rabbis, on age or education of the unbroken chain of tradition from the past...Authority for the Christians came immediately from God...and the voice of prophecy was alive in the community. The prayers of blessing shared by Christians with Judaism did not simply recall God's mercies of the distant past, in the hope of their renewal in the future. Christians gave thanks for God's present and continuing work among them, and prayed that what he had begun, God might complete in them.[290]

The ministry of Jesus was carried forward not only by the indwelling Holy Spirit within the lives of individual members of the community but also in the presence, power and authority of the apostles. The apostles who were the witnesses of the resurrection of Jesus the Christ exercised a predominant influence in shaping the early Christian community. Luke describes the apostles as continuing the work of Jesus – preaching, teaching, healing and baptizing.

Current understanding of this period of the Jerusalem church has been enlarged through information available from the Qumran scrolls, both in terms of the Jewish nature of the church and also common elements

---

[290] Op. cit., 95.

between the two groups. The separatist Essene religious community functioned between 150 B.C.E. and 70 C.E. mostly independent of outside social or religious influence. Their mission as a house or community of holiness was centered in the purity of their priesthood. Like the early Christians, they devoted themselves to *koinonia*, a Greek word meaning community, fellowship, participation or communion.[291] The Essenes exemplified this in being of one heart and mind in mutual fellowship and co-operation in communal decision-making. They were led by twelve men who had been set apart for this purpose. All men participated in the study of Torah and all ritual observances. The requirement for membership within this group was the offering of all resources and wealth to the community to be shared for the good of the group. Entrance into this community was voluntary, but the surrender of all material resources was not. Essenes believed that they alone were the people of God. They lived as family with communal meals that were described as being similar to Christian practices.

> The features of Essene tenets and practices...shed important light on passages of Acts that describe the early Jewish Christian church...one cannot prove from such points of contact that the early Jewish Christian church developed out of an exclusively Essene framework. The most that one can say is that the early Jewish Christian church was not without some influence from the Essenes. It is not unlikely...that among the "great number of priests" (Acts 6:7) who were converted some were Essene and provided the source of Essene influence.[292]

The coming of the Holy Spirit at Pentecost led to the fusion of principles of Jubilee with the vibrant freshness of

---

[291] McKim, 154.
[292] Fitzmeyer, 301-302.

the Holy Spirit among them. The word that describes their fellowship, *koinonia,* refers both to community among believers but also to the community of goods, "all things in common".[293] Sharing in the early church was not simply a one-time response to the spirit, it was the commitment to share in Jubilee, "the year of the Lord's favor," not only in worship, but also in the distribution of possessions so that all would have enough and that there would be no poor. This vision was clearly a fulfillment of the Mosiac Covenant of Shalom and Jubilee.[294] Not all possessions were surrendered, nor was there absolute equality, but they shared with each other and were unified in their belief and practice. They considered themselves alternate families or households, calling each other "brother or sister". Egalitarian church families even passed wealth among church family rather than the biological family of origin. The bond of the family was in the agape meal where all were invited.[295]

The question of possessions in the covenant community loomed large for the Jerusalem church. It is clear that they felt that the surrender of all earthly possessions was an important part of their commitment. "The demand to leave all earthly possessions was only normative for Jesus' followers; for the members of the church the willingness to part with possessions expressed by the community of goods was the norm."[296]

A prominent scholar has located the belief that one's property needed to be surrendered to the community of common goods to Greek thought and practice rather than to Hebraic sources.[297] Although the influence of Hellenism had been felt in Israel since before the establishment of the

---

[293] Acts 2:42-48. Kinsler and Kinsler, 142.
[294] Ibid., 142.
[295] Torjesen, 126-127.
[296] Johnson, *Possessions in Luke-Acts*, 130.
[297] Johnson, Writings, 62.

Essene community in Qumran, it is difficult to locate this practice in Greek philosophy since the Essene community consciously eschewed all foreign influence; for them, it would have been a reason *not* to do it.

The community of common goods has important precedent in Hebrew scripture. The miracle of manna in the desert was a part of their identity as well as other aspects of the Mosaic Covenant of Shalom described earlier in this work. In Deuteronomy, noting the legislation regarding the release of the land every seven years and also the duty of almsgiving, the author concludes, "Being without need therefore is a sign of God's blessing, a blessing of Israel on the land."[298] This was also a part of the ministry of both Jesus and John the Baptist who told their followers that they were to share their resources (Luke 3:11).

> Luke sees the sharing of all possessions as the natural corollary of life together. In perfect unity of mind and heart established by the Spirit, only a full sharing of good could function as an adequate expression of that interior oneness.[299]

If this practice had been rooted in Greek philosophy, it would have been likely that this cultural element would have come into Christian communities located in these gentile lands but there is no scriptural record of this.

Jewish Christians practiced the *voluntary* sharing of property at least for a short period of time. Luke records that the group was of one heart and soul. There was no private ownership of property, but all things were held in common; there was no need among them. It is not insignificant that at this time, there was great spiritual

---

[298] Ibid., 200.
[299] Johnson, Literary, Luke-Acts, 187.

power that was manifest among them, the time of spiritual refreshment spoken of by the prophets.

The apostles were in charge of many aspects of the early church. One of those ways was in the collection and disbursal of funds. Proceeds from the sale of property would be brought and laid at the feet of the apostles, symbolizing the authority of the apostles and also the submission of the people signifying their desire to live in unity within the community.

This is the context for the story of a couple from the community who sold their property and brought the proceeds to the church. Ananias and Sapphira decided to give themselves a financial "out" by reporting the amount that they gave as the total amount of the sale, not disclosing the amount that they had kept back as their secret funds. Clearly, they were not of one heart and mind in the community manifestation of spiritual unity. Their lie made a mockery of the dedication of others and was a direct challenge to the authority of the apostles. But the real injury was to the Holy Spirit, the source of blessing to the church. Ananias and Sapphira wanted the benefits of those who had sacrificed while keeping back financial security for themselves. The money was not the issue since all giving was voluntary, but their lie was of tremendous significance. Like Achan (Joshua 7:1) of old, their lie resulted in their death.

The story of Anaias and Sapphira is told in scripture because it was so contrary to the values of the community. Although their practice was not perfect, it is clear that the early Jerusalem church practiced Jubilee and the Mosaic Covenant of Shalom in their worship of God and egalitarian practices that provided the necessities for life and justice for the members of their community.

Chapter 17

The Church in Gentile Lands

By the time of Jesus, there were far more Jews living outside Palestine than within the confines of that state. Large numbers of Jews called the Diaspora (the dispersed) had lived outside the area of Palestine, at least initially for business and trade, for hundreds of years. The majority of those who left, although they might have made a pilgrimage to the temple in Jerusalem, were not tied to Jewish concepts of the promised land and the temple. Jews of the Disapora also had dealt with living as a religious minority in countries with a pluralism of religious belief and philosophy. Although they were a minority, at one time, fully ten per cent of the vast Roman Empire was Jewish.[300] A significant number of this population were called "Godfearers" – those who were not circumcised or did not observe the whole Torah but were believers in the God of the Jews and the high moral principles of that ancient religion.

Jews were able to retain their religious beliefs and way of life in the midst of different cultures with congregations of differing commitment to the religion. A major reason for this was that wherever they went, they established a synagogue. As a result, there was a network of synagogues, sometimes called "Houses of Prayer" scattered around the major cities of Mediterranean Sea.

The synagogues were the center for the maintenance of Jewish identity...as well as the steppingstone from

---

[300] Armstrong, History – God, 71.

which Christianity moved into the gentile world. Christianity inherited a long tradition of preaching and teaching and worship carried out in the midst of Greek culture...In the synagogue was read the Septuagint (i.e. Greek) version of Torah...The Septuagint...was the Bible of the Greek Diaspora and of the first Christians. It was the primary symbolic framework for the development of the specifically Christian self-understanding. The synagogue prepared for Christian evangelization by spreading through the gentile world an awareness of the peculiar exclusive Jewish monotheism, the high moral code of the Torah and the attractive claim to be God's people.[301]

Some of the very things that had made life in Palestine so difficult enabled the spread of Christianity. The Roman empire was experiencing a period of peace often called Pax Romana, that was marked by their freedom from major conflicts both internally and externally. There were good roads making travel relatively safe and rapid; this also enabled mail to be transported more efficiently. There was one universal language enabling preaching and teaching to be greatly facilitated to persons living within the Roman empire. Large urban areas were filled with a diverse population, many of whom were disaffected and looking for a new religion or philosophy among the many that were offered. The situation was far from ideal, but in this brief period, prior to the time of persecution that many Christians would later have to face, there were circumstances that initially enabled the message of Christianity to be heard.

Early Christian churches were seen as a movement within Judaism at first. This was particularly true of their form of worship. In the beginning of the movement, services consisted of the use of scripture, the Hebraic Bible (Old

---

[301] Johnson, Writings, 69.

Testament), songs, prayers, testimonies, and spiritual manifestations that were all based on Jewish tradition. The Hebrew Bible, including the Apocrypha – the books written after the Old Testament, had been translated into Greek about a century before the time of Christ and was in common usage. This was a tremendous aid to their worship and the spread of their faith. Their sermons or discourses were explanations of these scriptures. They studied scripture and even argued doctrinal points like Rabbis. But as time went on and people were converted from various cultures with various forms of worship, there were changes both in doctrine and practice.

Christianity had difficulties to overcome both externally and internally. Some of the external factors would later lead to persecution and martyrdom. From the beginning, Christianity was a very different religion that was not easily understood by the gentile pagan populace. The common perception was that this movement could be discounted because its members were only outcasts, slaves and women who were excitable and uneducated whose convictions certainly should not be taken seriously.

> The pagan perception of the first Christians was not totally inaccurate. These Christians did sing hymns to Christ as to a god (Phil. 2:6-11; Col. 1:1-15; Rev. 5:11-16). Some of them, at least, put their possessions into a community of goods (Acts 4:32-36) or generously contributed to the needs of other communities (Acts 11:27-30; Rom. 15:25-29). They did share common meals (Acts 2:42; I Cor. 11:18-34). They were stubborn in their convictions, even when persecuted (I Thess.2:14-3:10; II Cor. 11:23-29; Heb. 10:32-39). They expected to "live forever" (Rom. 6:23; Gal. 6:8;I Tim. 1:16; I John 5:11).[302]

---

[302] Ibid., 91-92.

There were also internal factors that created difficulty in the blending of people from groups that were normally antagonistic or who would never have come together to associate as equals. The religions appealed to women because its baptism formula stated that in Christ there was neither Jew nor Greek, bond nor free, or male nor female. All were one in Christ (Gal. 3:28). Pagans saw this people as compassionate in their care for the poor. But these differences with the main culture and its ways of social interaction also created problems. Baptism had not instantaneously changed them into a homogeneous loving family as the Body of Christ. Corinth was a case in point.

> In first-century Corinth the polarities between Jews and Greeks, slaves and free, rich and poor, men and women were more powerful than any that we face today. The body of Christ had to confront and overcome those polarities through the power of the Holy Spirit in the lives of all members...The grace of God in Christ is the same grace that God required of ancient tribes of Yahweh...Jubilee spirituality, which means that all God's people might have socioeconomic-spiritual fullness of life through sharing or solidarity.[303]

Like the church born in Jerusalem, the growth of the gentile church was enabled by the power of the Holy Spirit present among them as they worshipped. It is said that theirs was a Spirit Christology. Christology is a study of "the anointed one" sometimes called Messiah; Spirit Christology is a sense of the spiritual presence of Christ.[304] They sensed the active presence of Jesus' Spirit so vibrantly among them that the gifts of the Spirit both in corporate worship and also in their daily lives were a natural

---

[303] Kinsler and Kinsler, 145, 147.
[304] McKim, 48.

outgrowth. The loving presence of Jesus also made it possible for differences to be overcome through love. Because of this love, they became the body of Christ where Jesus Christ was their peace and the cornerstone of their belief (Eph. 2:14,17-20).

The letters of Paul identify Jubilee-Shalom principles but because they were in a different culture, the expression of beliefs and practices was not as clear as in the Jerusalem church. The central covenant concepts of God were manifest in Jesus Christ whose righteousness and compassion are evidenced through communal relationship of economic and political justice. The righteousness of God conveyed to humans through grace alone becomes the central motif of Pauline Christianity. The righteousness that comes to humans by the grace of God in faith is the product of that gift.[305]

Efforts toward economic and social justice were promoted in the early gentile church. The Roman letter echoes Jesus' teaching of the way of peace. Jesus and Paul acknowledged the human situation but also the grace of God that instructed persons to be reconciled. They were to love their enemies and work for justice without judgment of persons. Repentance on a continual basis was the essential personal and corporate preparation to do this work. They were to be bound together as a group.[306]

Paul was faithful to his Jewish heritage in his teachings that connected righteousness with justice, particularly evidenced in the care of the poor. Paul often asked that collections be taken up among those groups who were more affluent to be given to people in areas of great

---

[305] Marion L. Soards, *The Apostle Paul – An Introduction to his Writings and Teachings,* (Mahwah, NJ: Paulist Press, 1987), 165-168, 171. Book of Romans.

[306] Stassen, 56-57. Book of Romans.

need. The Macedonians were particularly commended because although they had little, they gave generously to help others. *They were able to do this because they first gave themselves to God.* When communities exercised care for each other, this was seen as a manifestation of the grace of God. Paul combined the concepts of gift, grace and blessing to teach them that the *very act of giving was a gift from God and the means of blessing both for the giver and receiver.*[307] They were told that Christ became poor for their sakes and that the miracle of manna was present for them. When they were asked to be generous in their alms or surrendering their possessions, it was in order that they might have greater treasure in heaven (I Cor. letter; II Cor. 8-9; Roman letter). In their life of discipleship,. they were also to manifest these principles.

> ...when the New Testament counsels people to abandon what they own, give their possessions as alms, be generous to their enemies, or cease defending their property rights, it is *in order that* they may do something else; find eternal life, have treasure in heaven, be the children of God, or enter the kingdom.[308]

The Mosaic Jubilee foundation was also further evidenced in Paul's discussion of the abuses of the Lord's Supper (I Cor. 11:23-26). The rich would arrive early and eat all the food so that there was nothing when poor workmen or slaves arrived. The poor not only experienced hunger and humiliation at the table of the Lord but also exclusion from this sacrament. Paul said that if they did not change their behavior, rather than the Lord's Supper being a means of spiritual empowerment, for them, it would be to their condemnation because of their treatment of the poor.

---

[307] Wheeler, 81.

[308] Ibid., 147.

Paul used Jubilee logic. Just as God had intervened in granting freedom to his people in slavery, it was unthinkable that they would practice debt extortion and slavery amongst themselves. The gift of God's grace expressed in manna was given freely for all. The people of Moses had been freed to create the alternate community of shalom with God. Paul connected not only the Jubilee vision, but also the sacrifice of Christ in his denunciation of this situation.[309] They were not to conform to the way of the world, but to pattern their lives after the reign of God's kingdom.

They patterned their lives on that kingdom as they perceived it, guided by what they knew of the teachings of Christ whose victory over death made all things possible. Their entire lives as communities of faith were based on the testimony of what Christ had done. They had freely received of the grace of God through Jesus Christ so sharing their resources was simply the way that they lived as Christians who had seen the vision of alternate community that was empowered and guided by the Holy Spirit.

Finally, it is the compelling power of the story of God's redemption in their own lives that sets Jesus' followers apart, and ground their sense of vocation as messengers and ministers of the good news of reconciliation through Christ. This conviction of distinctive mission, entrusted to them by God and supported by God's comprehensive care, gives force to the New Testament's exhortations to live out a distinctive life, embodying trust in God rather than in the protection afforded by worldly power and wealth.[310]

---

[309] Kinsler and Kinsler, 144-145.
[310] Wheeler, 148.

Chapter 18

The Vision of Shalom, Zion,

the Kingdom Changes

It has been said that the only constant is change; nothing endures except change. This would also be true of the sacred communal principle of being the people of God. There were profound changes in the vision of Jubilee Shalom that resulted both from the passage of time and also the circumstances of people in their world.

After the fall of Jerusalem, there was greatly increased persecution of both Jew and gentile communities that resulted in far more pervasive political pressure of the Christian churches to disavow any connection with Judaism. There had also been growing theological controversies that occurred because many pressing problems were not able to or just had not been resolved. The persistent problem of assimilation of converts to Christianity from diverse backgrounds with philosophies that were foreign to the Jewish roots of Christianity was also always a significant factor. Some of the theological changes made in adapting the gospel to a the very diverse body of Gentile believers struck at the heart of their former Hebraic beliefs, traditions and understandings of themselves as people of God.

Change also occurred because of the means of conveying the gospel, language itself. Jesus spoke Aramaic, a language related to Hebrew, but the documents of early Christianity were written in Greek. Words did not neatly transfer from one language to another since they described the understanding and experience of persons from diverse cultures and philosophies. For example, the Hebrew word, shalom, was very similar to the Greek word, eirene, but there were important differences as well. In addition to common meanings that dealt with well-being, the Hebraic meaning of shalom also included wholeness, harmony and balance. Greek philosophical dualism separated the superior spirit from the inferior bodily material existence. In the Hebraic sense, true thought or intention had to be wedded to appropriate action; thought was not complete or valid until it was actualized. Thus *righteousness and peace in the Hebraic sense meant doing the work of God's justice on earth* out of a heart attuned in praise to God. In the Greek sense, righteousness and peace were expressed in the life of the spirit, one's interior existence that was separated from material bodily existence. By using the Greek word, peace was spiritualized, rather than made concrete in activity in the cause of justice.

Life in a Greco-Roman world of dualism and the passage of time gave birth to other significant changes. By the end of the second century the distinct beginnings of *supersessionism*, the belief that Christ and the Christian church had replaced Israel as the chosen people of God, was being taught as biblical truth - although *the Bible does not in any way support this idea.*[311] The life of the spirit came to be affirmed over and *against* other aspects of life. The world of God's creation is no longer good. Their view was that the spirit was good, while the material world was evil. This was to be a persistent problem in the Christian church.[312] Faith was separated from action; "works" were seen in negative terms as the expression of an erroneous Jewish righteousness. *In the Hebraic Bible and more especially in the*

---

[311] Wilson, 88-90. Frymer-Kensky, et. al., 362, 358-368, 171-174.
[312] Wilson, 167, 174-178. Frymer-Kensky, et. al., 351-354.

teachings of Jesus, the two are not separated. The test of belief was always wedded to action.[313]

Over time, other changes were made. The location of both salvation and the kingdom was moved to a new address: heaven. Both ultimate salvation and the entrance into the kingdom of God would also occur at a new time, after death.[314] Justice was reserved for judgment after death in the punishment of an individual's deeds, not the activity that God's people were to be involved in on this earth, making the earth more just and righteous. Salvation was no longer communal, but individuals were to be saved based on the grace of God in Christ and also to a much lesser extent, on their exercise of personal acts of piety. *The Hebraic ideal of being a <u>people</u> mutually accountable for and to each other was lost.* The Mosaic Covenant of Shalom expressed in the wonder, beauty, joy, power, brilliance and compassion of Jesus called Christ who came to call us to the kingdom of God *on earth* was no more. This kingdom had been moved to heaven while life on the earth became the "vale of tears" to passively endure before being called to that heavenly abode.

These changes and other changes were made concrete with the conversion of Constantine, the Great, a Roman emperor who lived from 306-337 C.E..

With the conversion of the emperor Constantine…the Roman Empire took over from the church the role of God's providential agent in the world. Once Christianity became the religion of the empire…its success was linked to the success of the empire and preservation of the empire became the decisive criterion for ethical behavior….The church no longer saw the demonic as lodged in the empire, but in the

---

[313] Ibid., 182-185.
[314] Op. cit.., 178-182.

empire's enemies. Because society was now regarded as Christian, atonement became a highly individual transaction between the believer and God. The idea that the work of Christ involves the radical critique of society was largely abandoned.[315]

But the witness of scripture is clear. Our early brothers and sisters of the apostolic church understood that the gospel was both the message and the means, not of escape from this world to a heavenly realm, but to be enabled to work to make this world the place where the kingdom of God could be born, where all nations could come to worship and learn of his ways (Rev. 15:3-5). They did not understand eternal life as something reserved for the future, but as the quality of life that becomes transformed when persons come to know Christ (John 17:3).[316]

The first Christians clearly understood the concepts of the Mosaic Covenant of Shalom where the compassionate righteousness of God is the pattern for human relationships that are based on economic equity and justice. With the presence of the Holy Spirit, they lived these principles in their communal lives as the people of God.

The Holy Spirit that was present in the early church needs to be freed to call the contemporary church back to its task of proclaiming the compassionate righteousness of God. This righteousness needs to make Christ manifest in the world through their work on behalf of egalitarian access to the goods necessary for life and equal justice through the compassionate administration of power, sometimes called Jubilee, Zion or the Kingdom of God.

---

[315] Wink, Powers, 89-90.
[316] Ibid., 200.

Part III

Book of Mormon

Chapter 19

Some Considerations of the Book of Mormon's Influence on Early Restoration Concepts of Zion

Many authors have written about America's nineteenth century's revivalism, the formation of religious or secular communities, the Book of Mormon and the birth of the Restoration faith. Many of these ideas were a subject of vehement controversy and polarization from the very beginning, with very little middle ground for reasonable discourse. But no matter what position is taken, the work of Joseph Smith in the Restoration movement and the Book of Mormon cannot be easily dismissed or ignored.

All scholars generally agree that Smith became a remarkable, charismatic religious leader, and that the Book of Mormon as it flowed from his pen has taken its place among the world's most influential religious books.[317]

---

[317] Richard N. Ostling and Joan K. Ostling, *Mormon America – The Power and the Promise,* (New York: HarperSanFrancisco, 1999), 27.

Karen Armstrong has characterized the Book of Mormon as one of the most eloquent nineteenth century protests against the disparity of wealth and poverty, power and intellectual elitism that were extant at this time. In her view, this book functioned to bring tremendous hope with the ideals of democracy, equality and freedom of speech to the poor people on the American frontier.[318]

The Book of Mormon was an especially important factor prior to the actual birth or organization of the Restoration movement. Gunderson sees it in these terms.

> The Book of Mormon, more than any other factor, was the defining element in the establishment of the religious movement commonly known as Mormonism. Long before doctrine or organization, the focus of Joseph Smith Jr., and his close family and associates, was entirely on Joseph's sense of divine calling to procure and translate the plates and to publish the book.[319]

Some Restoration authors such as Richard Howard see the Book of Mormon as having a tremendous influence on the development of the Restoration faith in many ways. The coming forth of this book was seen as the *founding event* of the Restoration   movement. He outlines the following main themes in the Book of Mormon: America as the chosen land, the religious utopian ideal (Zion), a self-supporting lay ministry, the millennium and the gathering of the Jews, even seeing two Jerusalems including one for this continent, anti-secret society sentiment and a preference for democratic

---

[318] Karen Armstrong, *The Battle For God,* (New York: Knopf, 2000), 88-89.

[319] Robert A. Gunderson, "From Dust to the Dusty: The Rise and Pall of the Book of Mormon in the Life and Ministry of Joseph Smith Jr." *The John Witmer Historical Journal,* 2002, vol. 22, 75.

government. A powerful theme throughout the book was the distrust of wealth evidenced by reoccurring cycles of poverty with industriousness that brought prosperity, that brought about riches and pride followed by sinful, destructive behavior that brought poverty and the cycle would begin again.[320]

Vogel sees the message of the Book of Mormon as a protest against secret organizations while upholding the principles of strong centralized government where there is political and social equality. The themes he identifies are (1) a protest against secret organizations, (2) rejection against traditional forms of religious leadership, (3) concern for the loss of social and political equality and also (4) the fragmentation of centralized government. This summary examined both the time of King Mosiah and also the Golden Age of the Nephites as being times when a strong theocratic government ensured political and social equality for all.[321]

One of the most important things about the Book of Mormon was its clear vision of a righteous social order. It consistently upheld the ideal of groups with all things in common, although realizing that this vision was at best, very difficult to realize. Even in times of crushing poverty, the people of God shared their resources. Industriously working together enabled them to create prosperity and wealth. Most of the time, the periods of prosperity gave birth to a spirit of individualism rather than the consideration of the good of the community. This resulted in covetousness, pride and greed that became manifest in the separation of persons into classes, based on wealth or poverty. Extreme wealth for the few in the presence of the devastating poverty of the masses

---

[320] Richard P. Howard, *The Church Through the Years, Vol. 1* (Independence, MO: Herald Publishing House, 1992), 111-125.

[321] Dan Vogel, "Mormonism's Anti-Masonick Bible", *The John Witmer Historical Association Journal,* vol. 9, 1989, 24-26.

usually created civic unrest between the classes that was followed by war or the destruction of their society.

Joseph Smith spent more than two years translating or working on the manuscript of the Book of Mormon prior to the organization of the church. The principles of the Mosaic Covenant of Shalom – the righteousness of God as the focal point of all life and the guide for human conduct where relationships were characterized by equity in the distribution of power and the resources needful for life – was clearly present throughout the book in the mission, values and mores of the people. There can be no doubt that this communal principle evidenced throughout the Book of Mormon functioned as a birthright to the young church in its development of the idea of Zion.

Differences Between the Bible and the Book of Mormon in the Context of the Mosaic Covenant of Shalom and Zion

The similarities between the Bible and the Book of Mormon are both significant and numerous. But there are also important differences between the Mosaic Covenant of Shalom as expressed in the Old Testament and the vision of community in the Book of Mormon.[322] Although the tenets of the Mosaic Covenant of Shalom that would later add Davidic Zionic theology are present throughout the book,

---

[322] Sterling M. McMurrin, *The Theological Foundations of the Mormon Religion,* (Salt Lake City, UT: Signature Books, 2000). This book would not support LDS Mormon theology as being traditionally Christian. There are significant theological differences among other branches of Mormonism such as Community of Christ. Although the Book of Mormon comes from a Christian perspective, there are also differences within books of scripture, e.g. the Bible and the Doctrine and Covenants.

there are also some differences between later Restoration theology and the Book of Mormon. One of those differences is in the way that the term, Zion, is used.

Zion

There are two important considerations in regard to the word, Zion, that need to be understood. First, in the majority of instances, the Book of Mormon uses the word, Zion, in a common Judaic sense, often as another word for Jerusalem. I Nephi 3:187-189 pronounces blessing upon those who work for Zion in the future which could be understood as members of the church working for the return of Jews to form modern Israel, a common theme of the early church or the cause of Zion on this continent; both ideas were expressed in the Book of Mormon.[323] Second, the Restoration ideal of Zion that developed is not the traditional Christian concept of Zion. When Christians speak of Zion, it is usually in terms of "heaven" after death or in connection with the millennial reign of Christ. Sometimes it also means Jerusalem. Zion as an earthly community of righteousness is not normally thought to be a Christian interpretation. For most Christians, Zion is an image of heaven, while for Jews it is a metaphor for their whole ideal of life, Torah authority, the land of Israel, belonging to and being the people of God.[324] Reed Holmes summarizes various beliefs about Zion in this way.

> Historically, Zion is a place – Jerusalem. To some, Zion is a condition, a paradigm of the reign of God, the kingdom of heaven on earth. To others, Zion is neither a place nor a paradigm on earth but a

---

[323] Holmes, *Dreamers,* 35.
[324] McKim, 308. George A. Njeim, "Zion." Paul A. Wellington, ed., *Readings on the Concept of Zion,* (Independence, MO: Herald Publishing House, 1973), 71-72.

metaphor of a transcendent community, not of this world.[325]

The developing Restoration concept of Zion brought Hebraic concepts of communal rather than individual salvation to their ideal of the righteous society. Their understanding was that although God dealt with people on an individual basis in knowing them or answering prayer, God had always sought a people, not individuals or even a collection of persons, but a people, to make his will manifest in all aspects of their daily lives. This is a core principle that was espoused in the Book of Mormon.

Some Theological Considerations

Although the Book of Mormon could be thought of as having a part before the coming of Jesus Christ and another after his ministry that could be seen as similar to the Old and New Testaments, it is essential that the theology of these witnesses be considered before making this comparison. The theology of the Book of Mormon is Christian, although that term is not used until the time of Alma, from the vision of Lehi at the beginning of this witness through the entire book.[326] Unlike the Old Testament, there is almost no time when the prophecy of the coming Messiah is not known. While Hebrew prophets would have identified Messiah as an earthly king of the lineage and archetype of the heroic King David, the Book of Mormon would be clear in its language that Messiah would be Christ, the Son of God as presented in the New Testament.

---

[325] Reed M. Holmes, *Joseph Smith, Jr., and George J. Adams - Gentile Dreamers of Zion,*" (Ph.D. diss., University of Haifa, Israel, September, 1989), 3. Holmes, *Dreamers,* 2.
[326] I Nephi 3:4, Alma 21:43.

The witness of both the Old Testament and the New Testament / Book of Mormon is a vitally important source of Restoration theology. All parts of the canon have important insights to contribute. Both the Book of Mormon and the whole Bible contain necessary and vital truths. The Hebrew Bible (Old Testament) tends to use a "case law" approach, spelling out how principles are to be applied. For example, they were to treat the poor with consideration and dignity. In specific terms, this meant that wages must be paid to the poor on a daily basis, slaves must be freed at the end of seven years with ample provisions in order to begin a new life and food could not be withheld from anyone for any reason. On the other hand, the Book of Mormon tends to speak in more general terms but supports the principle that the poor are to be helped and that everyone is to be industrious in their labor, denouncing idleness. But inequity between persons - a disparity between wealth and poverty - is always seen as great sin on the part of those who have great resources that should have been shared with those in need.

In the New Testament, Jesus' first sermon announced Jubilee and almost resulted in his death.[327] The thread of Jubilee and the principles of the Mosaic Covenant of Shalom were at the heart of Jesus' message and ministry. The strongest statement of his kingdom theology was Matthew's Sermon on the Mount or the Lukan version, the Sermon on the Plain.[328] Both of these sermons outline how people could live as if the kingdom were present even in the midst of Roman oppression. The Book of Mormon also has these teachings with the addition of blessings for those who are humble and willing to be baptized.[329]

---

[327] Luke 4:18-19, 28-30; Isa. 61:1-2.

[328] Matthew 5:1-7:27; Luke 6:17-49.

[329] III Nephi 5:44-115.

The circumstances in the Book of Mormon were very different when Jesus began his ministry in the new world and thus, the story of the ministry of Jesus to the Jews, while having significant similarities, is also very different. In the opening chapters of the first writers, there was the idea of Messiah coming in the person of Jesus. There had been clear prophecies both of Jesus' birth and death; however, there were always those groups or individuals who did not believe in the coming Christ. The prophecies of his death were validated by cataclysmic disasters such as devastating earthquakes, storms and volcanoes, far greater than their world had ever known followed by three days of intense darkness. Many people had been killed in this dramatic fulfillment of prophecy. Thus the surviving people could not have been more ready to receive the ministry of Jesus, the resurrected Christ when he began his ministry with them.[330]

---

[330] III Nephi 1:1-28, 3:52-14:3.

Chapter 20

An Overview of the Text as
Seen Through the Lens of
the Mosaic Covenant of Shalom
The Approach - Narrative Theology

The approach to this scripture will be based on the tenets of narrative theology in *understanding* the text – that is *standing under the text.* The goal of this approach is not to impose various techniques of critical analysis but to allow the text to simply speak the powerful truths of the story that it tells.[331] Narrative theology presupposes dialogue with the text in which the reader becomes part of the story in the quest for greater understanding. The Book of Mormon speaks with power and eloquence, particularly in this context, in the telling of its story.

The Mosaic Covenant of Shalom – the righteousness of God as the focus of worship and praise and also as the model of our conduct in relationships between persons that are based on equity of access to the resources needed for life and justice – will be the lens through which we view the teachings of the Book of Mormon.

---

[331] Andrew Bolton, "The Book of Mormon: An Asset or Liability for Becoming a Peace Church?" *The John Witmer Journal,* 19:30-32.
Anthony Chvala-Smith, The Spirit, The Book, and The City: Retrieving the Distinctive Voice of the Restoration", *The John Witmer Historical Journal,* 19:25.

The Righteousness of God and the Human Response of Sanctification or Discipleship

The first principle is the righteousness of God as a focus for worship and also as a model for human conduct. The first examples of this principle are on the personal level. An example of the righteousness of God as a focus for worship and human conduct is Nephi's Psalm.[332] The author begins by praising God particularly for the scriptures, "my soul delights in scriptures...and in the things of the Lord". Then he recognizes his human failings at the same time seeing the ways that God has been manifest in his life in a multitude of blessings and experiences with the Holy Spirit. This moves him to a position of simple trust because he has had significant experience in coming to understand God, "I *know* in whom I have trusted". The author has confidence in coming before the Lord, the rock or foundation of his salvation and asks that he be encircled with the robe of the righteousness of God. Throughout this scripture, sublime experience with the divine is shared.

Another author also extols the importance of scripture, or food for the soul, as being of equal importance to food for the body. The people are encouraged to "feast on the words of Christ" and live in faithful expectation that God will bless the individual's desire for the indwelling Holy Spirit with the manifestation of the fruits and gifts of that Spirit. The role of the Holy Spirit in giving guidance is emphasized as directing the path of the believer.[333] It is never enough just to know the right things to do, obedience is at the heart of the life of the person or community that would come to know God.

---

[332] II Nephi 3:29-66.
[333] II Nephi 13:24-14:12.

Fasting and prayer, humility and repentance are continually emphasized. Fasting is often paired with prayer as complete focus of the whole person. Humility of spirit is essential and produces joy.[334] Many scriptures stress the importance of repentance, not just as a one-time or rare occurrence, but as a way of life. Enos prayed continually to be forgiven; when this happened he felt a deep concern and desire for the welfare of others.[335] Prayer is not complete until it produces change in the individual, being willing and ready to listen to what God would have them do.[336]

The importance of both personal and corporate worship is continually emphasized. An example of the worship of God is Jacob's hymn to the greatness, mercy and holiness of God who will come into the world to save mankind.[337] Alma is so filled with the ecstatic spirit of praise and thanks to God that his heart overflows, "brimming with joy".[338]

> ...let us glory in the Lord; we will rejoice for our joy is full; we will praise our God forever. Behold who can glory too much in the Lord? Who can say too much of his great power, and of his mercy, and of his long-suffering toward the children of men? Behold, I say to you, I cannot say the smallest part of which I feel.[339]

Although the term, sanctification, is not always used, the clear intention is that as persons begin to understand the love, mercy, righteousness, beauty and joy of God, they will know that they must also grow in these attributes. In the

---

[334] I Nephi 5:4.
[335] Enos 1:1-12.
[336] Alma 16:218-228.
[337] II Nephi 4:43ff.
[338] Alma 14:96-97.
[339] Alma 14:96-97.

Book of Helaman, there is the story of very poor people who were being continually harassed and persecuted by the rich elite of the church.[340] The poor people prayed and fasted and became stronger in their humility and ever more firm in their faith in Christ, many years before his ministry with them, so that their whole souls were filled with joy and consolation of the Holy Spirit. Their hearts became pure and sanctified because they continually yielded themselves to God. The very last part of the Book of Mormon contains the invitation to come to Christ and be perfected, loving God with one's whole soul, which is the goal of sanctification in Christ.[341]

Sanctification was not just a matter of individual piety or even personal righteousness; individuals were always inseparably linked to a community of faith. One's personal relationship with God was always important but it had to be lived out in community in order for it to be authentic. There are instances of leaders who prayed mightily for their people coupled with many who risked their lives to bring the gospel's good news to those who warred against them. Nephi said that he prayed continually for his people by day and at night his tears watered his pillow in his hopes and desires for his people.[342] Much later, another man also named Nephi, prayed all day that his people would not be destroyed for their faith in Christ. He received a wonderful message of encouragement, peace and assurance that the promised sign of Christ's birth would soon be given and the people sparred.[343]

The Book of Mormon is like the Bible in providing witness that some persons responded positively to God while others chose not to be involved. But for those who knew

---

[340] Helaman 2:31.
[341] Moroni 10:29ff.
[342] II Nephi 15:4.
[343] III Nephi 1:9-11.

God, there is no question that the righteousness of God was not only the focal point of their worship but also the model for their conduct.

Equity in the Distribution of Goods Necessary for Life and the Exercise of Power for Justice

The second part of the Mosaic Covenant of Shalom is the axis connection for the distribution of goods needed for life while the third component is the equitable distribution of power, seen as justice, that enables a relatively equal or egalitarian society to exist. This is where the Book of Mormon absolutely shines in its unfailing testimony that *the people of God are to be one, not divided by wealth, education, priesthood or any other sources of dominance and power.*

Although there seems to be no direct evidence of specific Jubilary practices – the provisions of the seventh or Sabbatical year and after seven cycles, the year of the Lord called Jubilee – that were to ensure the Mosaic Covenant of Shalom, there can be no doubt that they deeply understood the manna principle even if their practice was at times imperfect. The manna principle exemplified that everyone was to have the things needful for life and that God was the source of all good gifts. Like their Jewish brethren, they knew that everything belonged to God and that humans are stewards over these blessings of God.

"For behold, *are we not all beggars? Do we not depend upon the same being, even God, for all we have?*"[344] Like the Hebraic Testament's reminder that once they were slaves, these verses declare the reality of the human situation and also the folly of dependence upon riches or human

---

[344] Mosiah 2:32.

power. These powerfully spiritual verses also outline the justice of God in the condemnation of those who judge the poor as unworthy and withhold their support of them, thinking that the poor have brought their misery upon themselves. The people of God are to help others, not judge them. This scripture states in the strongest possible terms that there is absolutely no excuse for failing to help the poor and vulnerable. Like the message of the prophets and Jesus, the condemnation of those who fail to help the poor is certain.[345]

The value and importance of work was consistently upheld. Blessings would come to the people who were creative, industrious and willing to work.[346] The king also worked to support himself and stated that when we serve others, this is the way that we truly serve God.[347]

Obedience to the commandments of God coupled with industriousness in labor usually produced prosperity. It is important to note that wealth was not universally condemned but wealth could be a source of spiritual danger.[348] Everything depended on the hearts of people and how wealth was used. They were to always remember that they were all brothers and sisters together and lovingly share their resources accordingly. They were to first of all seek for the kingdom of God with all their might until they had received a hope in Christ that permeated their entire being. After their hearts were converted, they were to use their intellect and skills to seek for riches with the intent to use their resources to do good by clothing the naked, feeding the hungry, liberating the captive, and administering relief to the sick and afflicted.[349]

---

[345] Mosiah 2:13-50
[346] Jarom 1:19; Ether 4:78.
[347] Mosiah 1:48-50.
[348] Helaman 5:29.
[349] Jacob 2:22-24.

Long before Christ came, sharing with the less fortunate was both for one's personal spiritual practice and also for their churches.[350] Two churches were compared. One was a church where the abundance of God was celebrated in sharing with others in the spirit of joy and love while the other was a church of selfishness where the spirit of God could not dwell.[351]

The goal was that people would have the things that were needed, enough for their need, but not for their greed. This meant that those who had more were to share with the less fortunate. Great inequality between people was seen simply as the result of sin, selfishness and greed on the part of those who had more but did not share with the poor.[352] Pride was often at the root of sin and was a great hindrance to a sense of community that in turn resulted in classism and the persecution of the poor. When the people obeyed the commandments of God, there was relative equality among them. Everyone shared and attended to each other's needs and there was peace and abundance. They were industrious and did not have the desire for costly apparel that would set persons far above others. Their efforts resulted in great prosperity. This prosperity gave them more to share with all, not just "the church", because they had not set their hearts on personal riches but they first sought the righteousness of God.[353]

Other iniquities such as the lack of opportunity for education could also result in poverty and inequality. This made it important for those who had opportunity for learning to couple this with humility and listening to the

---

[350] Mosiah 9:51-64.
[351] Alma 1:37-49; Alma 2:17-22.
[352] Alma 15:50.
[353] Alma 1:33-48. See also II Nephi 11:90-99; II Nephi 12:16; Alma 2:19-22; Helaman 2:44-46.

voice of God; otherwise it could result in division and classism among the people.[354]

Questions of justice were constantly addressed. One of those concerns was the importance of the family and right social relationships. Most of the Book of Mormon is a comparison between "the good guys" and "the bad guys" – Nephites and Lamanites. During one shocking and condemning discourse, the people were told that their non-churched enemies were more righteous than they – the law-abiding church folk. This was so because the "supposed" good guys had not respected their marriage covenant and brought deep sorrow to their families because of their behavior while their enemies had good and secure families because of their right conduct with respect to their wife and children.[355] God would not be mocked by a show of piety nor were there to be family secrets that were destructive of family relationships. This scripture clearly supports monogamous marriage and the importance of the family, clearly standing in opposition to dehumanizing systems like polygamy (Jacob 2:33,35; Mosiah 7:3).

There are stories that deal with the themes of pacifism or military service. One group of Lamanites in particular had spent their lives in the most wild and egregious warfare against the Nephites. With lots of faith and prayer, they were converted by the Nephites and buried all of their weapons. They ultimately became martyrs for peace, allowing themselves to be killed rather than taking up arms again. Their testimony caused many other Lamanites to be converted to Christ.[356] There are additional powerful stories of those who sought to defend their homes, land and way of life and how they were blessed in their endeavors.[357]

---

[354] II Nephi 6:61.
[355] Jacob 3:50-63.
[356] Alma 14:9-54, 20:9-13.
[357] Alma 21:131-139.

Chapter 21

The Ministry of Jesus and the Golden Age

The Book of Mormon account of the ministry of Jesus is sublime (III Nephi 4:41-14:3). Unlike the gospels, the Book of Mormon account of the ministry of Jesus is marked by the lack of disbelief and controversy. The people of God, both Nephite and Lamanite, knew from the beginning that he was the Christ. The accounts of his teaching, preaching and healing after his resurrection were blessed by the powerful ministrations of angels and were also accompanied by mighty miracles. The ministry of Jesus and the period afterward is the culmination of the entire Book of Mormon. The 12th chapter of III Nephi begins by saying that the record does not contain even a hundredth part of the things Jesus taught. The III Nephi record closes the account of Jesus' ministry by saying that they were not permitted to write further things that were said and done. It is unfortunate that these things could not be written and known.

One of the things that *is* known from the scriptural record is that the power of these experiences with the living Christ transformed them and their community. An example of this is Jesus' blessing of the children. There was first the experience of rich, deeply spiritual prayer and then Jesus and the children were encircled with holy fire as angels were seen coming down from the sky and ministering to the children.[358] As these children, who had been so wonderfully blessed by Jesus and the angels, matured they were an important part of those who were enabled and empowered to form righteous community that carried on the ministry of Jesus after he left. These people, not only the children who experienced such a wonderful blessing but also the many that Jesus taught and healed, were transformed by the ministry of Jesus that enabled them to become powerful witnesses and carry on his work in important ways.

Surely, there could not be a happier people

The period after Jesus returned to heaven is often referred to as "the Golden Age of the Nephites". It was a time of wondrous joy and peace that extended for more than two hundred years where personal and communal life reached its zenith. This time was based upon the foundation of the wonderful ministry of Jesus among them and also the testimony of those who shared this experience.

After the ministry of Jesus there was equality among the people and great happiness with the vivid presence of the Holy Spirit with them. In this wonderful period that followed the ministry of Christ, they put into practice the things Jesus had taught them. They formed churches and all people were baptized. Not only had they received the Holy Spirit but they found ways to share and further the work by the process of conversion and identification, mentoring and training leaders to carry on the work after that first community was gone.

They were faithful in their worship of God both by their diligence in meeting together for worship and also in their personal lives marked by prayer and fasting. There

---

[358] III Nephi 8:23-26.

156

were no poor because they had all goods in common; this meant that there was also no crime. This is the manna principle where the resources of the community are made available to the people of the community. They extended this principle to spiritual aspects as well with everyone being made free and a partaker of the heavenly gifts. The spiritual gifts of all were honored and a blessing to the community. These people were intelligent, creative and industrious because they did not look at the wealth their labors produced as exclusively theirs, but as a means to bless the community.

They had no contention because they were humble and willing to resolve conflicts peacefully. It is not stated that there were never disagreements, but their commitment to be communities of love came first and ways were found to reconcile differences.

In such an atmosphere, their gifts of faith enabled many blessings of healings and miracles. They knew that the Holy Spirit was present among them. They knew that the spiritual gifts were part of the ministry of Jesus so it was their expectation that they would be blessed: the sick were healed, those who died before their time were raised, the lame walked, the blind could see, the deaf heard and all manner of miracles were performed. Everything they did was in the name of Christ and they were the recipient of many promises of God being fulfilled among them.

The blessings of God were extended to their personal health and well-being. They were healthy and strong people who were delightsome to God. Their community was stable and happy because they were faithful to their marriage covenant, and their families produced healthy secure children that lived the peace of God, shalom.

They lived under the banner of LOVE for God and Christ, each other and the created world. Thus, envy, strife, tumults, impure sexual relationships, lies, and murder had no place among them.

They also became prosperous and built cities and expanded their learning in many ways. Prosperity had not been their motivation but was the natural by-product of their way of life.

And surely there could not have be a happier people among all the people who had been created by the hand of God.[359]

After more than two hundred years of this peace, the same internal factors that had destroyed communities before them were able to gain entrance into their lives. Their prosperity resulted in pride with some wearing fine clothing and having the best of everything, while others began to suffer poverty. Communal things began to be controlled and finally completely privately owned, depriving others of access. They were divided into classes. Some of their churches were committed to Christ while others were against the teachings of Jesus. Secret organizations began to be formed, usually with destructive purposes.

There were also external factors that weakened them. Persecution arose and although they continually were "smitten" by enemies and those who would seek to destroy their way of life, for a significant period of time, they did not retaliate.[360] But because they had not maintained their community by spiritual vigilance, the same forces of greed, pride, and secrecy that had been so destructive in earlier times of spiritual empowerment increasingly became more prevalent against them.

---

[359] IV Nephi 1:1-28.
[360] IV Nephi.

Gradually, bit-by-bit and piece-by-piece they abandoned the vision of God for a righteous community, adopting instead a society based on classism, scarcity for the poor and abundance for the rich. Thus began the pattern of their destruction that followed and eventually resulted in their complete annihilation.

The Book of Mormon stands as a witness to the power of God that is present when individuals are willing to be transformed and live out the principles of shalom – Zion, the Kingdom of God – in their daily lives where the righteousness of God is the pattern of personal and corporate conduct and relationships are marked by equity in the distribution of goods necessary for life and in the exercise of power that enables justice for all life. The witness of the Book of Mormon's two hundred-year time of peace is that Zion is possible when people desire to live in righteousness.

Part IV

Historical and Theological Foundations of Zion of Community of Christ

Chapter 22

The Dream of Zion,

the Peaceable Kingdom

The dream of a beautiful holy city, of a place where the God of Israel reigned has been on the hearts and lips of people throughout the pages of scripture.[361] This dream has inspired people from the very beginning of Judeo-Christian history to this time. For many Christians, this was a dream of a heavenly beautiful city; for others, the dream was of an earthly place where people treated each other with justice and none was denied access to those things necessary for life because the righteousness of God was upheld as the model for human behavior.[362] The people would be of one heart and one mind, living in righteousness with no poor among

---

[361] Ps. 46:4, Ps. 48:1,8, Ps. 87:3, Isa. 65:17-25, Isa. 66:22, Heb. 11-12, Rev. 3:12 and Rev. 21.
[362] Micah 4:4; Zech. 3:10.

them.[363] For some, the heavenly dream was based on individual salvation. For others, although personal response to God was essential, their scriptural understanding was that God sought a *people*, a covenant community, living "the kingdom" that Jesus preached in their everyday lives.

The dream of that community has been elusive at best, always seeming to be just beyond the grasp of its hardy pioneers and yet there are records of persons who lived out the Mosaic Covenant of Shalom: the righteousness of God as focal point of worship and guide for human conduct with relationships characterized by equity in the distribution of power and resources necessary for life within the community. Although the dream of a just and equitable society is by no means confined to the Judeo-Christian faith, the focus of this part will be how a specific Christian community of faith struggled to create a just society built on the New Testament record of the apostolic Church in the new frontier of America.[364] They called these communities Zion.

This is a story of a group of people who were captured by their dream of Zion – for whom it became part of their corporate DNA, the organizing principle of the very life of each cell in the body. It is a witness to their heroic dreams and efforts to fulfill those dreams, of their hopes and fears born of almost relentless persecution, of sublime spiritual heights and struggles with individual and corporate sin, of boldness in their proclamation of God and also of their naivete, sorrows, mistakes and defeats. It is also a testament of their seemingly indomitable courage to persevere that arose from their powerful testimony that God had called them and was present among them in their continuing efforts to establish conditions ready for God to

---

[363] *Doctrine and Covenants*, 36:2h,
[364] Acts 2:44-47, 4:32-33.

bring Zion upon the earth. It was a dream for which some gave their lives and many repeatedly gave their assets in communities of "all things in common". None of these efforts to establish the Zion of their hopes and dreams was successful on a large scale or for long periods of time. Although these people experienced great loss, disappointment, and disillusionment that took some from the church, still the dream of Zion did not die. That dream was altered and revised through the years, but deeply within the hearts and minds of many people the dream of Zion still beckoned.

At the same time, in a post-modern western world awash in secularism, the dream of Zion is precariously dependent upon knowledge of that heritage and scripture that calls persons to this cause. The story of Zion does not resonate well in today's world of individualism, materialism, and continually increasing lack of concern for the poor and vulnerable. In a consumer-driven market economy with ever increasing disparity between the very rich and disparately poor, taking care of yourself - number one – is the primary goal. Many persons live in relative ease and safety but are constantly beset by fears for personal safety and driven by the desire to always accumulate more. Increasing privatization of former community responsibilities to care for its citizens, personal arsenals of firearms and "gated communities" are thought to provide insulation and security. In this atmosphere, for many, "community" has been reduced to television or the internet.

These values stand in stark contrast to the scriptural call to care for "the least of these". So it is to this time that the call of Zion must be heard. Today the world needs not just the *dream* of Zion, but its *manifestation* in community, the word must be made flesh and dwell among people. This dream needs to be given new birth and made relevant to the contemporary world.[365]

Zion, an important doctrine of the church that came to be known as Community of Christ, will be explored in terms of history and theology using the Mosaic Covenant of Shalom as the lens through which to view and assess this information.[366] Although there was effort toward the development of a systematic theology in the earliest days of the church, particularly in the education of the priesthood, this exploration was primarily pastoral or experiential theology as people struggled to understand not only what God had done through the pages of scripture but also what God was presently doing among them.[367] The early heritage of the church will receive the greatest attention, not only as the foundational base of the movement but also because of their persistence in the initial efforts to establish Zion.

---

[365] Sider, *Just Generosity, A New Vision,* 220. Hall, *The Steward – A Biblical Symbol,* 69. Meeks, 11-12. Thompson, 179-204.

[366] Other references to this movement include: Church of Jesus Christ, Church of Jesus Christ of Latter Day Saints, Mormon, Reorganized Church of Jesus Christ of Latter Day Saints or the Restoration

[367] Surviving examples include Parley P. Pratt, *A Voice Of Warning And Instruction To All People – The Faith and Doctrine of the Church of Jesus Christ of Latter Day Saints,* (Liverpool, England: F. D. Richards, 1854, reprint of earlier 1837), Parley P. Pratt, *Key To The Science Of Theology: Designed as an Introduction to the First Principle of Spiritual Philosophy; Religion: Law and Government; As Delivered By the Ancients, and as Restored in this Age, For the Final Development of Universal Peace, Truth and Knowledge,* (Liverpool, England: F. E. Richards, Publisher, 1855).

Chapter 23

The Setting – Important Influences to 1827

A thousand years prior to the Reformation, the doctrine of Supersessionism, the idea that the Christian Church had replaced Israel as the spiritual covenant people of God, was accepted as immutable fact.[368] The Jews were no longer the people of God and heirs of covenantal promises. During this time, the Catholic Church had also vested authority in its leaders to broadly interpret scripture or to develop whole new doctrinal understandings that had no foundation in the Bible. The Reformers rebelled against these ideas and enshrined the authority of the Bible, often with a new literalism; this was especially true in regard to the Old Testament prophets. Some of the followers of John Calvin in the Reform Movement came to understand prophetic statements about Israel and Zion literally with specific application to them.[369]

Communal life had been a characteristic of monastic groups within the Roman Catholic Church for many centuries. Now radical or reform Protestant congregations, such as the Anabaptists who defied threats of death by the Church in order to be baptized by immersion, began to form communities for freedom to worship according to the dictates of their conscience, commonly using the apostolic model of Acts 2 and 4. In addition to the Anabaptists were

---

[368] McKim, 273. Underwood identifies this as the Augustinian formulation of that doctrine. Grant Underwood, *The Millenarian World Of Early Mormonism,* (Chicago: University of Illinois Press, 1993), 63.

[369] Underwood, 63.

Familiests, Ranters, Quakers and Seekers. Some Seekers functioned within established churches, awaiting a time of greater spiritual truth and power, while others sought God apart from churches in their own experience.[370] "These groups believed in new revelations, the imminent appearance of Christ and the establishment of the New Jerusalem"[371]

The idea of religious communities spread not only to sects on the European continent but also to the new world in early groups such as the Puritans, Quakers and Unitarians.[372] Those who came to the new world did so not just for self-betterment, but also to be able to worship freely in community. They came with dreams of a regenerated society, with visions of America being a *new Zion*, "the city on the hill" in fulfillment of Old Testament prophecy.[373] John Winthrop, governor of the Massachusetts Bay Colony, referred to their glorious experiment as the New Jerusalem.[374] The communal impulse coupled with a growing sense of the dawning millennium was clearly an important factor in America that contributed to the divine sense of destiny felt by those first settlers - particularly in New England.

---

[370] Dan Vogel, *Seekers and the Advent of Mormonism* (Salt Lake City, UT: Signature Books, 1988), 2-3.

[371] Vogel, 3.

[372] Leonard J. Arrington, Feramorz Y. Fox, and Dean L. May, *Building The City Of God – Community and Cooperation Among the Mormons,* (Chicago: University of Illinois Press, 1992), 4.

[373] Examples include Isaiah 2:3, 33:20, 52:1, Micah 4:2 and Psalms 2:6 and 15:1.

[374] John Winthrop, "A Modell of Christian Charity, (1630)," *The American Intellectual Tradition, Vol. I 1630-1865,* ed. David A. Hollinger and Charles Capper, (NY: Oxford University Press, 1993), 7-16 and Samuel Willard, "Selection from A Compleat Body of Divinity (1688)," *The American Intellectual Tradition, Vol. I 1630-1865,* ed. David A. Hollinger and Charles Capper, ed. (NY:Oxford University Press, 1993),18-28.

In the nineteenth century on both sides of the Atlantic, there was a renaissance of what has been termed "New Testament Restorationism or Christian Primitivism" whose unifying force was in faith alone with "no creed but the Bible".[375] Christianity itself had begun as a restoration movement whose scripture was the Old Testament and claims were Judaic in nature. Mormonism would also begin as a radical restoration movement, reappropriating a Judeo-Christian past.[376]

The new world was an ideal place for newer religious ideas. From the seventeenth through the nineteenth centuries, there were more than 100,000 people who participated in communal ventures in several northern states.[377] Although their effort was to *simplify* theology by adopting the apostolic church model as they understood it, jettisoning centuries of Christian tradition, the result was a proliferation of doctrinal positions, not a unified New Testament faith. While there was not unity among these resulting sects, nevertheless in their appreciation of the scriptures, many groups saw the communal experience of the Apostolic church and the literal return of the Jews to Israel as important indicators not only of the spiritual presence of God, but also as immutable signs of the latter days.[378]

In the late eighteenth century, a movement called the Enlightenment also exerted great influence. Some of the ideas resulted in changes and dissatisfaction within existing churches while espousing belief in the *free agency of persons* and ethics as the chief aim of religion. An alternative

---

[375] Underwood, 90.

[376] Jan Shipps, *Mormonism – The Story of a New Religious Tradition,* (Chicago: University of Illinois Press, 1985), 68.

[377] Howard A. Snyder, *Models Of The Kingdom,* (Nashville, TN: Abingdon Press, 1976), 120.

[378] Ibid., 90.

approach was the primitive gospel movement that was a reaction against the dramatic revivals of Protestantism. Commonalities among the primitive gospel movement included: leadership by a man of limited training who was charismatic, a rejection of Calvinist election views, a belief in a communal, rather than only personal salvation, and belief in the second coming of Christ.[379]

Both millennialism and the great apocalypse were also important influences in established religions and these splinter groups. Millennialism was a unified world-view that dealt both with human history and also salvation seen in terms of the anticipated return of Christ. A movement would have been seen as millenarian if it believed that (1) salvation was collective for a faithful group, (2) terrestial - realized here on earth, (3) totally transforming the earth, (4) imminent – coming very soon, and (5) to be accomplished by divine intervention.[380] The great apocalypse was presented not just as hidden knowledge but also as the cataclysmic coming judgment of the world based on a literal interpretation of the Book of Revelations.[381] This was a tremendously powerful doctrine that would be felt in many ways.

The great apocalypse and coming judgment were powerful forces in the thinking of the eighteenth and nineteenth centuries. John Wesley's question to potential converts was "Do you desire to flee the wrath to come, to be saved from your sin?"[382] The Great Awakening relied heavily on this theme and came to the established denominations in a series of intense and frequent religious

---

[379] Leonard J. Arrington and Davis Bitton, *The Mormon Experience – A History of Latter-Day Saints* (NY: Alfred A. Knopf, 1979), 24-25.

[380] Underwood, 5.

[381] McKim, 14-15.

[382] Richard P. Heitzenrater, *Wesley And The People Called Methodists,* (Nashville, TN: Abingdon Press, 1995), 138.

revivals. Doctrinal distinctions of sponsoring churches often disappeared in the revival sawdust trail where the message was "hellfire and brimstone," intended to inspire fear and guilt with great moaning and weeping, while the person pleaded for a way to be saved.[383] It was not uncommon for persons to become "thunderstruck", falling to the earth in "strange fits".[384] Preachers used graphic terms, not only to cry repentance, but also to call the faithful to establish Zion in the wilderness.[385]

> "American Protestants...had long spoken of an American Zion, but they did so in the usual typological terms, never anticipating on their continent the actual presence of a glistening New Jerusalem."[386]

The World of Joseph Smith, Jr.

Persons are influenced by their environment, not only in terms of the collective traditions and moral attitudes of the larger geographical area, but also according to the value system and experiences of their family of origin. Joseph Smith, Jr. (1805-1844), the founding leader of the Restoration or Latter Day Saint movement, lived most of his young life in an area of northwestern New York that has been termed "the burned-over district" because of the deep spiritual hunger which seemed to be present.[387] This area tolerated a wider range of religious and social diversity and gave birth to many groups that practiced everything from

---

[383] Shipps, 57-58.   [384] Heitzenrater, 100.

[385] Milton Blackman, *American Religions And The Rise Of Mormonism*, (Salt Lake City, UT: Deseret Book Company, 1970), 237-238.

[386] Underwood, 176.

[387] Michael Barkum, *The Crucible Of The Millennium: The Burned-over District of New York in the 1840's, (*Syracuse, NY: Syracuse University Press, 1986) and Whitney R. Cross, *The Burned-over District: The Social and Intellectual History in Western New York, 1800-1850,* (Ithaca, NY: Cornell University Press, 1950).

varieties of vegetarian celibacy to millennialist communism whose common theme was the apocalypse.[388]

> Mormonism began in a cauldron of religious excitement....When in 1799 and 1800, the Second Great Awakening began to sweep the country, it struck a tinderbox in western New York.[389]

The influence of his parents and family life was also very important. His parents were examples of the two types of Seekers, a prominent religious movement in the area. His mother was attracted to the Presbyterian Church even though it did not conform to her image of the primitive church, while her husband chose not to be affiliated with a church until he found the one that in his mind was true.[390] Earlier in his life, Joseph Smith, Sr. had experienced a vision, being told that all existing churches were wrong.

Some conclusions that Shipps notes about the Smith family include the following: they were fascinated with religion, they knew the Bible well, Joseph Smith, Jr. probably had a vision or other non-rational experience in 1820 confirming his father's earlier experience not to join an existing church, and in the throes of revival excitement, he inquired about his first vision, resulting in a second vision in 1823.[391] Between the years 1823 and 1827, several critical spiritual experiences occurred including the knowledge of the existence of the Book of Mormon and his future role.[392]

---

[388] Jan Shipps, "The Prophet Puzzle: Suggestions Leading Toward a More Comprehensive Interpretation of Joseph Smith.," *The New Mormon History – Revisionist Essays on the Past* Salt Lake City, ed., D. Michael Quinn, (UT: Signature Books, 1992) and Vogel, 173.

[389] Cross, 3-13.

[390] Vogel, 8-25.

[391] Shipps, 61-62.

[392] "History of Joseph Smith," *Times and Seasons* vol. 3, no. 13 (May 2, 1842): 771-772. Oliver Cowdery and Joseph Smith, "Letter 8," *Latter Day Saints' Mesenger and Advocate* vol. 2, no. 1 (October 1835): 200.

Chapter 24

Church Organization and the Early Kirtland Period

Joseph Smith, Jr. was the first prophet and president of the church officially organized on April 6, 1830. In a period of only fourteen years, a church was organized, thousands of people were converted and communities were established to make concrete their belief in Zion as a contemporary expression of communal righteousness using the example of the apostolic church (Acts 4:32). It was a time of powerful spiritual experiences and insights that came to many people in the church but it was also a time of great devastation, disappointment and disillusionment. One dramatic event after another culminated in the assassination of Joseph Smith and his brother in 1844.

The first reference to Zion preceded the organization of the church. A revelatory message dated April 5, 1829 is the first time that the word Zion was used: "Keep my commandments, and *seek to bring forth and establish the cause of Zion*".[393] Further counsel was not to seek for riches, but for wisdom with the promise that the mysteries of God would be unfolded, which were the true riches of God. There is nothing to suggest that the idea of Zion was in any way clearly defined at this point, but the promise was that God

---

[393] The official record of revelatory messages for the church as a whole that are canonized is called the Doctrine and Covenants. *Doctrine and Covenants*, (Independence, MO: Herald Publishing House, 1992) 6:3a.

[394]Ibid., Section 6

would reward their search for this wisdom with unfolding truth.[394]

Another factor influencing the development of what came to be the church was more than two years that Smith had been spent working on or translating The Book of Mormon manuscript. This time was significant in the development of his understanding of ideas like the community of all things in common. The communal principle functioned as a birthright to the young church not only because of biblical references, but also because of the Book of Mormon.[395]

There were many concerns for the new movement but their strong foundational base was that God had initiated this movement by dramatic spiritual presence and would continue to guide them. This guidance was not only by the presence of the Holy Spirit in a general sense, but also by the direct, powerful encounter with God. From the beginning, the Saints gave enthusiastic testimony of spiritual gifts received like revelation, healing, vision, dreams, tongues and interpretation of tongues. For them, not only was scripture coming alive in the revelatory moment's understanding of the Bible but also in the encounter with divinity, illuminating additional insights.

Revelatory messages in the first year identified Zion in terms of "the *cause of Zion*;" establishing Zion was the *mission of the church*. As mission, Zion was both a goal and the process for attaining that end. Soon after the organization of the church, a vibrant hope of the second coming of the millennial reign of Christ based on a literal interpretation of biblical passages was wedded to the Hebraic communitarian ideal of the righteous community

---

[395] Howard, *Vol. I* 140. See also part III this book.

172

where the people of God could live in safety.[396] *The concept of Zion had been planted within the hearts and minds of the early church as part of the belief in the latter days.*

Zion and the Return of the Diaspora

As part of the message of the latter days, the return of the Jews to Palestine from their centuries of living as dispersed people, the Diaspora, had also begun to be a part of the preaching and teaching of the church. This would develop into a theology of two Jerusalems – one in Palestine and the other in the new world.

> He [Smith] believed that a renewed Israel and a church restored to its primal purpose shared a mandate to body forth in the organic structure of society the dream of the Kingdom of God. He called it the cause of Zion.[397]

> The Redemption of Zion has been in the hearts and on the lips of Latter Day Saints since the Restoration Movement was founded by Joseph Smith in 1830. "The cause of Zion," to use Smith's phrase, has been the primary focus from the beginning...It is the contention of this study that another dimension was of concern to Joseph Smith and his followers, the Redemption of Zion in the sense which has been primary in the estimation of the Jewish people during years of dispersion. This was the Redemption of Zion as the Return of the Jews from the Diaspora to the original place of Zion, Jerusalem.[398]

---

[396] Gary V. Smith, *Zionism: The Dream And The Reality, A Jewish Critique* (NY: Barnes and Noble, 1974), 66.
[397] Holmes, dissertation, iv.
[398] Ibid., viii-ix.

Smith believed that the restoration of the Jews to Israel was a part of the coming millennium.

> The expectation of Smith and the church was that the Jews would return to Jerusalem as Jews, to rebuild the Temple and to receive the Messiah. This expectation carried with it the conviction…that any converting would be between the Lord and his covenant people.[399]

He did not see this as the end of time or the destruction of the earth, but as a preparation for the glorious return of Christ. The vision for the righteous was glorious but quite another fate awaited those who rejected the gospel.[400] Nevertheless, a strong note of optimism was sounded in the earliest revelatory messages description of the "great and marvelous work" that was to come forth.[401] The *"great and marvelous work" that was about to come forth, the cause of Zion.* [402]

> Theologically central in Restoration cosmology, Zion was inextricably bound up in the Saints' millennial hope, for they also partook of the chiliastic fever of their times. And Zion, in its totality, had a role to play in the scenario of the Second Coming. In millennial chronology, Zion and its sister city Jerusalem had first to be built up: Zion established in the New Word, Jerusalem rebuilt in the Old….They saw themselves as recipients of the new dispensation. They were the latter-day chosen people, the

---

[399] Holmes, *Dreamers of Zion,* 38.

[400] Holmes, dissertation, v.

[401] Holmes, Dreamers, 166.

[402] *Doctrine and Covenants,* Section, 6:1a,10:1a, 11:1a and 12:1a.

[403] Elizabeth J. Higdon, "Eyes Single to the Glory: the History of the Heavenly City of Zion," in *Restoration Studies I – A Collection of Essays About the History, Beliefs, and Practices of the Reorganized Church of Jesus Christ of Latter Day Saints,* Barbara J. Higdon Ed.,

collectivity modeled on ancient Hebrew solidarity and vision.[403]

Zion had begun to take shape not only as mission and process but also as physical reality - a righteous people in a specific place living out the gospel in the ordinary events of their lives. Smith had been inspired to understand more of the meaning of Zion and had written (1830) what was to become one of the most important understandings of Zion. Zion was to be a condition of purity of the heart where people were of one heart and mind, living in righteousness with no poor among them.[404]

> Like other Restoration doctrines, the Zionic image did not spring full-blown but evolved organically. What evolved was not a single concept...Zion has a dual nature. It is at once both abstract and concrete, spiritual and physical, heavenly and worldly, until the totality of the concept reveals itself in Zion's cosmological and physical location at the intersection of man's earth and God's celestial kingdom.[405]

The beliefs about Zion that developed took the church further away from orthodox Christianity, even incorporating some Judaic beliefs. In the first place, the idea that God spoke to individuals was anathema, the most complete heresy, particularly among Protestants. Writing these insights was even worse; the canon had been closed with the Book of Revelation. "Understanding Joseph Smith will be facilitated if we see that his belief in an open canon of scripture is closer to the idea of the Living Torah than to customary Christian insistence on a closed canon."[406] Over a period of hundreds of years, Christians had also

Independence, MO: Herald Publishing House, 1980, 274-275.

[404] *Doctrine And Covenants:* Section 36:2h.

[405] Higdon, Op. cit., 270.

[406] Holmes, Dreamers xiv-xv.

175

reappropriated the Hebraic concept of Zion. For Christians, Zion was not an earthly city, but a heavenly one to be entered when we die or perhaps a metaphor of a transcendent community, not of this world.[407] It absolutely was not something that persons worked for lest they be guilty of "works righteousness" but would be a gift of God's grace for the faithful. Joseph's understandings were different.

> ...his concept of Zion was at odds with the prevailing Protestant notions of Zion and Jerusalem as the Church and not a city made with hands. Joseph echoed the Old Testament emphasis on Zion as a covenant people in tangible community.[408]

All things in common

The church of Joseph Smith, Jr., organized on April 6, 1830, soon drew into its midst a communitarian, Campbellite congregation led by Sidney Rigdon. In the initial months of the organization's life it successfully blended the doctrine of divine providence, the concept of restoring primitive Christianity, belief in a literal and earthly kingdom of God, and a specific communitarian endeavor mirroring the kind of social experimentation indigenous to Jacksonian America.[409]

Rigdon was a gifted leader, Bible scholar and fiery orator who strongly believed that these communities were

---

[407] George A. Njeim, "Zion", Paul A. Wellington, ed., *Readings on the Concept of Zion,* (Independence, MO: Herald Publishing House, 1973), 71-72. Reed Holmes, Dreamers, 2.
[408] Ibid., xv.
[409] W. Grant McMurray, "American Values for a "New Jerusalem": Formations of the First United Order of Enoch, 1860-71," *John Witmer Historical Association Journal,* Vol 8, 1988, 30.

the essential expression of the ancient Christian gospel.[410] He had established two "family" gatherings in the Kirtland area. These communities operated with *no ownership or private property* so "family" members were free to take things from each other as desired or needed. This was their understanding of the apostolic church's time of "all things in common."[411]

Communal religious groups were common. Many leaders in the new church were to come from religious movements that had some form of communal experience. They were based on Jacksonian communitarianism plus northeastern village democracy that valued a frugal lifestyle and honored the stewardship of the earth. The paradox of communitarianism and an authoritarian theocracy would be a source of conflict as the movement developed.[412] There were doctrinal differences such as Smith's with Rigdon on the issue of property ownership, but their common understanding included the formation of a community under God, sharing material goods and also banding together for security.

By 1831, a more definite understanding of Zion began to emerge including the designation of the place for the new Zion - Missouri, later to be further defined as Jackson County.[413] The "cause of Zion" thus became identified with a geographical place where Saints would colonize and attempt to build Zion. An essential part of their motivation was the promise and growing recognition of an endowment of spiritual power and the fruits of the spirit that would

---

[410] Richard S. Van Wagoner, *Sidney Rigdon – A Portrait Of Religious Excess* (Salt Lake City, UT: Signature Books, 1994), 73.

[411] Acts 2:44.

[412] McMurray, 33.

[413] *Doctrine and Covenants*, Section 52.

absolutely be necessary in order for their endeavors to be successful.[414]

The Law of Consecration

A fundamental component of Zion has always been stewardship that was understood as an individual and corporate lifestyle commitment to the revelation of Jesus Christ but this, too, has been an evolving concept whose practice was adjusted to circumstances.[415] The Law of Consecration, given to the church in 1831, was a "softening" of Rigdon's family system that had not allowed for any ownership of property and had many similarities to Shaker covenants.[416] The time was one of scarcity. Smith said that according to the divine economy of heaven, all persons were to be provided for according to their needs.[417] There is no evidence to indicate that he believed that this was the only or even the preferred economic system.[418] This plan was given to meet the circumstances present in terms of the larger goal of spiritual brotherhood and the encouragement of economic progress in order to create a surplus for the needy. The value of all work was upheld; there were to be no idlers in Zion.[419] The principles of this law were as follows:

1. All persons were equally *accountable* to God for economic resources and opportunities.

---

[414] I Cor. 12:9.

[415] . *Doctrine and Covenants,* Section 147:5.

[416] *Doctrine and Covenants*, 42.

[417] Ronald E. Romig, "The Law of Consecration: Antecedents and Practice at Kirtland, Ohio," in *Restoration Studies VI – A Collection of Essays About the History, Beliefs, and Practices of the Reorganized Church of Jesus Christ of Latter Day Saints,* Paul M. Edwards, Ed. (Independence, MO: Herald Publishing House, 1995), 191.

[418] Ronald E. and Anne L. Romig, *Stewardship Concepts And Practices – Studies in Restoration History,* (Independence, MO: Herald Publishing House, 1992), 8-9.

[419] Carter E. Grant, *The Kingdom Of God Restored* (Salt Lake City, UT: Deseret Book Co., 1955), 139-140.

Consecration of wealth was to be made to God in a lifelong covenant.

2. Consecration of surplus wealth would create a communal *storehouse for the poor.*

3. There was to be *relative equality* among consecrating stewards.

4. There was both *communal interdependence and individualism.* The community existed to help develop resources and talents in each person in a context of communal support.[420] [italics, author]

There would be no poor among them, if only they could find within themselves the charity and discipline to live up to the requirements of the new law. There is evidence that they tried diligently to implement the Law of Consecration, both at Kirtland and later in Independence, Missouri, where in a few months they would establish a new colony of the Restoration. Their lives were changed as a result, even though they did not fulfill their highest hopes.[421]

Eyewitness accounts state that although life in Kirtland was difficult, including internal problems, this was not of primary importance. The main issue was persistent external problems such as extreme poverty, complete economic boycott by the community, continual persecution, seventeen malicious lawsuits filed and acquitted, ever-present physical violence, destruction of property and death threats.[422] The problem with the Law of Consecration was not its practice among many dedicated members who saw this as their reenactment of the ancient church, but the fact that it was clearly at variance with civil law. The church was sued by a former member in regard to the Law of

---

[420] *Doctrine and Covenants,* 42.

[421] Howard, Vol. 1, 140.

[422] Karl Ricks Anderson, *Joseph Smith's Kirtland – Eyewitness Accounts* (Salt Lake City, UT: Deseret Book Company, 1989), 21-26.

Consecration and lost the case. Soon, groups of settlers left Kirtland to establish "Zion" in Independence, Missouri where some provisions of the Law of Consecration would be altered to make it more amenable to civil law.

> In both situations the general principle remained essentially the same: people are stewards over physical means entrusted to their care; their accountability is to God and to each other in community to seek the best possible good for each and all. The only thing that changed was the methodology that most responsibly might express the principle.[423]

Worth of Persons

One of the most cherished Restoration concepts was given voice at this time (1835), the worth of persons, the bedrock of the Hebraic faith and the teachings of Jesus.[424] Unlike many religions that emphasized doctrines of the depravity of humans, this revelation affirmed that the value of one human soul was so great that Christ willingly suffered humanity's pain, enabling all persons to come to him. Indeed, if the followers of Christ were to work all their lives and bring just one soul to Christ, their joy would be very great with that person in the kingdom of God. *Repentance would always be necessary for all of God's children, but the value of every person in the sight of God was inestimable.* This meant that the church was to honor that principle in all its relationships. This foundational belief has both inspired and challenged individuals and the church throughout its history.

---

[423] David Premoe, Ed., *Zion, The Growing Symbol – A Cases Study Approach on Images of Zion*, (Independence, MO: Herald Publishing House, 1980), 38.

[424] *Doctrine and Covenants* 16:3c-f. See pages 7-8, and footnotes 10-14 , Part I.

Chapter 25

Early Theological Considerations

Role of Joseph Smith

A discussion of theology during this early period is complicated at best. Theology can be defined in various ways, but if Anselm's general premise "faith seeking understanding" or the thoughtful reflection on experience with the divine is accepted, it can readily be seen that fourteen years of the most extreme crises with one-hundred thirteen canonized revelatory messages during the presidency of Joseph Smith, Jr. would not have been conducive to thoughtful reflection or the development of a systematic theology.[425]

The way that humans understand their encounter with God is always influenced by the circumstances of their lives both as individuals and corporately. The movement was young, not only in terms of the actual time since its inception, but also in terms of the age of the founding prophet and most of the leaders. Joseph was fourteen at the time of his first vision. When the church was organized, he was twenty-four; he was assassinated at the age of thirty-eight. Although he had great depth in primary religious experience and had knowledge of the Bible, he was not trained in theology or the basic doctrines of Christianity.

---

[425] This is according to the *Doctrine and Covenants*, the official canon of modern revelation. The process of creating canon is that revelation is received by the prophet but must be voted upon by the people in order for the message to be canonized or written as scripture in the *Doctrine and Covenants*.

Since both he and his father had spiritual manifestations indicating that existing churches had departed from the doctrine of the apostolic church, his theological stance was highly experiential (reliance on one's experience rather than external authority) and somewhat pastoral (an effort to mediate between the practical lives of people and the Word of God).[426]

For many people, the early church was centered in the person of Joseph Smith.[427] In the polity of a church with a Prophet/President, the character of that individual is very important. Some aspects of the temperament of Joseph Smith, Jr., particularly in these early years, are also significant to the understanding of the theology that developed in the early formative period. Howard lists three of his leadership characteristics that sometimes created tension, conflict and confusion within the church.

1. First was his capacity to see himself as human, capable of error and sin and his readiness to admit to such frailty to his own followers.
2. Second was his readiness to affirm the necessity of democratic process in church life and the expression of common consent. Specific inspired instruction to the church mandated this principle, as well as the creation of a unique priesthood system.
3. Third, Joseph believed deeply in his own (prophetic) credentials as a modern Moses.[428]

Draper lists the characteristics of a prophet in this way. They have an unusual sensitivity through the Holy Spirit to insights about such principles as love and justice and a sense of cosmic purpose in human life.

---

[426] McKim, 99, 203.
[427] Maurice L. Draper, "Prophets Are Human, Too," *John Witmer Historical Association Journal,* Vol. 11,7.
[428] Howard, Vol. 1, 86.

They have unusual courage in speaking about and living out these insights.

Their commitment to these insights enables them to give a high priority to their sense of call, the spirit of personal sacrifice, perhaps even to the point of martyrdom.[429]

The School of the Prophets 1833-1837

In 1832, the church received a commandment to engage in systematic comprehensive education accompanied by prayer and fasting.[430] To this end, the School of the Prophets was organized March 18, 1833 in Kirtland with an extensive curriculum including not only theology but also the Hebrew and Greek languages.[431] An effort was also made toward a systematic orderly arrangement of scripture in order to understand doctrine.[432] Another purpose of the school was to facilitate the development of ministers and their ministry within the church.

> In studying Hebrew in the temple, Joseph Smith believed he had erased the line of demarcation between the Hebrew Scriptures and the New Testament – and also the newest of scriptures, the Book of Mormon, and that which he was writing as new revelation. He saw past, present and future all within the time of the Promise.[433]

---

[429] Draper, 16.

[430] *Doctrine and Covenants* 85:21.

[431] President Joseph Smith and Apostle Heman C. Smith, *History Of The Church of Jesus Christ of Latter Day Saints,* Vol. 1 9th Edition, Lamoni, IA: Published by the Board of Publication of the Reorganized Church of Jesus Christ of Latter Day Saints, 1917, 282.

[432] Archival material includes Parley P. Pratt's *Faith and Doctrine, Principles of Spiritual Philosophy,* Joseph Smith, Jr., Oliver Cowdery, Sydney Rigdon and F. G. Williams's *Theology Lectures.* Original dates of publication were between 1835 to 1837.

[433] Holmes, Dreamers, 68.

Although, it is uncertain how the early Hebrew class fared, the later class taught by Rabbi Joshua Seixas is noted on several occasions in the time of building and the early occupation of the Kirtland Temple.[434]

They struggled to understand theology in comprehensive terms. Parley P. Pratt wrote the following definition of theology, reprinted from an earlier work:

1. Theology is the science of communication, or of correspondence, between God, angels, spirits, and men, by means of vision, dreams, interpretations, conversations, inspirations, of the spirit of prophecy and revelation.
2. It is the science by which worlds are organized, sustained, and directed and the elements controlled.
3. It is the science of knowledge and the key and power thereof...
4. It is the science of life – endless and eternal, by which the living are changed or translated, and the dead raised.
5. It is the science of faith, reformation and remission of sins, whereby a fallen race of mortals may be justified, cleansed and restored to the communion and fellowship of that Holy Spirit which is the light of the world and of every intelligence therein.
6. It is the science of spiritual gifts....
7. It is the science of all other sciences and useful arts...the very fountain from which they emanate. It includes philosophy, astronomy, history, mathematics, geography, languages, the science of letters; and blends the knowledge of all matters of fact...It includes all scientific discoveries and inventions, agriculture and the mechanical arts...All that is useful, great and good...originated by this

---

[434] J. Smith and H. Smith, Vol. 2, 20-22.

science alone, all other sciences being but branches
out of this – the root.[435]

The key to the science of Theology is the key of divine
revelation. Without this key, no man, no assemblage
of men ever did, or ever will know the Eternal Father
of Jesus Christ[436]

Early methods and materials for instruction included
a Catechism, the lesson and a series of questions and answers
to be memorized. An example of this is the *Theology
Lectures On The Doctrine of the Church of Latter Day Saints*
by Joseph Smith, Jr., Oliver Cowdery, Sidney Rigdon, and F.
G. Williams, 1835.[437] The purpose for this knowledge was
that the attributes of God could be known insofar as possible
so that the Saints in righteousness could offer praise and
glory to God. This worship would enable them to seek
further understanding pertaining to salvation until they had
a complete knowledge through revelation.[438] *It is important
to understand that worship was primary and foundational to
the study of theology.*

---

[435] The School of the Prophets was from 1833-1837. This was written for
the school. Most original printing plates and copies were destroyed in
mob action. A copy went with missionaries to England and was reprinted
there. Parley P. Pratt, *Key to the Science of Theology: Designed as An
Introduction to the First Principles of Spiritual Philosophy; Religion:
Law and Government; As Delivered By the Ancients, and as Restored in
this Age, For the Final Development of Universal Peace, Truth and
Knowledge,* (Liverpool, England, F. D. Richards Publisher, 1855), 1-2.
[436] Pratt, 27.
[437] Wilford C. Wood, ed., *Joseph Smith Begins His Work,* vol. II, Wilford
C. Wood, Publisher, 1962 (Certified photo copy of Joseph Smith, Jr.
Oliver Cowdery, Sydney Rigdon, and F. G. Williams, *Theology Lectures
On The Doctrine of the church of Latter Day Saints,* Kirtland, Ohio,
1835).
[438] Wood, 50-51.

During this period, there was a strong belief in essential Christian doctrines such as grace and salvation only through Jesus Christ.

> ...Mormon theology is set in the classical Christian framework defined by the fall of man in Adam and the atonement in Jesus Christ. But the Mormon character developed against a background of American dissent and rationalism. And above all it had its beginnings in an atmosphere of optimism that rejected the life-denying qualities of traditional Puritanism. The biblical literalism that fed it was characterized less by the negative theology of Paul than by the life affirmations of Jesus and the prophets. Inevitably it was a central task of the Mormon theologians to accommodate their liberal concept of man to the limitations imposed by the doctrines of the fall and the atonement that had for fifteen hundred years dominated Christian orthodoxy with a somewhat negative appraisal of man and his predicament. The history of Mormon theology, therefore, has been at many points a recasting of Pelagianism, Socinianism or Armininianism in a nineteenth-twentieth-century role where reason and theological subtleties have counted for less than common-sense insights, practical necessities, and dogmatic certainties. [439]

Mormonism has been described as being syncretic "never fully reconciling contradictory tenets and opposing organizational structures, but rather allowing extremes to balance each other."[440] McMurrin noted theological difficulties in the adoption of orthodox systems of Christology, the way that Jesus is understood, and

---

[439] McMurrin, 67.
[440] Vogel, 216.

soteriology, a study of salvation, while at the same time denying original sin's doctrine of the depravity of man. He noted that Mormonism's tendencies toward Pelagianism's doctrine that salvation comes not just by grace, but also by obedience to the law is yet another evidence of Hebraic influence.[441] For Restorationists, salvation was based on the gracious act of God toward humankind but human response was also a necessary part of the equation.

Mormon theology also included the willingness to live with *mystery* beyond human comprehension partly based on the expectation that God would continually reveal more light and truth. All the answers have not yet been given.

The culminating high point of this early period was the dedication of the Kirtland House of the Lord, sometimes called the Mormon Pentecost, on March 27, 1836. This edifice, later called a temple, had been built at great financial sacrifice and the whole endeavor was fraught with considerable and constant danger. But the saints believed that God had called them to this task and persevered. When the edifice was finished, they prepared themselves for the dedication of the House of the Lord. The awesome beauty, wonder and power of the spiritual gifts experienced by the congregation on the dedication day and also other occasions was attested to by hundreds of people. For many people, this edifice continues to play a significant role not only in terms of the Restoration heritage but also because of the continuing spiritual presence experienced within its walls.

---

[441] McMurrin, 74.

Chapter 26

Dilemmas of a Gathered People

The history of the early church was fraught with trials and problems. One problem had always been the influx of the massive numbers of people coming into a given area that completely overwhelmed and changed communities.[442] Not only did their neighbors have to deal with increasing numbers of Saints, they were communally-minded and actively participated in politics and could easily change the power structure. But this was not the only problem.

Often their value system was in conflict with prevailing community norms; examples of this include their acceptance of both Native Americans and Black people. An initial missionary effort to the Native Americans was, at best, not well received by their neighbors. A more critical issue involved their acceptance of former Africans as persons, not as slaves. The Saints had baptized and ordained black

---

[442] There were 15,000 Mormons located by percentage in the following counties: Jackson 57%, Daviess 70%, Caldwell, virtually 100% where there were 30 town sites, hundreds of homes, businesses. Wayne J. Lewis, *Mormon Land Ownership as a Factor Evaluation the Extent of Mormon Settlements and Influence in Missouri, 1831-1841,* MA Thesis, Brigham Young University, 1981, 72-72, 230. Roger D. Launius, "Alexander William Doniphan and the 1838 Mormon War in Missouri," *The John Witmer Historical Association Journal, Vol. 18, 1988, 63.* Launius reports the number of Mormons at 10,000 with 100 non-Mormons in the country but this population spilled over into other counties. . Michael S. Riggs, "The Economic Impact of Fort Leavenworth on Northwestern Missouri 1827-1838 and "Yet Another Reason for the Mormon War?" Joni Wilson and Ruth Ann Wood, Ed. *Restoration Studies VII,* 172. Economic opportunity to trade with the US government in the adjacent Indian lands in Kansas was an additional factor, 172.

members in Ohio as fully part of the worshiping community of faith.[443] In Missouri, slaves sold for as much as $500 – five times the price of a good horse.[444] According to the 1830 census of Jackson County, there were 193 slaves, and many farmers were looking forward to having slaves.

The Saints were never accepted by Gentile residents who regarded them as self-righteous zealots, abolitionists, and communitarians who laid claim to Jackson County as a land divinely chosen for them. The original settlers, on the other hand, were perceived by the Saints as irreligious, individualistic, and amoral. Neither conception was entirely correct; nonetheless, these differences precipitated a violent confrontation between the two groups in the summer and fall of 1833. This led to the forced expulsion of the Saints from their holdings and land to their exile from the county.[445]

The 1833 expulsion came about by a secret constitution signed by 80 prominent citizens of Jackson County who accused the Saints of "tampering" with slaves and "blasphemy", usually defined as expressing through speech or writing that which is contemptuous of God.[446] Church leaders were made to execute the decisions of the secret group under dire threat of violence. In 1836, the Missouri legislature designated Caldwell County as a permanent home for the Saints. Many church members had already consecrated all their assets and lost everything.[447] But again, they pooled resources and bought 250,000 acres of

---

[443] Howard, Vol. 1, 219.

[444] Ibid,, 152.

[445] Roger D. Launius, *Zion's Camp - Expedition to Missouri, 1834,* (Independence, MO: Herald Publishing House, 1984), 7.

[446] McKim, 31.

[447] Romig and Romig, 18-19.

land from the federal government.[448]   Twelve hundred members returned to Kirtland, Ohio, the headquarters of the church.

Communication was always slow and often unreliable. Various means of persecution had afflicted the church from the beginning; often it was severe. Sidney Rigdon almost died in an early beating and "tar and feathering" and suffered ill effects from that experience throughout his life. Many of the church members had endured similar incidents. Although the Saints could be faulted for being exclusionary, not establishing good relationships with their neighbors, nonetheless, they had not retaliated. When word came to Kirtland about the dire conditions in Missouri with the level of persecution greatly intensified, it was decided that further persecution would not be tolerated. Makeshift weapons were gathered and the group called Zion's Camp left for Missouri.

Prior to reaching their destination, they were stopped by a hailstorm at a place called Fishing River. A revelation was received that was a reprimand to them. They were told that they had *not learned to be obedient to God's commands particularly in terms of the care of the poor,* a lack of unity of spirit and commitment to the laws of God. The people would be chastened until they learned obedience even by the things that they suffered. They were not spiritually, emotionally, physically or intellectually prepared to act for God. There were many things that they needed to learn but most of all, *they needed to wait until they were endowed with the spiritual power that God had for them.* They were to be faithful and humble – not boasting of the blessings or the judgments of God, and take into consideration the understanding of other people. Gathering was to be done carefully. The people of God were to understand that they were not to fight, but to

---

[448] Lewis, MA Thesis, 72-80.

remember a former commandment when they were promised that God would fight their battles. They were to *seek justice*, but to do this by *suing for peace from those who had smitten them*. The Saints were to *lift up an ensign of peace, always proclaiming peace*. Zion could not be built unless it was done according to God's principles.[449]

An earlier revelation had also addressed stewardship, particularly in terms of the poor. One of the most important principles of the movement was that *every person was accountable to God as a steward*. All things belonged to God. God had decreed how the poor would be cared for and stewardship laws were the means that God had designed for this purpose. The Saints were to be more equal particularly in monetary resources..."for the earth is full, and *there is enough and to spare*."[450] The earth has the capacity to bring forth abundance but because of the human choice, there is covetous greed for some in the presence of grinding poverty for others. A modern theologian has discussed the issue of *abundance and scarcity as a deeply spiritual issue* that cuts to the heart of the righteousness, or lack thereof, of the people of God.

> ...the biblical faith teaches that there is enough *if* the righteousness of God is present and acknowledged as the source of life. In biblical traditions it becomes clearer over and over again that the crucial issue is not how many goods are present, but whether the righteousness of God is present.[451]

That passage was concluded with a warning of the judgment that awaits those who do not share with the poor according to the law of the gospel. Observation of the law of stewardship and the care of the poor were of utmost

---

[449] *Doctrine and Covenants,* Section 102.
[450] Ibid., Section 101:2.   [451]Meeks, 174-175.

importance. In spite of the fact that the provisions of the Law of Consecration changed according to the circumstances or legal challenges, the basic principles had not changed. Zion could only be a reality if these principles were obeyed.

In 1838, Joseph Smith prayed, "O Lord, show unto thy servants how much thou requirest of the properties of thy people for a tithing."[452] The following was received.

> 1a. Verily thus saith the Lord, I require all their surplus property to be put into the hands of the bishop of my church of Zion for the building of mine house, and for the laying of the foundation of Zion, and for the priesthood and for the debts of the presidency of my church;
>
> b. and this shall be the beginning of the tithing of my people; and after that, those who have thus been tithed, shall pay one tenth of all their interest annually; and this shall be a standing law unto them forever, for my holy priesthood, saith the Lord.
>
> 2 a. Verily I say unto you, It shall come to pass that all those who gather unto the land of Zion shall be tithed of their surplus properties, and shall observe this law, or they shall not be found worthy to abide among you.
>
> b. And I say unto you, If my people observe not this law, to keep it holy and by this law sanctify the land of Zion unto me, that my statutes and my judgments may be kept thereon, that it may be most holy,

---

[452] *Doctrine and Covenants*, introduction to section 106.

c. behold, verily I say unto you, It shall not be a land of Zion unto you; and this shall be an ensample unto all the stakes of Zion. Even so. Amen.[453]

---

[453] Ibid., 106.

Chapter 27

The Mormon Wars and the Effects of Severe Trauma

Although much has been written about this segment of history, it is still hard to believe and much more difficult to imagine what it would have been like to have lived through this time. The Saints had been driven from Jackson County in 1833. Many lived in the areas around, particularly in Caldwell County, the location of the community of Far West. This county had been designated as a place for the Saints. Joseph Smith had moved his family to this area in 1838. He was not a pacifist. However, he believed that it was the duty of a man to defend his family, but even this was restricted. Although there are some exceptions in practice, his belief was that aggression was never justified.[454] There was consistency in his belief that restraint was always preferable to war and no act of resistance justified self-motivated destructive acts but there were also limits to this restraint. Smith thought it was legitimate to defend their rights.[455]

The following are accounts of a legalized massacre of citizen church members at a place called Haun's Mill and the terror afterward. Those who were not killed had to

---

[454] The intention of the failed Zion's Camp noted earlier is an exception to this.

[455] Graham St. John Stott, "Just War, Holy War, and Joseph Smith, Jr.," in *Restoration Studies IV – A Collection of Essays About the History, Beliefs, and Practices of the Reorganized Church of Jesus Christ of Latter Day Saints,* Maurice L. Draper, Ed., (Independence, MO: Herald Publishing House, 1995), 134-136.

sacrifice property in order to save their lives by forced eviction.

The two militia commanders had been ordered to take the field, with their commands, against the Mormons by Governor Lilburn W. Boggs on October 27, 1838, in what has been derisively called the "Extermination Order." It commanded the militia to treat the Mormons as enemies of the state and to either expel them by force or exterminate them for the public good. With what amounted to a license to kill, some of the militia attacked the Mormon settlement of Haun's Mill on Shoal Creek on October 30, 1838. They killed about twenty Mormons and wounded several others in the surprise attack. The Mormons quickly fled to Far West following the massacre at Haun's Mill and Clark and Lucas surrounded and laid siege to the Mormon stronghold on November 1, 1838...The militia demanded the taking of Joseph Smith and his leading church officers as prisoners in return for the safe passage of the rest of the church body from the state. Hinkel accepted these demands and turned over several religious leaders to the Missourians, who took them, threatened execution, but eventually placed them in jail to stand trial for treason.[456]

When Missouri Governor Boggs issued his extermination order it was executed vigorously. Imprisonment, sacking of homes in the communities of the church members, murders at Haun's Mill, loss of property in Jackson County and elsewhere, and forced removal by wagon, horseback, and on foot

---

[456] F. Mark McKiernan and Roger D. Launius, *An Early Latter Day Saint History: The Book of John Whitmer Kept by Commandment,* (Independence, MO: Herald Publishing House, 1980), 166.

were all part of the experience of those who fled Missouri to Illinois during the winter of 1838-1839.[457]

After living six months in prison with the constant threat of a military death sentence without any civil trial or protections of the law, Joseph Smith escaped and arrived in Nauvoo, Illinois in April of 1839.

> Nauvoo, Illinois began as a wretched refugee camp peopled with five thousand Mormons who survived the holocaust in northwest Missouri in 1838-39. They were broken in spirit, sick, maimed, dying, possessed only of the goods they carried with them.[458]

Saints were also arriving then, having "sold" their property at sacrifice prices or having been required to abandon their property without legal protection. The church petitioned the United States government for redress of these wrongs dating back to 1831 – expulsions, land purchases with illegal loss of property, mob attacks, the extermination order of Governor Boggs and the illegal imprisonments of church leaders – to no avail.

> It is interesting to note that, even in the midst of some of the most difficult experiences, the published position of the church leaders was that corporate decisions should be made in the church according to common consent and that personal decisions are based on personal agency. Both of these doctrines have persisted through more than 150 years.[459]

---

[457] Launius, *Zion's Camp*, 161.
[458] Robert Bruce Flanders, "Dream and Nightmare Revisited," in *The New Mormon History – Revisionist Essays on the Past,* D. Michael Quinn, Ed., (Salt Lake City, UT: Signature Books, 1992), 77.
[459] Launius, 169.

Survivors of great trauma are often scarred. "Never again!" frequently becomes not only the way to survive on a day-to-day basis, but also the foundational principle of life afterward. Although seeds of many of the great social and theological changes that occurred in Nauvoo might be discovered earlier, nonetheless, the church individually and corporately was to be marked in powerful ways by the trauma it had experienced.

Never again would Joseph Smith be in a position of powerlessness.[460] The changes that were based on this foundation were dramatic and far-reaching. At times, this was expressed as institutionalized paranoia that became articulated in flagrant militancy and many forms and levels of secrecy.[461]

> In the midst of all of these difficulties, Joseph Smith became more defensive, perhaps even paranoid, frequently speaking of his possible demise...In leadership style he became more autocratic, not brooking dissent.[462]

Ironically, this could have been the most potentially successful opportunity to establish Zion.

---

[460] Gary James Bergera, "Joseph Smith and the Hazards of Charismatic Leadership," *The John Witmer Historical Association Journal,* vol. 6, 1986, 34.

[461] The authors state that maladjusted behavior can be traced to circumstances like great trauma (among other things) wherein people become sensitized in reactions that they make to life challenges. If it even appears that these circumstances are again being encountered, the feelings of initial trauma can block an objective understanding of the situation. "...the more sensitized one is to life threats, the more difficult it is to adapt in conventional ways." (p21) Fear is the filter through which the world is seen. Paranoia always has an a greater or lesser element of reality but because it does not allow other information or the consideration of other courses of action, it is not an accurate assessment of the situation. 321-323
Norman Cameron and Joseph F. Rychlak, *Personality Development And Psychopathology.* (Boston: Houghton Mifflin Company, 1985), 321-23, 326.

[462] Holmes, Dreamers, 60.

Chapter 28

Nauvoo

Nauvoo was "...possibly the epitome of the Mormon spiritual and temporal society, but also replete with the seeds of tragedy and disaster."[463] Most of the saints had arrived there in the dead of winter, destitute, having purchased the land with borrowed money. By spring, they discovered that they had purchased a swamp that needed to be cleared and drained. It was also a breeding ground for mosquitoes that spread malarial fever from which many people soon died.

But in spite of all of these difficulties, Nauvoo shortly became the second largest city in Illinois with industrious citizens – veterans of other communal establishments - and immigrants gathering to the new Zion from successful missionary efforts in this country and from nations abroad. There was a period of peace where the rapid expansion even included a university, but it all happened too fast, not allowing time for people to become assimilated into the community. The doctrinal divisions that resulted would never be healed.[464]

Church leadership at Nauvoo instituted many changes. Tithing had replaced the Law of Consecration in Far West since most of the citizenry had nothing left to consecrate. Payment of one-tenth allowed for some inequalities in personal ownership and distribution of the resources of the community. There were greater differences

---

[463] McMurray, 32.
[464] Holmes, *Dreamers,* 59.

between the people than before. Justice and peace were considered solely in terms of the welfare of Nauvoo and would be enforced by a grand and well-armed militia. Perhaps the saddest change was in the amassing of almost regal power by Joseph Smith. Nauvoo "forsook a society egalitarian for one authoritarian and hierarchical."[465] Not only were there vast changes in the belief system including new sacraments and ordinances, former leaders of unquestioned faithfulness to the movement who dared to question or voice opposition were cast out of the organization. There were also positive things that happened because of the efforts of good people, but the Mosaic Covenant of Shalom that had been in evidence earlier in their dreams of Zion had faded away into oblivion.

> The ultimate failures of the early Mormon economic experiments are explained by a confluence of factors: internal dissent, national economic conditions, frequent adjustments in the community plan, the inner workings of greed and power, among others.[466]

This period is ended by the murders of Joseph and his brother Hyrum by mob violence in 1844 and the dispersal of almost all of the community of Nauvoo by 1846. The largest group went to Utah while small, scattered groups of Saints waited for young Joseph (then only twelve years old) who had been chosen by his father as his successor, to take leadership of the church. This occurred at a conference in Amboy, Illinois in 1860.

---

[465] Flanders, *Nauvoo,* 83. It could be argued that there are exceptions to this statement from earlier church history but this was mainly true of an earlier time. Amassing personal power is also another effect of trauma. When persons have been traumatized and stripped of power, this will be protected at all costs. See footnote 87.
[466] McMurray, 32.

Perhaps the single abiding objective of the members of the Church of Jesus Christ of Latter Day Saints during the lifetime of Joseph Smith, Jr. was the establishment of a viable Utopian community on earth, a place to which the righteous might gather for protection from the evils of the world and the sanctuary from which the gospel might be carried to the nations of the globe. Ultimately this society would serve as the vehicle for the establishment of an earthly kingdom of God and as the catalyst for the millennium.[467]

They sought to bring together the faithful in common locales, establish a spiritual/temporal society in preparation for the millennium, and build an earthly kingdom in a place they believed was designated by God.[468]

[467] Roger D. Launius, "Quest For Zion: Joseph III and Community-Building in the Reorganization, 1860-1900, in *Restoration Studies III – A Collection of Essays About the History, Beliefs, and Practices of The Reorganization Church of Jesus Christ of Latter Day Saints* 1986, Maurice L. Draper, Ed., 314.
[468] McMurray, 31.

Chapter 29

The Early Reorganization –1860-1914
Joseph Smith III

The Reorganization actually began when a small group of scattered Saints whose belief systems were more aligned with American Christianity gathered in conference in 1852.[469] Despite their disappointment and frustration in Zion, they could not reject the belief and waited for the time when a prophet would arise and call them to establish Zion. But the conference of 1852 said that it was neither the time nor the place for the gathering of Saints toward Zion.

> The conference did not reject the "sacred goal of bringing forth Zion in America," but it adopted a more cautious policy that asked the Saints to wait until a more opportune time before beginning a settlement. The policy proposed that the Saints be satisfied for the present "to turn their hearts and their gazes towards Zion, and supplicate the Lord God for such deliverance." [470]

Joseph Smith III, "young Joseph," assumed leadership of the church on April 6, 1860. Both in terms of longevity of wise and devoted service and also in terms of his placement as the first leader of the Reorganization, his role

---

[469] Shipps characterizes the Reorganization as a very different form of Mormonism, more a reformation movement than a radical restoration within Christianity. However, the Reorganization would be very different than more evangelical forms of Christianity. Shipps, xiv.

[470] Launius, *Quest.*, 315.

in the church was critical. He was a reformer and moderating influence to the church and made it possible for the church to return to a more moderate respectable Christianity while attempting to preserve unity.[471] The scattered Saints were dependent on their neighbors and needed to establish roots by being a positive influence wherever they were as "leaven" rather than a separated community. Initially he discouraged efforts to gather into separate communities, sensing that time was needed to abandon some doctrines from the Nauvoo period.[472] A side effect of this effort was that the Saints gradually lost some of the communitarian values from the earlier period and took on the beliefs of the predominant culture around them.[473]

> Joseph Smith III served as President/Prophet of the RLDS Church for 54 years. He was keenly aware of the continual strife between the Mormons and their neighbors during the life of his father, felt it was unproductive, and urged the development of stability, good neighborliness, and credibility wherever there were branches. There was less emphasis on gathering to a center. Nevertheless they retained the goal of Zion, took half a century to become reestablished in Independence, Missouri, and were grateful for evidences of the Return of the Jews, still feeling that this was part of the divinely ordained process of Restoration.[474]

---

[471] Jean-Christophe Bouissou, "Evolution of Institutional Purpose in The Restoration Movement," *Restoration Studies VI – A Collection of Essays About the History, Beliefs, and Practices of the Reorganized Church of Jesus Christ of Latter Day Saints,* Paul M. Edwards, Ed., Independence, MO: Herald Publishing House, 1995, 119.

[472] Bouissou, *Restoration Studies VI,* 118.

[473] Conversations with Wallace B. Smith, the former leader of the church, on May 16 and May 30, 2000.

[474] This dissertation tells the story of a group from Nauvoo (who later affiliated with the RLDS) under the leadership of George J. Adams who left from Maine to establish a colony in Jaffa to assist in the return of

Although he was regularly pressured to establish Zion, he made it clear on numerous occasions that he would not instruct persons to gather until compelled by the Lord to do so; in the meantime they were to develop spiritual maturity and virtues, and live peaceably with their neighbors. Over and over again, he emphasized the deeply spiritual aspects of Zion both in terms of individual conduct and as congregations. He counseled that the church had not yet engaged in the purification necessary to establish Zion and truly be a people of peace.[475] People were to demonstrate their faith, avoiding persecution and conflict. His message to the church was that *as long as there was contention and disobedience, the gospel of peace was not working.* Those who worked for Zion would do so by confronting the evil in society, the primary barrier to the establishment of Zion. He did this by working in both political and social arenas for reform of American society. "Despite Joseph III's consistent advice, the Saints' penchant for Zionic gathering flourished."[476] Quietly, several families moved back to Independence in 1879.

> While convinced that his father's approach toward organizing righteous communities was basically correct, Smith realized that the early Mormons had tried to accomplish too much too quickly. He believed that neither the early church members nor the non-Mormons had been sufficiently prepared to overcome their fundamentally selfish human nature and accept an all-sharing lifestyle. Smith noted that

Jews to Israel in the early 1860s. Holmes, dissertation, 264. Reed M. Holmes, *The Church In Israel,* Independence, MO: Herald Publishing House, 1983, chapters 1-7.

[475] Roger D. Launius, "Quest For Zion: Joseph Smith III, , *Restoration Studies III*, 320.

[476] Richard P. Howard, *The Church Through The Years* – Vol. 2, (Independence, MO: Herald Publishing House, 1993), 36.

besides selfishness, the Saints had never exhibited the respect for each other that made possible a communitarian society nor had they shown the personal piety and striving for perfection crucial to the successful establishment of such a Christian Utopia...Smith soon came to believe that the Reorganization's Zion-building effort should be more liberal and all-encompassing than it had been during his father's lifetime.[477]

Development of Stewardship Theology

Like many people of that time, church people were mostly poor farmers and like many Americans of the time, not well educated. Missionaries went "without purse or script" and would be gone for indefinite periods of time while church members pledged support to their families. It was a time of sacrifice on the part of church members. "In such an age of 'making do', the 'spiritual' aspects of life came to be emphasized while the 'temporal' were downplayed."[478] There were always urgent problems due to lack of funds. Because there had been three stewardship systems prior to 1844, there was also confusion as to how to support the church locally, the paid appointee ministry, the staff and other expenses of the headquarters organization.

One of the first actions of the Reorganization was naming a Bishop and initially clarifying that role. The church needed to discover what it believed about stewardship of resources particularly in the present circumstances. The people no longer lived in separate communities where sharing of resources was the expectation so it was important to see how sound scriptural principles could be applied in the new circumstances. Basically, the

---

[477] Launius, "Quest for Zion: Joseph III,"*Restoration Studies III,* 315.
[478] Romig and Romig, 31.

church taught tithing. The Saints were asked to tithe themselves of one-tenth of their total worth and then one-tenth of the yearly increase or surplus thereafter.

It took a long time for members to accept a unified perspective of stewardship leading to systematic and consistent payment of tithing. As a result, there were seldom funds to support church goals...The year 1867 was a turning point...While endorsing Section 106 terminology, the Twelve demonstrated their internal uncertainty by printing a resolution along with their 1867 epistle...This perspective became, in effect, the church's operative tithing policy...This early reemphasis of stewardship accounting practices in the Reorganization affirmed its significance as part of the church's emerging financial system.[479]

At first, tithing was not required of all church members, but by 1895 the General Conference adopted a resolution stating that tithing was to be required of all members. This gradually became the accepted basis of giving for the support of the General or World Church.

The Second United Order of Enoch and Lamoni

The United Order of Enoch reemerged at the General Conference in 1869. The original United Order of Enoch had begun in Kirtland, Ohio in 1832 but was disbanded in 1834 because of the community's economic boycott of all business activity of church members. The economic activity of the new United Order was not to be an official Zionic project of the church, but hopefully a step in that direction to be taken by a stock company, legally constituted to do

---

[479] Ibid., 32.

business, procuring lands where church people might settle. The location of Decatur County, Iowa was chosen. Joseph's concerns were that there be balance among the economic, ethical and spiritual aspects of this venture and an avoidance of the apocalyptic language that had characterized the earlier ventures. He did not want any venture to become economically exclusive or have people gather based on hopes or fears of the imminent apocalypse with the Saints fleeing to Zion to escape the burning of the wicked.[480]

> RLDS people sometimes felt that they wavered between two worlds touching the kingdom-building theme. They sought to honor the apocalyptic vision of the early Latter Day Saints, to nourish their hope in being the generation to usher in the kingdom of God. They also leaned, however, toward practical, down-to-earth communal experimentation. The goals here were to alleviate immediate injustice and want, and to build up an ordered social and economic system. Whether some tended toward apocalypticism while others embraced the more practical work of the United Order, their prophet seemed able to hold them together against major schism. His power to do this lay in his consistent view that building up the kingdom of God was a long-term and multifaceted work. Such an enterprise demanded the devotion and gifts of all.....RLDS Zionic development during the late nineteenth century was remarkable considering the size, poverty, and wide disbursement of the saints. The United Order of Enoch emerged and resulted...in the establishment of Lamoni as church headquarters and center of much cooperative economic and social endeavor.[481]

---

[480] Howard, Vol. 2, 39-40.
[481] Ibid., 44-45.

The community that developed in Lamoni, Iowa is of critical importance to the church. It was both an outgrowth of the early-cherished concepts of Zion and also the evolution of change and growth in the Zionic ideal. Along with many others, Joseph Smith moved there with his family and greatly enjoyed harmonious relationships and the peaceful life there. Many people saw this as the first time they could be a gathered community with peace and harmony within the context of freedom of worship without persecution. Industry, business, agriculture, education and the arts blossomed in an atmosphere of a growing, stable and secure community. Lamoni was evidence that the Zionic ideal works, even imperfectly. The community of Lamoni is of critical importance for many reasons. The spiritual foundation of community with good relationships with the greater community enabled this endeavor to be successful. The church learned a great deal from this enterprise. It was from this base of stability and confidence that the church would be able to eventually return to Independence.

The United Order of Enoch played a valuable role both in the establishment and the ongoing community of Lamoni. Joseph still understood that the eventual place of the ideal society was to be Independence and said that if they worked carefully, the day would come that the church could return, but success in establishing Lamoni gave them a sense of assurance and promise for the future.

Although peace has often been elusive throughout the development of the church, shalom has remained at the heart of belief in Zion. It was during this time of shalom that the visual theology expressing the dream of peace became adopted as the official church seal by conference action in 1874. The theme of the seal is taken from Isaiah 11:6 and features a lion and lamb being led by a little child.

Throughout the artistic revisions of the seal, the word, peace, has always been the theme of the seal.[482]

Independence and the Third United Order of Enoch

Joseph moved his family and church headquarters to Independence in 1906 signaling that the gathering back to Independence should begin. The Saints were also encouraged to purchase land and property in Jackson County. The General Conference of 1909 asked the prophet to seek divine guidance in the matter of Zion. Some of the important parts of the message received included the following: Zion was not to be limited to any one location, many vocations and organizations needed to play vital roles in the Zionic process, the form of Zionic activity needed to be determined by the context, the Saints would need to depend on their neighbors to be a part of the process and must always be sensitive to them.[483]

The third United Order of Enoch was formed in 1909, again to secure property and assist in the development of the community. Another purpose of this group also was to work toward taking care of the poor.

> Philosophically, the guiding principle behind the organization of the united Order of Enoch in Independence was to provide a means to care for the poor of the church through the temporal contributions of active church members and then to re-distribute assets and aid according to the needs of the poor. Theoretically this group stewardship concept was consistent with the previous Orders of Enoch in Kirtland, Ohio and Lamoni, Iowa. The

---

[482] Mark A. Sherer, "The Theme of Peace in Church History," *Saints Herald,* 145: no. 5:18.

[483] *Doctrine and Covenants*, 128:5-9.

organization was another noble attempt to apply the gospel to the temporal aspects of the life of the church.[484]

The United Order took on the task of property acquisition and management with great zeal to the exclusion of significant work in caring for the poor. The mission of this group became changed to the acquisition and management of real estate resources while the World Church assumed responsibility for the care of the poor by the means of a storehouse and also oblation offerings both at the local and World Church level.

In the 1914 General Conference, the First Presidency and Quorum of Twelve issued a lengthy statement that identified Independence as a gathering center. They admonished the Saints to use economy, frugality, and good judgment in gathering and issued the need for a "people whose main desire is to glorify the name of God in the best and noblest service to their fellows." The United Order of Enoch was ideally positioned to facilitate gathering Saints. Too many Saints, however, wished to answer the call who were not financially able to support themselves, and the First Presidency warned that those Saints gathering would need to be well prepared.[485]

Although the Independence United Order of Enoch provided little help for the poor, they developed neighborhoods and assisted greatly in the gathering process. Perhaps their finest contribution was their assistance in enabling the process of gathering by land procurement and

[484] Gregory Smith, "The United Order in Independence," *John Witmer Historical Association Journal,* Vol. 22, 2002, 100.
[485] G. Smith, 102. Quotation from RLDS History, vol. 6, (Herald Publishing House, 1970), 619.

planning communities thereby keeping the dream of gathering to Zion alive in the hearts of the people.

Chapter 30

The Beginning of the Modern Era
1914-1946

Frederick Madison Smith grew up as the "heir apparent" to presidency in the church and assumed that role at his father's death. His preparation included a Ph.D. with extensive study with G. Stanley Hall, one of the nation's leading social psychologists. The church often heard the slogan - "Zionize the church and Evangelize the world".[486] He re-emphasized the earlier communitarian principles of Zion as taught by Joseph II, strongly encouraging people with economic resources, training and education to be involved in Zionic projects.[487] He deeply wanted the church to be able to confront the evils in the world by being more righteous, wise, compassionate and just than the world around them, not just an assimilated mirror of culture. Another goal was the modernization of church administration to accomplish these purposes. This modernization involved great change that resulted in a more efficient administration; this in itself was a very important contribution to the church.[488]

As a powerful articulator of Zion, he kept the vision alive in many and various ways like his hymn, "Onward to

---

[486] Pastors Reference Library, *Rules and Resolutions, Rules of Order,* (Independence, MO: Herald Publishing House, 1980), 102. Publishing Board, *Priesthood Manual.* (Independence, MO: Herald Publishing House, 1934), 5. The very first statement in the book referred to these ultimate goals of the church.

[487] Conversations – Wallace B. Smith, May 16 and May 30, 2000.

[488] Paul M. Edwards, *The Chief: An Administrative Biography of Fred M. Smith,* (Independence, MO: Herald Publishing House, 1988), 271-272.

Zion...Zion the beautiful beckons us on".[489] He called for the Saints to gather funds to purchase land in Jackson County for the gathering.[490] Concerning "the gathering to Zion," he wrote: "Shall we teach gathering? Yes. In effect now? Emphatically YES! Shall we advise the Saints to gather? YES! The Lord has told us to gather! Be Prepared!"[491]

He held this vision with great passion. It was a vision of a community not only of theory, but of buildings, streets, and places to work and play. It was a vision with a physical presence. As strong as the abstraction was about the kingdom of God, the gathering of Zion he envisioned had to do with people, places, and things. But unfortunately, within his relationship with the community, he was an outsider.[492]

Dr. Smith was the quintessential paradox, "a good man. But like most men he was paradoxical. He held a passionate belief in democracy but matched it with a commitment to unified command and supreme control".[493] He spoke and wrote voluminously, yet felt misunderstood. He upheld the grand brotherhood of persons, yet treated his brother, Israel, with less than respect.[494] He believed in servant ministry, yet always seemed to be dominant. He devised wonderful social programs promoting Zionic ideals that could not be launched because of the social unrest in the church. Democracy was within his value system, yet he saw

[489] Hymns of the Saints, 316.

[490] Mark Scherer, "Historic Views of Zion and Changing Prophetic Understandings," Saints Herald 146:1, (1999) 21.

[491] Frederick M. Smith, "Gathering to Zion," Saints' Herald, Vol. 75, 929.

[492] Edwards, Biography, 20. Paul M. Edwards, "Beating Plowshares into Swords: The Community of Christ and War," The John Witmer Historical Association, Vol. 22, 2002, 25.

[493] Ibid., JWHA, 15ff.

[494] Norma Derry Hiles, Gentle Monarch: The Presidency of Israel A. Smith (Independence, MO: Herald Publishing House, 1991), 64-76.

the democratization of American life in terms of the dissolution of civilization, the breakdown of respect for law and order. The danger that he sensed was *individualism, a spirit of selfishness and lack of concern for the community.* He taught that the only solution to this situation was obedience to stewardship principles recognizing that God is true owner of all that exists.[495]

The problem he wrestled with throughout all his tenure was common consent, an important part of church polity that required the vote of a representative body in matters of governance and doctrine. He saw this as the worst manifestation of individualism. In his view, being a good church member was equated with loyalty that honored authority, the center of which was the prophetic office. His answer to common consent was theocratic democracy, the interplay between theocracy being the rule of God and democracy, the voice of the people.[497] Common consent had been an important principle of the church since its inception (although at times, this practice was imperfect at best), but Dr. Smith placed far greater emphasis on the theocratic rather than the democratic aspect.

This was not a question of persons or relationships, but simply a question of who was in ultimate control. For him, the answer was obvious; it was the responsibility of the presiding officer. Smith had already had major disagreements with the Presiding Bishopric and Quorum of Twelve Apostles, the leading officers of the church.[498]

---

[495] *Foundations of Zion: Social Needs and Divine Purposes,* Pamphlet written by F. M. Smith and published by Israel A. Smith, Independence, MO: Herald Publishing House, 1951. F. M. Smith's writings were published during his lifetime and also afterward by his brother, I. A. Smith.

[496] Howard, Vol. 2, 223.

[497] McKim, 278.

[498] Howard, Vol. 2, 225-238.

This was not a formula for Zion but for major conflict. These issues came to a head at the General Conference of 1925 with the presentation of a document outlining Supreme Directional Control wherein the Presidency appropriated some of the authority of the Bishopric. This was seen by some as a negation of the traditional leadership that had provided for separation between the presidency and bishopric with a system of checks and balances. This was also seen as a violation of the legal structure of the church. The Presidency "won," but the cost was that hundreds of gifted leaders and members were either "ousted" or lost in this debacle. His brother, Israel A., stands as an illustration of these policies. He had been under appointment serving as a member of the Presiding Bishopric. At the conclusion of the conference not only was he not in the Bishopric or under appointment, he was even replaced on church boards and committees. In spite of these things, he remained a faithful member of the church.[499]

In addition to internal conflict, there were massive considerations from the interplay of economic disaster in the United States and also the world. Difficult external challenges were greatly exacerbated by the lack of internal unity. There had been problems beginning with the First World War, the Great War for Democracy. Now in the time of the Great Depression, the church was also systemically affected and had to literally struggle for its financial life. Many programs were cut, valuable and irreplaceable assets were sold and many gifted and able ministers had to be released from appointment. Nor was it soon to be over. Great financial problems continued until the time of the Second World War. Devoted church members and those who served in the bishopric during these difficult times served the

---

[499] Norma Derry Hiles, *Gentle Monarch: The Presidency of Israel A. Smith,* Independence, MO: Herald Publishing House, 1991, 72-76.

church with sacrificial devotion and great wisdom, making it possible for the church to eventually be able to retire it indebtedness.

Although other parts of the Mosaic Covenant of Shalom were not as easily identified, the church made progress in their understanding of the law of stewardship. The 1923 conference had passed legislation that clarified the stewardship responsibility of members. The guiding principle was to tithe the "increase" after the initial tithing of one's total assets; a form was produced to help determine the surplus or increase after necessary living expenses. Church members were to (1) file an inventory, (2) pay tithing, (3) contribute from their surplus, (4) make offerings and (5) give an annual accounting "as required by the law of God".[500]

There were many positive aspects to the leadership of F. M. Smith that need to be remembered. One of these is that he inspired a whole generation of young people to be excited about the dream of Zion. Many of these people have spent their lives working in many diverse areas in that cause. Some formed communities or cooperative endeavors while others took advanced work in the fields that could assist in the development of Zionic communities. These contemporary pioneers for Zion have also influenced others to be committed to the Zionic ideal in a variety of ways.[501]

---

[500] Presiding Bishopric, *Stand In Holy Places – THE ForGIVING HEART*, (Independence, MO: Herald Publishing House, 1992), 76.
[501] James A. Christenson, *Zion In Our Neighborhood – The Story of Harvest Hills (1970-1995)*, Leawood, KS: A Leathers Publishing Production, 1997

Chapter 31

Post-war Years – 1946-1958

The church has always been influenced by the time and cultural situation in which it lives out its witness of Christ. The leadership and authority, particularly of those ordained to the office of President and Prophet, the Bishopric and the Apostolic Quorum balanced by the common consent of the people, have attempted to give witness to Christian principles including the vision of Zion.

Zion was first identified as the "cause of Zion," not a finished perfect community, but a desire or aspiration for which to strive and also the means of attaining that goal. Like other aspects of church polity, the cause of Zion was also influenced by the insights and priorities of leaders and also the concerns and social environment of the people expressed in common consent. There seemed to be an alternating pattern of aggressively pursuing communal aspects of Zion and then attention to the need of greater unity and spiritual depth. This pattern could be seen in the leadership of the first two prophet presidents of the church and was also true of the differences in administrative goals and styles of Frederick M. and Israel A. Smith.[502]

Israel A. Smith served as president from 1946 to 1958. Like other prophet presidents of the church, one of the most important parts of his leadership was his inner affirmation of the call of God to prophetically lead the people. This was balanced by his education, training, and

---

[502] Conversation with Wallace B. Smith previously cited footnote 125.

work experience as a lawyer and politician, enabling him to give credence and attach importance to the voice and concerns of people. His administrative style was horizontal rather than vertical; he gathered competent men, worked with them in the understanding of what they were to do and then gave them freedom to do it. Many gifted leaders emerged at this time. He also spent time with the people, listening and creating an atmosphere of genuine trust.

Israel was deeply concerned about spiritual issues. Zion for him was first and foremost about the spiritual condition of the people. A prophetic message promised an endowment of spiritual power through the elders if and when they were willing to study and prepare to receive it.[503] He held conferences of general officers and priesthood leaders at Kirtland Temple for the deepening of spirituality. He worked for reconciliation and brought the church to greater unity with a renewed spiritual emphasis.

It was a time of newness, promise and change. There was an explosion of knowledge in almost every aspect of human existence. Ordinary Americans had discovered the rest of the world. The work of the church was opening in Japan, Korea and India, cultures far different than previous missionary work in Europe or Christian nations. It was also time to begin the painful process of shedding narrow institutional parochialism and discovering not just new and challenging historical insights, but also grappling with theology and its relationship to other areas of learning, science in particular.[504] Higher education was becoming possible for more people than ever. This was also true in the church, particularly among the leadership of the church; ministerial preparation for leaders and appointee ministers in the local areas received heightened attention. People

---

[503] *Doctrine and Covenants*, 142:4-5.
[504] Howard, Vol. 2, 358-62.

throughout the world were looking to America, including her churches, for leadership and assistance.[505]

When the church went into non-Christian countries, Saints also were required to wrestle with hard questions about Zion in relationship to the basic tenants of Christianity. Our "distinctives" like a belief in the reality of Zion or our history could never be as important as the basic message of Christianity, the love of God made manifest through Jesus Christ. Now, more than ever the center of our message needed to be Jesus Christ, not our history or even Zion.[506]

Jesus Christ had always been the center of faith but sometimes that center had been obscured. Earlier emphases had included millennialism that had largely faded around the end of the nineteenth century. The social gospel was emphasized by the religious world that also influenced church leadership. Now church leaders began to give expression to Zion as a network of leavening processes that the church uses to transform social systems of the cultures of the world into the kingdom of God.[507] Previously Zion had been defined as an actual community of persons dedicated to God where relationships were marked by social righteousness but now, Zion was being seen in terms of a motivating principle of human conduct in every situation, time or place.

The implications of being a more diverse world church also affected concepts of Zion. Former assumptions and practices were being challenged in many ways within the once basically Euro-American church. It was also clear that

---

[505] Bouissou, *Restoration Studies*, VI, 121-123. Herald Publishing House, 1994, 129.
[506] Roger Yarrington, "What Is Zion?" *Saints' Herald*, 1955, Vol. 102, 980.
[507] Howard, , Vol. 2, 416-418.

the church had much to learn about and from new brothers and sisters of diverse cultures who had their own gifts and insights to share with the greater church. Concepts of Zion were being enriched by the contributions of Saints from around the world. Some of these insights offered new questions or challenges in regard to Zion.

Some of this change was very difficult for the church. At the base of many issues was the understanding of scripture. Although the church had never held a view of scriptural inerrancy, for many people there was an implied assumption of a more literal interpretation of scripture of which their view of Zion was a part.

There is no way to know what might have been. There can be no doubt that the leadership of the church struggled valiantly with very difficult issues, some of which involved an accumulation of questionable or erroneous ideas about Zion that had built up over the years. But it seems that in the process of de-emphasizing of past understandings, when Zion became a "principle of all Christian life" rather than actual communities of Christian witness, many people experienced a loss of focus and the unique mission that had once defined the church. When Zion became Zionic and morphed into a principle of every part of Christian life that often was not that different from the status quo, the call of Zion was muted into metaphor.

Chapter 32

Going into the Storm – 1958-1984

W. Wallace Smith was ordained to leadership in the church in 1958 at the death of his brother, Israel. In some ways, the early part of Wallace's tenure was the calm before the storm that gave birth to a period of unprecedented social and religious change. No part of society was immune. The church was also significantly influenced by transformations and even revolutions that altered the entire national social fabric with issues like the civil rights struggle and war in Viet Nam. Nor were these only national issues, the maelstrom could be felt in some ways throughout the world.

Although leaders or World Conference Resolutions had issued statements from time to time concerning social issues in the past, the church had not substantially dealt with these matters. The atmosphere of civil unrest affecting the national scene was also apparent within the church in the controversy and polarization of the membership. The historic early church had been on the forefront of issues like race relations, but the contemporary church more often mirrored culture, rather than taking the courageous stands that had been so very costly to the church in the past. In the midst of all the confusion, clear direction was needed.

The Joint Council Statement of Objectives for the Church in 1966 was an attempt to deal with some of the issues. Our belief in Zion was also affected. The following is a summary statement outlining the understanding of World Church leadership in regard to Zion.

223

The introduction of these objectives clearly stated that Zionic communities could exist all over the world, when appropriate spiritual conditions are present. It also stressed the need to articulate the faith in relevant terms. The church needed to "Interpret the Zionic concept for our day in world terms and aggressively pursue the implementation of Zionic development"....Zion was no longer defined in geographical terms, but on spiritual conditions within a given community.[508]

The prophetic ministry given during this time is particularly significant. Several messages dealt with the *deeply spiritual aspects of stewardship.* One of the most profound insights simply states that *stewardship is our response to the ministry of Jesus Christ.* The message goes on to say that *stewardship response is required* of those who would be involved in building the peaceable kingdom, Zion. Echoing an earlier message, the church was reminded of their responsibilities as stewards in the repression of unnecessary wants. Acquisition and materialism were to be de-emphasized for the sake of Christ and the kingdom.[509] A message stated that the "hastening time" was at hand when the principles of stewardship accounting and Zionic procedures must be practiced more fully than in times past.[510]

Doctrine and Covenants Section 149 gave the church direction in two important ways. First, the saints were called to grow in their knowledge, ever seeking more light and truth by study and faith and not cling to words, phrases and understandings of an earlier day that were at best incomplete. Secondly, the Lord gave guidance to begin the

---

[508] Quoted by Bouissou, *Restoration Studies VI,* 123.
[509] D*octrine and Covenants* 147: 5, 130:7.
[510] Ibid., 148:9.

process of building the temple in Independence by using one of the tenets of stewardship, the consecration of surplus.

The church's work in the world was to be governed by the recognition of God's prevenient grace, that grace that had come to people before they knew anything about God or Christ. Previenient grace was simply the love of God that had enabled people to understand and respond to the gospel. The case in point was in regard to the conversion of polygamous tribes in India. The church was told to bear their sins and teach them the ways of the Lord. All aspects of corporate and individual Christian life were to be governed by the principle of "worth of persons." The church was to be guided by the principle of the inestimable value of persons. This section(150:6-12) also expanded the call of stewardship to include active engagement in working against the forces of destruction in the lives of people and the desecration of the land.

Although the leadership changed in 1978 when Wallace B. Smith came to the presidency, both the direction of the church and brewing problems remained. One of the most difficult issues involved the deconstruction of former ideas and systems of belief in areas like theology and history. This process was also going on in other parts of contemporary culture and exacerbated doubt within the church. The result was that many people were no longer sure of what the church believed and looked for certainty.

There were a host of divisive issues and concerns in regard to the practice and beliefs of the church, but for many people, they all seemed to coalesce around the issue of the ordination of women. This issue would be the defining point from which there could be no compromise or accommodation. While most church members would not have denied the spiritual giftedness or even leadership qualities of women, the primary question was whether those gifts could find expression in priesthood ministry.

Some of the most stirring messages in regard to Zion came during the presidency of Wallace B. Smith, 1978-1996. These revelatory messages were powerful, exhorting the Saints to reach out to those who had not been able to hear the message. The Temple, women in the priesthood and the nearness of God to assist people as they moved out in service were all clearly articulated. The importance of seeking peace and reconciliation in the midst of war and greed was lifted up as well as the responsibility for the care and protection of the earth. Stewardship of the earth became a more important issue as the desecration and pollution of the earth was increased.

> ...the personal-universal community is never simply that of human beings joined through God. It is a community of creation. It is the community of human beings bound to the birds of the air, the teeming life of the seas, and, indeed, to the acid-rained lakes and polluted atmosphere...Our slow awakening to the environmental, ecological crisis should make us realize that Francis of Assisi...was a thorough realist when he spoke of "Brother Cloud" and "Sister Moon."....that community which is, in God's intention, inclusive of all being.[511]

Members were to find their place working with others in organizations that recognize the worth of all persons, one of the enduring foundations of the Restoration.[512] All the prophetic messages spoke of the wonderful promises of God and are a continuing blessing and challenge to the church.

---

[511] James B. Nelson, *Moral Nexus – Ethics of Christian Identity and Community,* (Louisville, KY: Westminster John Knox, 1996), 165.

Stewardship was to also provide the means for continued mission to the world. The Bishops were to teach stewardship principles in stirring new ways to touch the hearts of the people so that they would understand and live in the fullness of life as stewards.[513] The call was always for the unity and greater spiritual depth among the people that would be necessary to accomplish these goals.

[512] *Doctrine and Covenants 16:3c-f.*
[513] Ibid., 147:5, 149:4-6, 150:6-7, 151:9-10.

Chapter 33

Back to the Future 1984-2000

The World Conference of 1984 was critical to the church in many ways. The Revelation that came to the conference pointed both back to the witness of scripture and the essential purpose of the Restoration movement and also forward to an exciting and challenging future. A prophetic message was brought to the church that called its people to build a temple dedicated to the pursuit of peace, reconciliation and healing of the spirit, a place for strengthening faith for witness and education for empowerment echoing an earlier admonition to "seek learning by study and also by faith".[514] The temple was to be a place where the essential meaning of the Restoration as healing and redeeming agent is given new life, inspired by the life and witness of Jesus Christ.[515] Clearly this was also a message urging the church to be more committed to mirror the *righteousness of God* as known in the incarnate one, Jesus Christ.

A temple dedicated to peace, reconciliation and the healing of the spirit was constructed to not only house church offices but also provide places for its ministries to take place. This beautiful edifice hosts the continuing and very successful Peace Colloquys begun in 1993 that have challenged the church and larger community to focus on complex and difficult issues of peace and justice. Two important centers were inaugurated in 1994: the Temple

---

[514] *Doctrine and Covenants,* 156:5; 85:36a

[515] Ibid., 156:5.

Peace Center that worked in the area of peace and justice ministries and the Abundant Life Center which developed personnel and resources in the area of spiritual formation.

Doctrine and Covenants 156 also clarified the call to priesthood, allowing for the first time in the church's modern history, the ordination of women.[516] But the main emphasis of this message was peace. The irony of this message's proclamation of peace was that a significant schism caused by differences centering in the call of women to priesthood that had been fomenting in the church for several years took place. As the situation developed, the possibility of reconciliation seemed more and more remote. But this message of peace also spoke to the very real difficulties in establishing not just boundaries of toleration and ethical dissent but also ways to live with respect for difference within that framework.

The irony of the resulting schism is that within this religious community, there are resources for this difficult and sometimes painful process of reconciliation, such as openness to more light and truth, recognition that persons are at different and valid stages of growth and the importance of common consent, listening to the voices of others.[517] We have been people who have known threat, persecution and violence from without and also debilitating polarization from within but all these factors were not enough to withstand schism.

But in spite of – or even because of – these factors, this religious community has begun to look at the deeper

---

[516] Op. cit., 156:7-9. There was clear biblical and historical warrant for women's ordination. Campbell, "Women," 141-151. Torjesen, The focus of the entire book.

[517] Andrew Bolton, "Blessed Are...Developing a Christ-Centered Theology of Peace, Justice, and Sustainable Environment", *Saints Herald,* vol. 145, no. 10, 12.

questions of peace and justice and know that justice understood by scriptural witness always needs to inform the ways of peace. As a people we are called to always sue for peace – lifting up the ensign of peace and always seeking peace - even from those who have "smitten" us. When this is done, the promise is that God will act on behalf of those who have followed these commandments.[518]

---

[518]   *Doctrine and Covenants,* 102:11, 3f.

Chapter 34

Contemporary Theological Considerations

The recent past has witnessed the deconstruction of systems of belief and values in many institutions, sacred and secular. Two main responses were elicited to the various theological questions and concerns that had been raised: opportunity for significant prayer, collaboration and study to find new ways to address the current situation or stringent literalism that found the solution in remaining faithful to former understandings, relentlessly resistant to change.

In the process of pursuing change, some positive things were birthed, but underlying problems also became more apparent and persistent. For the church, this has also included the painful confrontation with our history; bringing with it questions regarding the Restoration scriptures and the whole process of creating the canon as well as opening a multitude of other issues pertaining to our belief and practice. For many, the shock waves from this exercise made the "Rock of Revelation" – a former description of the immutable foundation and belief system of the church - seem more like amorphous bits of shifting sands caught in the winds of change.

The process of questioning former assumptions in the light of contemporary understandings was also important in coming to new and deeper understandings and beliefs about Zion, that are based on our heritage and a solid scriptural foundation. This study has placed that foundation at the beginning of the formation of God's people in the Mosaic

Covenant of Shalom. It was carried throughout the Old Testament into Jesus' mission statement of Jubilee and the communities of "all things in common" established in the apostolic church. The Hebraic symbol of sacred community with its promise and possibility was always greater than the realities of everyday life, but the call was to *live Shalom* or Zion.

Although community has always been fraught with conflicts and difficulties, it has always been an essential Jewish value. Indeed, Judaism is fundamentally communal. Jewish spirituality is most fully realized in community: Certain significant prayers...require a *minyan* (prayer quorum); they cannot be said in ascetic isolation....Not only prayer, but Jewish study has also been communal....Jews have shared a communal history, a common fate and a commitment to a collective mission...God's reign on earth.[519]

The communal principle or symbol was also necessary to guide the formation of Christian ideals but without some demonstration - something to do - acting on the belief, Zion seemed to fade from consciousness of many members of the church.

In its essence, belief in Zion has always been about salvation. Those who only believe in personal salvation – that Zion just does not relate to life in this world – are like those who see people in a burning building and set out to rescue people, one by one, as opposed to those who work to put out the fire so that all may be saved. Zion is not only about working to save the building, it is also about establishing those procedures of maintenance and prevention that would ensure a higher quality of life for the community.

---

[519] Debra Orenstein and Jane Rachel Litman, *Lifecycles – Jewish Women on Biblical Themes in Contemporary Life,* (Woodstock, VT: Jewish Lights Publishing, 1997), 228.

Biblically, the kingdom involves all areas of life....The theme is best understood in the light of Old Testament promises of shalom (peace, health, harmony); of a coming age of reconciliation, a fulfillment of Jubilee promises. The legal code or the Sinai Covenant and ...biblical wisdom literature both point toward the new order of the kingdom. Every area of life falls within the purview of God's concern and, therefore, of holiness and wisdom....The kingdom is ecological in this sense. It brings everything into view and is concerned with a proper ecological harmony throughout all of life, including matters of the spirit, the mind, the arts, the family, and all economic and political concerns...In this sense we may say that the kingdom is not only God's reign but that it is also concerned with *where that reign is effected in space and time.*[520] (italics by author)

Whether it was in the Hebraic covenant or Jesus' vision of the kingdom, there was always the sense of the present kingdom and yet, the kingdom to be. Although the final kingdom is a gift of God, it is a social order, not hidden or independent of the will of humans who have direct involvement. It belongs to the pardon and repentance of Jubilary obedience preached by Jesus but first begun in the time of Mosaic Covenant that opens up a new order where grace and justice are linked.[521]

In the Restoration, Zion is first mentioned as "the cause of Zion" indicating the on-going mission of the church and later with *conditions* of righteousness, unity, love and peace with no poverty. Zion is often spoken of in terms of a

[520] Snyder, 149.
[521] John Howard Yoder, *The Politics of Jesus:Vicit Agnus Noster,* (Grand Rapids, MI Eerdmans, 1994), 105, 109.

place, (not limited to one place, but Zion has an address here on this earth), condition and process. Equally true is the paradox that Zion is also a mindset or lifestyle that influences all of life.

> ...Zion has to do with the "how." In an age of specialization, individualism, and mechanization, Zion is the insistence upon a holistic approach to every sector – health care, welfare, counseling, architecture, education, legislation, administration, family, sexuality...Zion is a holistic, incarnation method of transforming every segment of social and personal life...Wherever the movement found itself – Kirtland, Nauvoo, Far West – came the Zionic call: to drain the swamp, to house the people....In this time of rampant self-gratification, there is much need for this witness to disciplined faithfulness.[522]

[522] W. Paul Jones, "Demythologizing and Symbolizing the RLDS Tradition," in *Restoration Studies V – A Collection of Essays About the History, Beliefs, and Practices of the Reorganized Church of Jesus Christ of Latter Day Saints,* Paul M. Edwards, Independence, MO: Herald Publishing House, 1993.

Chapter 35

The Call – Zion The Beautiful Beckons Us On

Early church members, like their brothers and sisters in the apostolic church and the Old Testament, were called saints not because they were perfect or even exemplary but because as baptized members, theirs was the journey of sanctification or discipleship, and they were committed to that struggle in their daily lives together as a family of faith.[523] Today the call and the creation of sacred peaceable community, Zion, must also elicit our response.

We are also called to claim our birthright as children of the Restoration where a movement began because men, women and children were called by the Holy Spirit and could not turn away but followed the light of that Spirit that empowered them to move forward. They joined Spirit and intellect together in coming to powerful new understandings about the work of God in the world. They joined heart and hand to work together in the cause of Zion. Their response was dependent upon taking the first step; they had to choose to respond – to be open to the call, to allow the Spirit to fill them and go forward into an uncertain future with God.

The Reorganized Church of Jesus Christ of Latter Day Saints is facing the greatest challenge in its

---

[523] Carol Cease Campbell, "Whither the Saints? The Bible, Saints, and Sanctification," *Restoration Studies IX: A Collection of Essays about the History, Beliefs, and Practices of Community of Christ,* edited by Joni Wilson (Independence, MO: Herald House, 2004), 147-152.

history. It is no less than whether we shall rise to the opportunity of a spiritual awakening that is global in its dimensions and intended for the blessing and salvation of all, or whether we shall be satisfied with the blessings that have already been ours and content ourselves with business as usual.[524]

Our people from all around the world responded magnificently to the building of the Temple in Independence, Missouri. The Temple, connecting the early church's hopes and dreams with the church of today, was built by the sacrifices of Saints around the world as a place dedicated to the pursuit of God's peace, wholeness and healing of the spirit, which is Shalom or Zion. The world today is experiencing an unprecedented period of spiritual renewal – along with increasing problems of evil.

Newer research has shown that Zion or the Mosaic Covenant of Shalom dates back to the time of the Pentateuch, goes throughout the Bible, the Book of Mormon and has been given to the Restored Church. Salvation is about a righteous people, not just a righteous person. Zion is not just our adaptation of a passing phase of an earlier era of Restoration history but is an integral part of salvation for ourselves, all humankind and the created earth itself.

Our salvation requires that we respond to the call of God in Christ. Zion means that all aspects of our lives are spiritual, including our commitment to peace with justice and also the way we care for others and the earth itself. One of the clearest ways that the call must be heard is in our understanding of stewardship. If *stewardship is our response to the ministry of Christ and is required,* then it is also true

---

[524] Velma Ruch, *Summoned To Pilgrimage: The Temple as Focus of a Pilgrim People* (Independence, MO: Herald Publishing House, 1994), 129. This book was written prior to the church's name change to Community of Christ. Ruch.

that our response to the ministry of Christ must include stewardship in order to be authentic. Everything belongs to God. The way we use these resources is often a truer indication of our hearts than the things we say or even what we do. In our contemporary consumerist world, fewer and fewer people know or observe stewardship principles although those who do support the churches at higher levels.

> Though all spiritual disciplines ...are relevant to the concept of Zion, the one that is fundamental is stewardship. It is response to the ministry of Christ. To be co-creators with the Divine is the basic meaning of stewardship...Our commission as stewards is stated in the first chapter of Genesis...We, both women and men, are given rulership. All are responsible. We all, in one way or another, are stewards of God's gifts...Not only are we called to stewardship but we are called to accounting as to how we handle all the gifts at our disposal.[525]

The benefits of life as a steward must be taught and shared more fully. Stewardship principles not only bring us into a truer and more honest relationship with God, but stewardship also makes it possible for us to be brothers and sisters to each other and the world at a whole new level. The oldest scriptures in the Bible deal with stewardship, God's eternal way of life for us.

There are issues that we must confront. Many religious leaders around the world are warning of *the dangers of individualism, materialism and a theology of consumption as demonic forces in our world that threaten the very existence of the Christian faith.*[526] Since 1980, religious and secular ideology have glorified "radical individualism"

---

[525] Ruch, 129.
[526] Walter Brueggemann, "The Liturgy of Abundance, the Myth of Scarcity," in *The Christian Century,* March 24-31, 1999, 342.

that has resulted in a serious decline in civic participation, voluntary associations, labor unions, churches and political parties. The powers and social responsibilities formerly the province of the federal government have either been dismantled or assigned to other forms of government (state or county) or to business concerns that are increasingly "merged, conglomerated, pyramided and multinationalized, responsible only to their shareholders not the community.[527]

This does not even address the fact that *our selfishness on an individual and corporate level* means that those persons whom God loves, the poor and vulnerable, will not even be able to live. They are deprived of those things necessary for life because most of us are not willing to live according to our just wants and needs in the repression of unnecessary wants but equally or perhaps more important is the fact that often we unwilling to make our voice be heard politically to act for the masses of those in want and need with the political avenues open to us to advocate for the sharing of the resources of the earth with justice

Many people have become caught up in the unceasing acquisition of wealth and the accumulation of things. For many, belief and trust in capitalism or market economic theory profoundly and systemically affects life's decisions and can even occupy a *dominant* position in life; this is a form of idolatry.

Stewardship, particularly in the context of Zionic relationships is God's antidote to this form of idolatry. Stewardship is not first of all about getting the things that we want; stewardship is about living in accordance with the will of God, seeking the kingdom of God first in all ways in our lives. The guidance of the Book of Mormon is particularly important in this regard.

---

[527] Geyer, 99, 101-102.

Think of your brethren as being like yourselves, and be familiar with all, and free with your substance, that they may be rich like you. Before you seek for riches, seek for the kingdom of God. And after you have obtained a hope in Christ, you shall obtain riches, if you seek them; and you will seek them, for the intent to do good, to clothe the naked, and to feed the hungry and to liberate the captive and administer relief to the sick and the afflicted.[528]

Wealth is not the problem; it can be used for wonderful purposes by those whose hearts are dedicated to Christ and the kingdom. God has given talents to some to be able to see opportunities and benefit financially. The "rich, and the learned, the wise and the noble" have an important role to play in enabling Zion to become a reality.[529] It is a matter of the heart. Who or what is our first love?

Over and over again, the scriptural witness is that righteousness and justice do not exist without stewardship. We cannot be serious about Zion until we are serious about stewardship.

Our Message

The people of God have always needed to understand their spiritual foundation, applying those principles to speak to both the present and the future. This process results in both message and mission. The current prophet president defines the message in these terms:

1. the centrality of Christ within a prophetic restoration tradition;

---

[528] *Book of Mormon,* Jacob 2:22-24.
[529] *Doctrine and Covenants,* 58:3

2. the movement from exclusive, gathered nineteenth-century community to inclusive, global twenty-first century community;

3. a theology that began with uneducated frontier thinkers and speculators and now seeks clarity and focus in a pluralistic society, while avoiding stifling orthodoxies and creedal formulas;

4. the Zionic imperative that once caused the founders to build cities and create militias and now calls the movement to face down the powers of injustice and violence through peaceful engagement with the communities and cultures of our world;

5. the worth of persons, with its profound implications for lay ministry and non-hierarchal structures within a movement that was founded by a teenager with questions;

6. a search for the spiritual in a church which began with one who defined himself as an oracle of heaven, but now finds itself sharing the prophetic task with visionaries and mystics and explorers of all types and cultures.[530]

Sharing Zion with others

The Saints have understood from the Reorganization onward that they were not to withdraw from their neighbors but were to work with them, particularly in those causes and organizations that support the worth of persons and the stewardship of the earth. This study has traced the development of the idea of Zion within the Reorganization. While it has been difficult for those within the movement to fully comprehend, Zion has been much harder for the larger Christian community to understand. Yet, if we are to work

---

[530] "American Values," McMurray, 45-46.

with them, it is essential that we be able to explain the things that define us as a movement *and do so in common biblical terms.*

This study places the belief in sacred community at the beginning of the time that God called a people together in the Mosaic Covenant of Shalom, giving them the means to sustain community, and traces that covenant into the ministry of Jesus and through Paul's mission to the gentile world using recognized scholars and the Bible itself. Thus, the Mosaic Covenant of Shalom, Jesus' vision of "the kingdom" or Zion resonates throughout the Bible; this enables our community of faith to explain our belief in Zion using both the Old and New Testaments.

Going forward

This exploration should also stir different or deeper questions to ask ourselves in regard to Zion. One of the ways that the Bible can be understood is as the answer to the question of Cain, "Am I my brother's keeper?"[531] As people who honor the voice of scripture, we have not one witness but three powerful, compelling testimonies that answer the question of Cain absolutely and unequivocally. YES! We are our brother's keeper and are meant to care for each other, sharing with the world in sacred community. The issues could not be more clear in a world where greed and war have been painted in positive or even "Christian" hue while the suffering and the poor are portrayed as the enemy within.

While it is true that we do not have all the answers as to how the principles of the Mosaic Covenant of Shalom - Zion - is to be adapted for our diverse world today, our heritage is that of a people of strong faith and courage who

---

[531] Genesis 4:9.

dared to venture out, doing impossible things and were blessed beyond measure. We believe that God does not change. What reason would there be that God would not also bless us today to be able to find ways to powerfully and prophetically live Zion in the here and now? The question is not the capacity or readiness of God to guide and bless us, but our willingness to be engaged in the task.

The poet T. S. Eliot has expressed the importance of life in community in a poem called "Choruses from 'The Rock'" in these lines:

> What life have you if you have not life together?
> There is no life that is not in community,
> And no community not lived in praise of GOD.[532]

Like the people in the time of the prophet Jeremiah, we also stand at the crossroads and need to make clear choices as to the direction we will take.

> Thus says the Lord: Stand at the crossroads, and look, and ask for the ancient paths, where the good way lies; and walk in it, and find rest for your souls.[533]

The choices are clear - to rise to the challenges of making Zion a reality in our time - or to do nothing toward this cause. We would be a part of the problem, not the strong and courageous people of our heritage. We have the opportunity to choose life in righteous community with wonderful promises of God to bring unprecedented spiritual renewal – the "great and marvelous work" – the kingdom of God on earth, ZION – or not. What will we do?

---

[532] T. S. Eliot, *Collected Poems, 1909-1962* (NY: Harcourt, Brace & World, 1963), 101 Quoted in Nelson, 197.

[533] Jeremiah 6:16.

We are called to the Peaceable Kingdom – the Mosaic Covenant of Shalom, the Kingdom of God – Zion on earth.

Glossary

Acceptable year of the Lord – an alternate term for the year of Jubilee

Agape meal – a fellowship meal in the apostolic church that could be a part of the Lord's Supper or held separately

Alms – gifts of charity to the poor; receiving alms became a part of worship in the early church

Alternate consciousness – a way of explaining a whole different way to think

Anathema – one of the strongest terms of denunciation

Ancestral land – a reference to the original tribal divisions of the Promised Land

Apocalypse – a Greek term meaning the revelation or disclosure of divine mysteries

Apogee – the culmination or highest point

Apostolic – referring to the church or work of the original New Testament Apostles

Appointee Minister – a term used in the Reorganization of the Restoration church under Joseph Smith III to denote a minister employed by the General or World Church as opposed to the vast majority of ministers who were self-sustaining

Aramaic – a Hebraic language that was spoken by Jesus

Baptism, Baptizer – Baptism - a sacrament of the early church in which the believer was immersed as an initiation into the Christian faith. Baptizer usually refers to John the Baptist

Bat qol – a Jewish term meaning daughter of the voice – that referred to a process of divine revelation that had replaced more direct prophetic utterance

Catechism – a means of Christian instruction characterized by memorized questions and answers

Chiliast – a person who believes in the thousand-year reign of Christ

Christology – the study of the work and ministry of Jesus Christ

Conference, General or World – the highest legislative body of Community of Christ; it is elected by proportional membership

Corban – a sacrifice or offering to God among ancient Hebrews that was broadened to include the often forced "gift" of property to the temple rather than the ordinary expectations that land would be used to support elderly parents or children

Corvee – the conscription of forced citizen labor under King Solomon, often seen as a form of slavery

Cosmology – a term meaning the study of the universe that is often used to denote the worldview of a particular people or time

Covet, Covetousness – the envious wish or desire for possessions of another, the state of unbridled greed warned against in the Ten Commandments

Creationism – *in this work,* this word is used as the doctrine of God as creator of all, order and the belief that what exists is good, a part of God's will

Cult, cultic – sometimes cult refers to the forms and practice of worship of a people while at other times, this word refers to sects or heretical groups that are marked by strong inner social control of it membership

Davidic theology – a combination of Israel's earlier faith plus the incorporation of the divine promises of a Davidic dynasty with the ideal of the king as being the servant of the covenant

Day of Atonement – Yom Kippur – the day that the High Priest offers the sacrifice of atonement for the sins of Israel

Debt slaves – when people could not pay a debt, they were taken for a specific period of time to serve as repayment for the debt

Decalogue – another term for the Ten Words or Commandments

Diaspora – the Jews who were dispersed or living outside Palestine

Distributive justice – a part of the Mosaic system where sharing and relative equality were the goals

Divine Providence – the belief that God was continually guiding and involved in human affairs for divine purposes

Dualism – a view that has two opposing forces such as spirit and matter or good and evil

Egalitarian ideal – a social philosophy that would advocate the removal of the extremes of wealth and poverty in order for everyone to have the things needed for life

Election, Predestination – Election is the belief that God chose a people to enjoy the benefits of salvation and carry out the purposes of God in the world; Predestination – can be used in terms of God's foreordination of salvation or damnation of persons or as a synonym for election

Endow - endowment – a term commonly used by those of the Restoration faith to indicate a particular divinely enriched ministry or period of enhanced spiritual gifts

Enoch – a biblical prophet, significant in the Restoration faith whose righteous city was taken to heaven, a way to describe the ultimate in righteousness

Eschatology, eschatological consummation – a study of last things, usually seen as the end of the world that relies heavily on the vision of John the Revelator

Essenes – a reform movement in the time of Jesus, characterized by life in an inclusive community of all goods in common for which the entry requirement was surrender of all property to the good of the order.

Experiential theology – a theology based on one's experience with the Divine rather than relying on external authority such as the tradition and authority of the Church, the Bible or traditional interpretation

Father's house – the tribe or extended family that was ruled by the patriarch; this was the unit of work, consumption and justice where members lived in smaller households that were subject to the larger, father's house

Gathering – an important term in the Restoration indicating the importance of being together in groups; initially, at least, this referred to coming to Zion, Jackson County, Independence, MO.

Godfearers – Gentile men who believed in Israel's God but had not undergone circumcision

Great Awakening(s) – Great religious revivals that swept through much of the United States with great fervor

Hebraic Covenant – This term can be used in several ways as the Old Testament or more specifically to the covenants of the Old Testament

Hebrew Bible – another name for the Old Testament

Hellenist - Greek

Herod, Herodians – King Herod who lived in the time of Jesus or the political party who supported the king, the Herodians

Homily – a sermon or discourse

House of prayer – one of the names for ancient synagogues, also given to the Kirtland Temple

Idolatry – the act of placing someone or something in dominance rather than God

Incarnation – to give bodily form or actualization to a concept or non-materialized form

Inerrancy – the theological conviction that the Bible is completely truthful and accurate, written by God or "God breathed"

Judeo-Christian – Christianity that consciously uses both the Old and New Testaments for its scriptural base.

Jubilee – the fiftieth year when after seven Sabbatical years, the fields were left fallow, debts forgiven, slaves freed and the land returned to the original tribal division

249

Kingdom of Heaven, Kingdom of God – Jesus' term for the time of God's reign when heaven and earth would be as one, the will of God being done on earth as in heaven

Koinonia – deep bonds of fellowship and communion experienced by the first Christians with each other, God, Christ and the Holy Spirit

Logos – an ancient Greek word for reason or the principle that guided the universe that was manifest in creation and the redemption of the world, usually identified by Christians as Jesus

Maccabees, Macabean – a religious/political group first under the leadership of Judas Maccabaeus, a part of a priestly family, who led a revolt against Greek and Syrian rule of Palestine from 142-63 BCE

Manna – sometimes called the bread of heaven, the food that sustained the people of the exodus in the desert, manna also means those ways that we are sustained by the gracious gift of God

Melchizedek – high priest and king of Salem, later to be known as Jerusalem, and the leader that Abram visited and to whom he paid tithing

Messiah – the anointed one, for Jews this would have been a king of the lineage of David who would be prophet, priest and king, the one who would deliver Israel and establish the rule of God while for Christians – this is another name for Jesus, the one in whom the promises of God are fulfilled

Midrash – commentaries and explanations of scripture by Jewish rabbis, often as the result of additional revelation of God, officially written down from the time of Babylonian captivity until 1200 CE

Mikvah – ceremonial cleansing according to purity laws, facilities for complete immersion in cold water, accompanied by prayer and introspection

Millennnium – a thousand years, used by Christians for the period of time when Christ is to reign on earth (Rev. 20:1-7) Those who do not believe in the millennial reign of Christ are called A-millennialists. Post-millennialists believe that Christ will come after the thousand years while Pre-millennialists believe that the coming of Christ will be the beginning of the millennial reign.

Monotheism – belief in one God

Motif – a dominant or essential idea or theme

Mount Sinai – also called Mt. Horeb, the holy mountain on which the Ten Commandments were received making them binding upon all people for all time

Myth – a story that is used to explain a religious belief, the story can contain powerful truths without needing for the details of the story to be factual

Nahala – the original division of the Promised Land into ancestral lands given to tribes and families, sometimes called one's inheritance in Zion

Narrative theology – the conscious use of religious story without the tools of criticism or analysis, the goal is to allow the story to speak and interact with the reader to convey its truths

Nazarenes – the first name given to Christians in Jerusalem, a way of dismissing the movement

Oracle – associated with receiving wise or authoritative advice or divine revelation

Oral Torah – the framework for expanding the Torah (first five books of the Old Testament) based on the study and meditation of the Rabbis as they received continuous revelation that God had first given Moses at Sinai, Oral Torah is written for others to study

Ordination – the act of setting a person apart for ministerial service and conferring sacramental powers

Original Blessing – a term used for the blessings given at creation

Original Sin – the belief that all persons share the human sinfulness caused by the sin of Adam and Eve, resulting in the fall from grace, loss of righteousness and distortion of the image of God from original creation

Passover – the Jewish commemoration of the angel of death that spared ancient Hebrew slaves prior to their exodus from Egypt

Pastoral theology – practical theology that deals with the relationship between scripture and the lives of people

Patriarchal – male dominance over all aspects of the lives of women and children

Penance – sorrow for sins that is expressed by contrition, confession and positive acts

Pentecost – one of the first fruits ancient Hebrew harvest festivals fifty days after the resurrection, the time when the Holy Spirit first came to the church

People of the land – term used for people without land or a home in the Roman period

Pilgrimage – a journey to a religious site to enrich one's faith

Pentateuch – another name for Torah, the first five books of the Hebrew Bible or Old Testament

Pharisees, Phariasaic – a reform branch of Judaism associated with the synagogue movement in the time of Jesus, the only branch of Judaism to survive the Roman destruction of Jerusalem and environs

Prevenient grace – the grace of God that comes before persons know anything of God that enables them to hear and understand the gospel message, God has gone before, loving and drawing persons into relationship

Primitivism – a belief in the superiority of the apostolic church and desire to restore that church and belief systems rather than reliance upon the tradition and dogma of established Christianity

Procedural Justice – the importance of preserving the status quo, law and order to insure a stable society

Prophet, Prophecy – the person who speaks for God, the message delivered

Purity Codes, Laws and/or Systems – the ancient Levitical laws that were intended to protect Yahweh God from unworthy, unprepared human approach

Purification – the process of outer and inner cleansing involving both repentance and water cleansing, the mikvah

Qumran – the desert location of the main colony of the Essenes

Rabbi – Hebraic meaning: my master, a teacher of Jewish law, a spiritual leader or a leader of a congregation or synagogue; usually a rabbi would need to be ordained

Restoration, Restorationism – a movement like primitivism that sought to go back to the ancient apostolic church, this term is also used for the Joseph Smith movement in the nineteenth century

Retributive justice - a part of wisdom literature, the righteous prosper while the idle and wicked must also suffer their just rewards, persons shape their own destiny so it is right that persons become extremely wealthy while others suffer poverty, God simply assures the consequences

Sabbath Day, Sabbatical Year – the Sabbath was the seventh day and the commandment to honor this day is an important part of the Ten Commandments; the Sabbatical year is the seventh year at which time the land is to be rested while the land owner lives in solidarity with the poor and Hebrew slaves are to be released, the purpose of all Sabbath observance was to always keep in mind that God was the true owner of all

Sadducees – the ruling religious faction of wealth and power located in Jerusalem

Saints – a term used throughout the Bible for the people of God; it was also used in this way in some of the early names of the Restoration churches: Church of Jesus

Christ of Latter Day Saints or Reorganized Church of Jesus Christ of Latter Day Saints

Salvation – the activity of God in bringing humans back into right relationship with God and Christ

Sanctification – the life of faith of a believer used throughout scripture, sometimes termed, discipleship, by Christians

Sanhedrin – the ruling body of the Hebrew people from the time of Moses when he was told to find seventy men to rule Israel so these bodies always consisted of seventy-one men – the seventy chosen by Moses plus Moses; this was also the main judicial body during the time of the Roman occupation

Schism – a formal division of a group

Scribes – an important group in the time of Jesus, the traveling interpreters of the law

Second Temple Judaism – the Jewish religion in the time of Jesus

Septuagint – the Greek translation of the Hebrew Bible (Old Testament) completed a century before the time of Christ; it was the Bible of the early church and included the apocrypha, writings from the period between the Old and New Testaments

Shalom Community – a community based on the covenant of peace and right relationships between God, within one's self – health, ever expanding circles of human contact (spouse, family, church, state, nation, world), and the created world

Shechem Convocation – a conference of those who had gone into the Promised Land, prior to the time of the monarchy, where they recited the promises and pledges of living in that land as well as addressed matters of concern to themselves

Shekinah – a Hebraic personification of the divine spiritual presence that dwelt in a tabernacle near their desert communities, the hovering spiritual presence

S'hma – the first word of the foundation of monotheism, hence another term for it: Hear, O Israel, the Lord, our God is one.........Deuteronomy 6:4ff

Sophia – a Hebrew word meaning wisdom, an Old Testament personification of God as the agent of creation and guide for the world; in the New Testament, Jesus is called the Sophia of God

Sojourner – a resident alien without rights in the land

Soteriology – the doctrine of salvation

Substantive Justice – the main concern is for the transformation of communities for the equity of all those who live there; laws are important, but underlying justice needs to supercede the law enabling laws to be changed

Suffering Servant – Isaiah's description of the power inherent in undeserved suffering, Christians identify these passages as the description of Jesus Christ

Supersessionism – the belief that with the coming of Jesus, the covenants of God with Israel were superceded and transferred to the Christian church, hence the Jews are no longer the people of God

Systematic theology – an orderly arrangement of scripture and doctrine that presents a unified frame of reference

Tabernacle, Tent of Meeting – the desert dwelling of God

Theocratic Democracy – a Reorganization concept of the rule of God as manifest in the leadership of a religious body balanced by the voice of the people in common consent

Theophany – an appearance of God visible to humans

Tikkum olam – Jewish term, participation with God toward the repair of the world, the peaceable kingdom

Tithe – the ten per cent of one's possessions that belongs to God

Torah – the first five books of the Old or Hebraic Testament, sometimes called the Law

Untouchables – those persons who could not be touched without making the other person unclean, persons who fell into this category were women, those with sores or leprosy; generally the term would also include those who would not be included in "polite company" such as tax collectors, shepherds, prostitutes or other people of the land

Utopia, utopian – the ideal society that is meant for this earth (as opposed to the Christian idea that the kingdom Jesus preached was for heaven)

Wisdom theology – the belief that God established order, humans are to choose wisdom – the product of human reason accompanied by divine discernment, individuals are more important than communities since a community exists to serve persons, there is no thought or concern for salvation since a wise person will be rewarded, generosity will be rewarded by God but there is no thought for the poor and vulnerable beyond the good that will then come to the giver

Yahweh, Yahweh God – JHWH, a way to speak the ancient name for God, another way is the word, Jehovah

Year of God's favor – Jubilee, also called the acceptable year of the Lord

Yoke of Torah – a description of a person directed by and walking in obedience with Torah, giving meaning, purpose and direction in life

Zealot – term could be used for a Jew who rigorously kept the law but more commonly denoted a nationalist group that saw revolution as the only way to be free of Roman occupation

Sources used for definitions

Bruce C. Birch, *Let Justice Roll Down – The Old Testament, Ethics and Christian Life*

Tikva Frymer-Kensky, David Novak, Peter Ochs, David Fox Sandmel, Michael A. Signer, *Charistianity in Jewish Terms*

Donald K. McKim, *Westminster Dictionary of Theological Terms*

Selected Bibliography

Anderson, Bernhard W. and Steven Bishop. *Contours of Old Testament Theology.* Minneapolis: Fortress Press, 1999.

_____ and Katheryn Pfisterer Darr *Understanding the Old Testament.,* Upper Saddle River, NY: Prentice Hall, 1997.

Anderson, Karl Ricks. *Joseph Smith's Kirtland – Eyewitness Accounts.* Salt Lake City: Deseret, 1989.

Andrus, Hyrum L. *Doctrines of the Kingdom.* Salt Lake City: Bookcraft, 1973.

Antonelli, Judith S. *In The Image of God: A Feminist Commentary on the Torah.* Northvale: Jason Aronson Inc., 1995.

Armstrong, Karen. *The Battle for God.* New York: Knopf, 2000.

_____ *In The Beginning – A New Interpretation of Genesis.* New York: Knopf, 1996.

_____ *The History of God – The 4000-year Quest of Judaism, Christianity and Islam.* NY: Ballentine Books, 1993.

Arrington, Leonard J., Feramorz Y. Fox, and Dean L. May. *Building The City Of God- Community and Cooperation Among the Mormons.* Chicago: University of Illinois Press, 1993.

_____ and Davis Britton. *The Mormon Experience.* Chicago: University of Illinois Press, 1992.

Barkun, Michael. *Crucible Of The Millennium: The Burned-over District of New York in the 1840s.* Syracuse: Syracuse University Press, 1986.

Barrett, C. K. ed., *The New Testament Background: Writings from Ancient Greece and the Roman Empire That Illuminate Christian Origins.* New York: SanFrancisco, 1995.

Bergera, Gary James. "Joseph Smith and the Hazards of Charismatic Leadership," *John Witmer Association Journal,* edited by Peter Judd, vol. 6, 1986.

Birch, Bruce C. *Let Justice Roll Down—The Old Testament, Ethics, and Christian Life.* Louisville, KY: Westminster John Knox, 1991.

_____ "A New Heart and a New Spirit," *Stewardship Worship Resource.* Indianapolis: Ecumenical Center for Stewardship Studies, 1992.

_____ and Larry L Rasmussen. *The Predicament of the Prosperous.* Philadelphia: Westminster, 1978.

_____, Walter Brueggemann, Terence E. Fretheim, and David L. Petersen. *A Theological Introduction to the Old Testament.* Nashville: Abingdon Press, 1999.

Borg, Marcus J., ed. *Jesus At 2000.* Boulder: Westview Press, 1997.

_____*Jesus, A New Vision: Spirit, Culture, and the Life of Discipleship.* New York: HarperSanFrancisco, 1991.

_____*Meeting Jesus Again For The First Time: The Historical Jesus and the Heart of Contemporary Faith.* New York: HarperSanFrancisco, 1995.

Blackman, Milton. *American Religions and the Rise of Mormonism.* Salt Lake City: Deseret Book Company, 1970.

Block, Peter. *Stewardship: Choosing Service over Self-Interest.* San Francisco: Berrett-Koehler

Boff, Leonardo. *Cry of the Earth, Cry of the Poor.* Maryknoll: Orbis Press, 1997.

Bolton, Andrew. *Sermon on the Mount: Foundations for an International Peace Church.* Independence: Herald Publishing House, 1999.

Bouissou, Jean-Christophe. "Evolution of Institutional Purpose in The Restoration Movement," *Restoration Studies VI – A Collection of Essays about the History, Beliefs, and Practices of the Reorganized Church of Jesus*

Christ of Latter Day Saints, edited by Paul M. Edwards Independence: Herald Publishing House, 1995.

Brock, Carolyn and David Brock. *The Gift of Peace.* Independence: Herald Publishing House, 1993.

Brown, Richard A. *Temple Foundations: Essays on an Emerging Concept.* Independence: Herald Publishing House, 1991.

Brown, Robert McAfee. *Saying Yes and Saying No – On Rendering to God and Caesar.* Philadelphia, PA: John Knox Press, 1986.

Brueggemann, Walter. *The Bible Makes Sense.* Winona, MA: St. Mary's Press, 1997.

_____ *Biblical Perspectives on Evangelism: Living in a Three-Storied Universe.* Nashville: Abingdon Press, 1993.

_____ *The Land: Place as Gift, Promise and Challenge in Biblical Faith.* Philadelphia: Fortress Press, 1977.

_____ *Living Toward A Vision: Biblical Reflections on Shalom.* New York: United Church Press, 1982.

_____ *Old Testament Theology: Essays on Structure, Theme, and Text.* Minneapolis: Fortress Press, 1992.

_____ *The Prophetic Imagination.* Minneapolis: Fortress Press, 1978.

_____ *Texts Under Negotiation: The Bible and Postmodern Imagination.* Minneapolis: Fortress Press, 1993.

_____ *Theology Of The Old Testament: Testimony, Dispute, Advocacy.* Minneapolis: Fortress Press, 1997.

Bushman, Richard L. *Joseph Smith and the Beginnings of Mormonism.* Urbana: University of Illinois Press, 1984.

Cahill, Lisa Sowle. *Discipleship, Pacificism, and Just War Theory.* Minneapolis: Fortress Press, 1994.

Cahill, Thomas. *The Gift of the Jews – How a Tribe of Desert Nomads Changed the Way Everyone Things and Feels.* NY: Doubleday, 1998.

Cameron, Norman and Joseph F. Rychlak. *Personality Development and Psychotherapy.* Boston: Houghton Mifflin Co., 1985.

Campbell, Carol Cease. "Whither the Saints? The Bible, Saints, and Sanctification," *Restoration Studies IX: A Collection of Essays about the History, Beliefs, and Practices of Community of Christ,* edited by Joni Wilson. Independence, MO: Herald House, 2004.

_____ "Women in the Apostolic Church and Their Demise," *Restoration Studies VIII: A Collection of Essays About the History, Beliefs, and Practices of the Reorganized Church of Jesus Christ of Latter Day Saints,* edited by Joni Wilson, Independence MO: Herald Publishing House, 2000.

Capon, Robert Farrar. *The Parables of Grace.* Grand Rapids: Eerdmans, 1988.

_____ *The Parables of Judgment.* Grand Rapids: Eerdmans, 1989.

_____ *The Parables of the Kingdom.* Grand Rapids: Eerdmans, 1985.

Capra, Fritjof. *The Turning Point: Science, Society, and the Rising Culture.* New York: Simon and Schuster, 1982.

Carter, William G., ed. *Speaking Of Stewardship – Model Sermons on Money and Possessions.* Louisville: Geneva Press, 1998.

Cartlidge, David R. and David L. Dungan. *Documents for the Study of the Gospels.* Minneapolis: Fortress, 1994.

Ceresko, Anthony. *Introduction to the Old Testament: A Liberation Perspective.* Maryknoll: Orbis Books, 1992.

de Chardin, Pierre Teilhard. *The Future of Man.* Translated by Norman Denny. New York: Harper and Row, 1964.

_____ *The Phenomenon of Man.* Translated by Bernard Wall. NY: Harper and Row, 1965.

Chilton, Bruce. *Rabbi Jesus – An Intimate Biography – The Jewish Life and Teaching That Inspired Christianity.* NY: Doubleday, 2000.

Chilton, Bruce and Jacob Neusner. *Judaism in the New Testament – Practices and Beliefs.* NY: Rutledge, 1995.

Chvala-Smith, Anthony. "The Spirit, The Book, and The City: Retrieving the Distinctive Voice of the Restoration," *John Witmer Historical Journal,* 19:25.

Christenson, James A. *Zion in Our Neighborhood-- The Story of Harvest Hills (1970-1995).* Leawood, KS: A Leathers Publishing Production, 1997.

_____. *Zion in our Time.* Independence, MO: Published by the Center for Zionic Studies, 1980.

Clothier, Louita, ed. *Heritage and Horizon: Our Story Illuminates a New Century.* Independence: Herald Publishing House, 2000.

Cohn-Sherbok, Dan. *A Dictionary of Judaism and Christianity.* Philadelphia: Trinity Press, 1991.

Cook, Lyndon, W. *Joseph Smith and the Law of Consecration.* Provo: Grandin Book Company, 1985.

Cross, Whitney R. *The Burned-over District: The Social and Intellectual History in Western New York, 1800-1850.* Ithaca: Cornell University Press, 1950.

Crossan, John Dominic. *The Essential Jesus: Original Sayings and Earliest Images.* New York: HarperSanFrancisco, 1994.

_____ *Who Killed Jesus? Exposing the Roots of Anti-Semitism in the Gospel Story of the Death of Jesus.* New York: HarperSanFrancisco, 1995.

Draper, Maurice L. *The Founding Prophet: An Administrative Biography of Joseph Smith, Jr.* Independence: Herald Publishing House, 1991.

_____ "Prophets Are Human, Too," *John Witmer Historical Association Journal,* edited by Imogene Goodyear, vol. 11, 1991.

Edwards, F. Henry. *Commentary on the Doctrine and Covenants.* Independence: Herald Publishing House, 1977.

Edwards, Paul M. "Beating Plowshares into Swords: The Community of Christ and War," *John Witmer Historical Association* edited by Joni Wilson, vol. 22, 2002.

_____ *The Chief: An Administrative Biography of Fred M. Smith.* Independence: Herald Publishing House, 1988.

_____ *Our Legacy Of Faith: A Brief History of the Reorganized Church of Jesus Christ of Latter Day Saints.* Independence: Herald Publishing House, 1991.

Egan, Eileen. *Peace Be With You: Justified Warfare or the Way of Nonviolence.* Maryknoll: Orbis Books, 1999.

Flanders, Robert B. "Dream and Nightmare Revisited," *The New Mormon History – Revisionist Essays on the Past,* edited by D. Michael D. Quinn Salt Lake City: Signature Books, 1992.

_____ *Nauvoo: Kingdom on the Mississippi.* Urbana: University of Illinois Press, 1965.

Fiorenza, Elisabeth Schussler. *In Memory Of Her: A Feminist Theological Reconstruction of Christian Origins.* New York: Crosssroad Publishing, 1994.

Fitzmyer, Joseph A. *The Semitic Background of the New Testament.* Grand Rapids: Eerdmans, 1997.

Forest, Jim. *The Ladder Of The Beatitudes.* Maryknoll: Orbis, 1999.

Fox, Matthew. *Breakthrough: Meister Eckhart's Creation Spirituality in New Translation.* New York: Doubleday, 1991.

_____ *Creation Spirituality: Liberating Gifts for the Peoples of the Earth.* New York: HarperSanFrancisco, 1991.

_____ *A Spirituality Named Compassion and the Healing of the Global Village, Humpty Dumpty, and Us.* New York:HarperSanFrancisco, 1990.

Frymer-Kensky, Tikva, David Novak, Peter Ochs, David Fox Sandmel, and Michael A. Singer. *Christianity In Jewish Terms.* Boulder: Westview Press, 2000.

Geyer, Alan. *Ideology in America – Challenges to Faith.* Louisville, KY: Westminster John Knox Press, 1997.

Goldingay, John. *Theological Diversity and the Authority of the Old Testament.* Grand Rapids: Eerdmans, 1987.

Grant, Carter E. *The Kingdom of God Restored.* Salt Lake City: Deseret, 1955.

Gregg, Samuel. *Economic Thinking for the Theologically Minded.* Lanham, Maryland: University Press of America, 2001.

Grimsrud, Ted and Loren L. Johns. *Peace And Justice Shall Embrace – Power and Theopolitics in the Bible.* Scottdale: Herald Press, 1999.

Grenz, Stanley J. *A Primer on Postmodernism.* Grand Rapids: Eerdmans, 1996.

Gunderson, Robert A. "From Dust to the Dusty: The Rise and Pall of the Book of Mormon in the Life and ministry of Joseph Smith Jr." *The John Witmer Historical Journal,* 2002, vol. 22, 75.

Hall, Douglas John. *The End of Christendom and the Future of Christianity.* Valley Forge: Trinity Press International, 1997.

_____*The Steward: A Biblical Symbol Come of Age.* Grand Rapids: Eerdmans, 1990.

_____ *The Stewardship of Life in the Kingdom of Death.* Grand Rapids: Eerdmans, 1985.

_____ *Thinking the Faith – Christian Theology in a North American Context.* Minneapolis: Fortress Press, 1991.

Hamma, Robert W. *Landscapes of the Soul: a Spirituality of Place.* Notre Dame: Ave Maria Press, 1999.

Harris, Maria. *Proclaim Jubilee!* Louisville: Westminster John Knox Press, 1996.

Hauerwas, Stanley. *The Peaceable Kingdom: A Primer in Christian Ethics.* Notre Dame: University of Notre Dame Press, 1983.

Heitzenrater, Richard P. *Wesley And The People Called Methodists.* Nashville: Abingdon Press, 1995.

Higdon, Elizabeth J. "Eyes Single to the Glory: the History of the Heavenly City of Zion," *Restoration Studies I – A Collection of Essays About the History, Beliefs, and Practices of the Reorganized Church of Jesus Christ of Latter Day Saints,* edited by Barbara J. Higdon. Independence: Herald Publishing House, 1980.

Higdon, Barbara J. *Committed To Peace.* Independence: Herald Publishing House, 1994.

Hiles, Norma Derry. *Gentle Monarch: The Presidency of Israel A. Smith.* Independence: Herald Publishing House, 1991.

Hill, Marvin S., C. Keith Rooker, Larry T. Wimmer. *The Kirtland Economy Revisited: A Market Critique of Sectarian Economics.* Provo: Brigham University Press, 1977.

History of the Reorganized Church of Jesus Christ of Latter Day Saints, vol. 1. Independence: Herald Publishing House, 1951.

Hoge, Dean, Patrick McNamara, and Charles Zech. *Plain Talk About Churches And Money.* Washington: Alban Institute Publication, 1997.

Hollinger, David A. and Charles Capper, ed. *The American Intellectual Tradition,* 2 Vols., New York: Oxford University Press, 1993.

Holm, Francis W. Sr. *The Mormon Churches – a Comparison from Within.* Kansas City, MO: Midwest Press, 1970

Holmes, Michael, ed. *The Apostolic Fathers.* Grand Rapids: Baker Book House, 1989.

Holmes, Reed M. *Dreamers of Zion.* Portland, OR: Sussex Academic Press, 2003.

_____ *The Church In Israel.* Independence: Herald Publishing House, 1983.

_____ *The ForeRunners,2nd edition* Pepperell, MA: Jean and Reed Holmes, 2003.

Howard, Richard P. *The Church Through the Years*, vol. 1. Independence: Herald Publishing House, 1992.

_____ *The Church Through the Years*, vol. 2. Independence: Herald Publishing House, 1993.

Hymns of the Saints. Independence: Herald Publishing House, 1981.

Janzen, David. *Fire, Salt and Peace: Intentional Christian Communities Alive in North America.* Evanston: Shalom Mission Communities, 1996.

Jennings, Theodore W. Jr., *Good News To The Poor: John Wesley's Evangelical Economics.* Nashville: Abingdon Press, 1990.

Johnson, Luke Timothy. *Living Jesus: Learning the Heart of the Gospel.* New York: HarperSanFrancisco, 1999.

_____ *Religious Experience in Earliest Christianity.* Minneapolis: Fortress Press, 1998.

_____ *The Writings Of The New Testament: An Interpretation.* Philadelphia: Fortress Press, 1986.

Jones, Bruce, ed. *Becoming Makers of Peace: The Peace Symposium at Kirtland, Ohio.* Independence: Herald Publishing House, 1987.

Jones, D. Paul. "Demythologizing and Symbolizing the RLDS Tradition," *Restoration Studies V – A Collection of Essays about the History, Beliefs, and Practices of the Reorganized Church of Jesus Christ of Latter Day Saints* edited by Paul M. Edwards Independence: Herald Publishing House, 1993.

Judd, Peter A. *Transformed By the Spirit: Reflections on Jesus' Proclamation in the Synagogue at Nazareth.* Independence: Herald Publishing House, 2000.

Kee, Howard Clark. *Understanding the New Testament.* Englewood Cliffs: Prentice Hall, 1993.

Kinsler, Ross and Gloria Kinsler. *The Biblical Jubilee and the Struggle for Life.* Maryknoll: Orbis Books, 1999.

Kraftchick, Steven J., Charles D. Myers, Jr., and Ben C. Ollenburger, eds., *Biblical Theology: Problems and Perspectives.* Nashville: Abingdon Press, 1995.

Kraybill, Donald B. *The Upside-down Kingdom.* Scottdale: Herald Press, 1990.

Kuttner, Robert. *Everything for Sale: The Virtue and Limits of Markets.* New York: Knopf, 1998.

Launius, Roger D. "Alexander William Doniphan and the 1838 Mormon War in Missouri," *John Witmer Association Journal,* vol 18, 1988.

_____ *Joseph Smith III - Pragmatic Prophet.* Urbana: University of Illinois Press, 1998.

_____ "Quest for Zion: Joseph III and Community-Building in the Reorganization, 1860-1900," *Restoration Studies III – A Collection of Essays about the History, Beliefs and Practices of the Reorganized Church of Jesus Christ of Latter Day Saints* edited by Maurice Draper Independence: Herald Publishing House, 1986.

_____ *The Kirtland Temple: A Historical Narrative.* Independence: Herald Publishing House, 1986.

_____ *Zion's Camp: Expedition to Missouri, 1834.* Independence: Herald Publishing House, 1984.

_____ and John E. Hallwas, ed., *Kingdom on the Mississippi Revisited: Nauvoo in Mormon History.* Urbana: University of Illinois Press, 1996.

Learning to Build a Peaceful World, A Working Conference. Independence: Herald Publishing House, 1990.

Liturgy Committee of the Central Conference of American Rabbis. *Gates of Prayer – The New Union Prayerbook.* NY: Central Conference of American Rabbis, 1982.

Mackender, Lisa and Brad Martell. *Jubilee – A Cycle of Justice.* Independence: Herald Publishing House, 2000.

McKiernan, F. Mark and Roger D. Launius. *An Early Latter Day Saint History: The Book of John Witmer Kept by Commandment.* Independence: Herald Publishing House, 1980.

_____, Alma Blair, and Paul M. Edwards, eds. *The Restoration Movement: Essays in Mormon History.* Lawrence, KS: Coronado Press, 1973.

McKim, Donald K. *Westminster Dictionary of Theological Terms.* Louisville: Westminster John Knox Press, 1996.

McMurray, W. Grant. "American Values for a 'New Jerusalem:' Formations of the First United Order of Enoch, 1860-71," *John Witmer Historical Association Journal* edited by Imogene Goodyear, vol. 8, 1988.

McMurrin, Sterling M. *The Theological Foundations of the Mormon Religion.* Salt Lake City: University of Utah Press, 1965.

Meeks, M. Douglas. *God, The Economist: The Doctrine of God and Political Economy.* Minneapolis: Fortress Press, 1989.

_____ *The Portion Of The Poor: Good News to the Poor in the Wesleyan Tradition.* Nashville: Abingdon Press, 1995.

Meeks, Wayne A. *The Moral World of the First Christians.* Philadelphia: Westminster, 1986.

Murphy, Frederick J. *The Religious World Of Jesus: An Introduction to Second Temple Palestinian Judaism.* Nashville: Abingdon Press, 1991.

Nelson, James B., *Moral Nexus – Ethics of Christian Identity and Community.* Louisville, KY: John Knox Press, 1996.

Neusner, Jacob and Bruce D. Chilton. *God In The World – Christianity and Judaism, the Formative Categories.* Harrisburg, PA: Trinity Press International, 1997.

Newell, Linda King and Valeen Tippetts Avery. *Mormon Enigma: Emma Hale Smith.* New York: Doubleday, 1984.

Niebuhr, Richard. *The Kingdom of God in America.* New York: Harper and Row, 1959.

Njeim, George A. "Zion", *Readings on the Concept of Zion, edited by Paul A. Wellington.* Independence: Herald Publishing House, 1973

Nyce, Dorothy Yoder. *Jesus' Clear Call To Justice.* Scottdale: Herald Press, 1990.

Ollenburger, Ben C. *Zion, The City Of The Great King: A Theological Symbol of the Jerusalem Cult.* Sheffield, England: Sheffield Academic Press, 1987.

Orenstein, Debra and Jane Rachel Litman. *Lifecycles – Jewish Women on Biblical Themes in Contemporary life.* Woodstock, VT: Jewish Lights Publishing, 1997.

Ostling, Richard N. and Joan K. Ostling, *Mormon America – The Power and the Promise,* New York: HarperSanFrancisco, 1999.

Outler, Albert C. and Richard P. Heitzenrater. *John Wesley's Sermons: An Anthology.* Nashville: Abingdon Press, 1991.

Plevnik, Joseph. *What Are They Saying About Paul?* Mahwah: Paulist Press, 1986.

Premoe, David, ed. *Zion, The Growing Symbol: A Case Study Approach on Images of Zion.* Independence: Herald Publishing House, 1980.

Priesthood Manual. Independence: Herald Publishing House, 1934.

Riggs, Michael S. "The Economic Impact of Fort Leavenworth on Northwestern Missouri 1827-1838" and "Yet Another Reason for the Mormon War?" *Restoration Studies - A Collection of Essays About the History, Beliefs, and Practices of the Reorganized Church of Jesus Christ of Latter Day Saints VII* edited by Joni Wilson and Ruth Ann Wood Independence, MO: Herald Publishing House, 1996.

Romig, Ronald E. "The Law of Consecration: Antecedents and Practice in Kirtland, Ohio," *Restoration Studies VI – A Collection of Essays About the History, Beliefs, and Practices of the Reorganized Church of Jesus Christ of Latter Day Saints,* Paul M. Edwards, Editor, (Independence, MO: Herald Publishing House, 1995.

_____Ronald E., and Anne L. Romig. *Stewardship Concepts and Practices-- Studies in Restoration History.* Independence: Herald Publishing House, 1992.

Ruch, Velma. *Summoned To Pilgrimage: The Temple as Focus of a Pilgrim People.* Independence: Herald Publishing House, 1994.

Rules and Resolutions, Rules of Order. Independence: Herald Publishing House, 1980.

Ruoff, Norman D., ed. *The Writings of President Frederick M. Smith,* vol.1. Independence: Herald Publishing House, 1978.

Russell, Letty M. *Church in the Round: Feminist Interpretation of the Church.* Louisville: Westminster John Knox Press, 1993.

Ryan, John A. *Economic Justice – Selections from Distributive Justice and A Living Wage.* Louisville, KY: Westminster John Knox, 1996.

Saliba, John A. *Understanding New Religious Movements.* Grand Rapids: Eerdmans, 1995.

Schneebeck, Harold Jr. *The Body of Christ – A Study of the Nature of the Church.* Independence, MO: Herald Publishing House, 1968.

Schrage, Wolfgang, *The Ethics Of The New Testament.* Translated by David E. Green, Philadelphia: Fortress Press, 1988.

Shipps, Jan, *Mormonism--The Story of a New Religious Tradition.* Chicago: University of Illinois Press, 1985.

Sider, Ronald J. *Just Generosity, A New Vision for Overcoming Poverty in America.* Grand Rapids: Baker Book House, 2000.

_____*Rich Christians In An Age Of Hunger.* Dallas: World Publishing: 1990.

Smith, Frederick M. *Foundations of Zion: Social Needs and Divine Purposes.* Independence: Herald Publishing House, 1951.

Smith, Gary V. *Zionism*: *The Dream and the Reality, A Jewish Critique.* New York: Barnes and Noble, 1974.

Smith, Gregory. "The United Order in Independence," *John Witmer Historical Association Journal* edited by Joni Wilson, vol. 22, 2002.

Snyder, Howard A. *Models of the Kingdom.* Nashville: Abingdon Press, 1976.

Soards, Marion L. *The Apostle Paul: An Introduction to his Writings and Teaching.* Mahwah: Paulist Press, 1987.

Stand In Holy Places – The ForGIVING HEART. Independence: Herald Publishing House, 1992.

Stassen, Glen H. *Just Peacemaking: Ten Practices for Abolishing War.* Cleveland: The Pilgrim Press, 1998.

_____ *Just Peacemaking: Transforming Initiatives for Justice and Peace.* Louisville: Westminster John Knox Press, 1992.

Stern, Chaim, ed., *Gates of Prayer, The New Union Prayerbook.* New York: Central Conference of American Rabbis, 1985.

Stott, Graham St. John. "Just War, Holy War, and Joseph Smith, Jr. *Restoration Studies IV – A Collection of Essays about the History, Beliefs, and Practices of the Reorganized Church of Jesus Christ of Latter Day Saints* edited by Maurice L. Draper. Independence: Herald Publishing House, 1988.

Tanakh – The Holy Scriptures – The New Translation According to the Traditional Hebrew Text. New York: Jewish Publication Society, 1985.

Tillich, Paul. *A History of Christian Thought.* New York: Harper and Row, 1968.

Thompson, J. Milburn. *Justice And Peace: A Christian Primer.* Maryknoll: Orbis Books, 1998.

Thompson, Rhodes. *Stewards Shaped By Grace: The Church's Gift to a Troubled World.* St. Louis: Chalice Press, 1990.

Torjesen, Karen Jo. *When Women Were Priests – Women's Leadership in the Early Church and the Scandal of Their Subordination in the Rise of Christianity.* New York: HarperSanFrancisco, 1993.

Troeh, Marjorie B. ed. *Restoration Studies IV.* Independence: Herald Publishing House, 1988.

Thurow, Lester C. *The Future Of Capitalism: How Today's Economic Forces Shape Tomorrow's World.* New York: Penguin, 1996.

Tyree, Alan D. ed. *Exploring The Faith.* Independence: Herald Publishing House, 1987.

Underwood, Grant. *The Millenarian World of Early Mormonism.* Urbana: University of Illinois Press, 1993.

Vallet, Ronald E. *The Steward Living In Covenant: A New Perspective on Old Testament Stories.* Grand Rapids: Eerdmans, 2000.

Van Voorst, Robert E. *Jesus Outside the New Testament.* Grand Rapids: Eerdmans, 2000.

Van Wagoner, Richard S. *Sidney Rigdon – A Portrait of Religious Excess.* Salt Lake City: Signature Books, 1994.

Vogel, Dan "Mormonism's Anti-Masonick Bible", *The John Witmer Historical Association Journal,* vol. 9, 1989.

Vogel, Dan. *Seekers and the Advent of Mormonism.* Salt Lake City: Signature Books, 1988.

Vogt, Virgil. *Treasure In Heaven – The Bible Teaching About Money, Finances, and Possessions.* Ann Arbor: Servant Books, 1982.

Waterman, Bryan, ed. *The Prophet Puzzle: Interpretive Essays on Joseph Smith.* Salt Lake City: Signature Books, 1999.

Wellington, Paul A., ed. *Readings on the Concept of Zion.* Independence: Herald Publishing House, 1973.

Wheeler, Sondra Ely. *Wealth as Peril and Obligation: The New Testament on Possessions.* Grand Rapids: Eerdmans, 1995.

Will, James E. *A Christology of Peace.* Louisville: Westminster John Knox Press, 1989.

Wilson, Marvin R. *Our Father Abraham: Jewish Roots of Christian Faith.* Grand Rapids: Eerdmans, 1989.

Wink, Walter. *Engaging The Powers: Discernment and Resistance in a World of Domination.* Minneapolis: Fortress Press, 1992.

_____ *The Powers That Be: Theology for a New Millennium.* New York: Galilee Doubleday, 1998.

Wright, N. T. *The Climax of the Covenant: Christ and the Law in Pauline Theology.* Minneapolis: Fortress Press, 1991.

Wuthnow, Robert. *Acts Of Compassion: Caring for Others and Helping Ourselves.* Princeton: Princeton University Press, 1991.

_____ *The Crisis in the Churches: Spiritual Malaise, Fiscal Woe.* New York: Oxford University Press, 1997.

Ziesler, John. *Pauline Christianity (The Oxford Bible Series).* New York: Oxford University Press, 1991

Yoder, John Howard. *The Politics Of Jesus: Vicit Agnus Noster.* Grand Rapids: Eerdmans, 1999.

_____ *When War Is Unjust: Being Honest in Just-War Thinking.* Maryknoll: Orbis Books, 1996.

Yoder, Perry B. *Shalom: The Bible's Word for Salvation, Justice and Peace.* Nappannee: Evangel Publishing House, 1987.

Zehr, Howard. *Changing Lenses: A New Focus for Crime and Justice.* Scottdale PA: Herald Press, 1995.

Scriptures

The New Oxford Annotated Bible with the Apocrypha, New Revised Stand Version. NY: Oxford University Press, 1991.

Book of Mormon – Revised Authorized Version. Independence, MO: Herald Publishing House, 1966.

Doctrine and Covenants. Independence, MO: Herald Publishing House, 1990.

Encyclopedias

The Interpreter's Dictionary of the Bible – An Illustrated Encyclopedia, vol. 2. Nashville TN: Abingdon Press, 1962

Dissertations and Theses

Holmes, Reed, M. "Joseph Smith, Jr., and George J. Adams – Gentile Dreamers of Zion." Ph.D. diss., University of Haifa, 1989.

Lewis, Wayne J. "Mormon Land Ownership as a Factor Evaluation the Extent of Mormon Settlements and Influence in Missouri, 1831-1841." Master's Thesis, Brigham Young University, 1981.

Roberts, Forest. "The History And Development Of The Stewardship Idea." Master's thesis, State University of Iowa, 1922.

Periodicals

Bolton, Andrew. "Blessed Are...Developing a Christ-Centered Theology of Peace, Justice and Sustainable Environment." *Saints Herald*, 145: no. 10:12-13.

Brueggemann, Walter. "The Liturgy of Abundance, the Myth of Scarcity." *Christian Century,* March 24-31, 1999, 342-347.

Campbell, Carol Cease. "Jesus Third Way." *Herald,* 149: no. 7:12-15.

Johnson, Luke T. "The Literary Function of Possessions in Luke-Acts." *Scholars Press – The Society of Biblical Literature,* 39, (1977).

McMurray, W. Grant. "A Transforming Faith: A Call to Discipleship." *Saints Herald,* 145: no. 6:7-15.

Scherer, Mark. "Historical Views of Zion and Changing Prophetic Understandings." *Saints' Herald,* 146: no. 1:21.

_____ "The Theme of Peace in Church History." *Saints Herald,* 145: no. 5:18.

Smith, Frederick M. "Gathering to Zion." *Saints Herald*, 75: no. 32:929.

Yarrington, Roger. "What Is Zion?" *Saints Herald*, 102: no. 41:16-17.

Archival Material

Cowdery, Oliver and Joseph Smith, "Letter 8," *Latter Day Saints' Messenger and Advocate*, vol. 2 no. 1, October 1835

Pratt, Parley P. *A Voice of Warning and Instruction To All People – The Faith and Doctrine of the Church of Jesus Christ of Latter Day Saints.* Liverpool, England: F. D. Richards, Publisher, 1854 (first published in *Cincinnati,* 1837). Temple Archives, Independence, MO.
_____ *Key to the Science of Theology: Designed as an Introduction to the First Principles of Spiritual Philosophy; Religion; Law and Government; As Delivered By the Ancients, and as Restored in this Age, For the Final Development of Universal Peace, Truth and Knowledge.* Liverpool, England, F. D. Richards Publisher, 1855. Temple Archives, Independence, MO.

Smith, Joseph and Heman C. Smith. *History Of The Church of Jesus Christ of Latter Day Saints, 1805-1835.* vol. 1. Lamoni, IA: Board of Publication of the Reorganized Church of Jesus Christ of Latter Day Saints, 1917.
_____ *History of the Church of Jesus Christ of Latter Day Saints, 1836-1844,* vol. 2. Lamoni, IA:Board of Publication of the Reorganized Church of Jesus Christ of Latter Day Saints, 1920.
_____ *Synopsis of the Faith & Doctrines of the Church of Jesus Christ of Latter-Day Saints, Compiled from the Bible, Book of Mormon, Doctrine & covenants, and other publications of the Church with an Appendix Containing an Epitome of Ecclesiastical History and a Chronology of Important Events in the History of Latter-*

Day Work. Plano, IL: The Reorganized Church of Jesus Christ of Latter Day Saints, 1865.

Times and Seasons, vol. 3 no. 13, May 2, 1842.

Winchester, B. *Synopsis of the Holy Scriptures, and Concordance in which the synonymous Passages are arranged together – Chiefly Designed to Illustrate The Doctrine of the Church of Jesus Christ of Latter-Day Saints to which is added as an appendix and Epitome of Ecclesiastical History, etc.* Philadelphia, PA: United States Book and Job Printing Office, 1842. Temple Archives, Independence, MO.

Wood, Wilfred C., ed., *Joseph Smith Begins His Work,* vol. II. Wilfred C. Wood, Publisher, 1962. (Certified photo copy of Joseph Smith, Jr., Oliver Cowdery, Sidney Rigdon, and F. G. Williams, *Theology Lectures On The Doctrine of the Church of Latter Day Saints, Kirtland, Ohio, 1835.)* Temple Archives, Independence, MO.

Unpublished Works

Livingston, H. L. *A Compilation on the Gathering in Three Volumes,* Unpublished photocopies of *Saints Herald* articles: 1863-1971.

Indexes

Scripture

Bible

Authors cited

Yoder, Perry –
34,36,37,38,43,46,47,48,5
0,56,66,72,87,102

Subjects

inclusive global community – 201

Community of common goods – Essenes –91; sharing in early church106-109; Based on manna principle – 107; meaning – the desire to live in unity with brothers and sisters of the church - -108; story of Ananias and Sapphira – 108; Book of Mormon, Golden Age – 135-138; Restoration movement – 135-162; all things in common – Restoration – 151-153; Law of Consecration, means of achieving – 155-157

Conditional Covenant, Mosaic – based on the obedience of the people – 25-26

Covenant – 8-9; Abrahamic – 16; Mosaic Covenant of Shalom 22-25; Jubilee – God's

protection for the Mosaic Covenant – 29; Davidic Covenant - 49

Covenant People – 21; process - 21

Creation process, change – 6; God connected with forces of creation – 6

Curse model – life apart from God, evidence of continuing sin – 13

Desert laboratory for community – 23

Diaspora – during Roman rule – 77; pilgrimage to Jerusalem – 77; role of in bring gospel to gentile lands – 110; return of, latter days – 149-151

Dualism – role of in early church116-117;

Education, importance of – 37; Book of Mormon – not to cause division among people – 130-131; See School of the Prophets – 158-162; post-war

286

education boom, leaders becoming seminary, professionally trained – 186; church mandated to deeper levels of education and interaction with scripture – 190; Independence temple – provide place and means for education – 193; call of Zion and education – 198

Essenes 80; role of in early church 105-108

Exile – lessons learned – 61-62

Father's house – promised land – 42

Gathering, the – JSIII moved family to Independence, 1906, signaling the gathering to Independence – 178; stressed by FM Smith – 180-181

God – redeemer – 5; righteousness, source of – 5; steadfast love, justice, righteousness and compassion – 8; personhood of God – 9; world created for love and communion – 10; Owner of the land –30; Jewish belief in vs Babylonian – 76; purity system – 85-86; compassionate righteousness taught of, taught by Jesus – 87; righteousness of, central theme of Pauline Christianity – 113; righteousness of God, model for human conduct affirmed in Book of Mormon – 122; nearness of God emphasized – 191

Godfearers – role of in spread of Christianity - 110

Grace – God's gift –13; human need to accept; in Old and New Testaments – 65; Restoration – prevenient to tribes of India – 190

Holy Spirit – see Shekinah for Old Testament; in the apostolic church – 104-105; gentile church – 113; Book of Mormon – experiences Spirit – 128-130; beginning of Restoration movement, evidences of – 144; call for greater unity and depth of Spirit – 192; Abundant Life center – focus – spiritual formation – 193

Houses of prayer – synagogues in Roman empire - 110

Idolatry - 29

Image of God, humans created in – 7-8; image as meaning stewards, 8

Independence, MO (Jackson, County) – place for Zion – 150; problems with gathering – 163-167; expulsion and extermination order – 168-170; a few families move back,

1879 – 175; JSIII moves to Independence – 178; FM Smith stressed gathering to Zion – 180-181

Jethro – wise counselor, organizer – 23

Jesus – suffering servant – 63; God's shalom – 70; the World become flesh – 70; declared Jubilee – 70; spirit person, healer, wisdom teacher, social prophet and founder of a movement, personification of Sophia, agent of creation – 72; victor over death, divine teacher, personification of divine reason, the shepherd, savior – 73 world of Jesus; the kingdom – 73; knowing him – 74; Jewish son – 75; the teacher – 76; ministry of in terms of Mosaic Covenant of Shalom – 84-96;

Jubilee principles – 84; unique – 84-85; attack on the purity system - 86; authority – 86-87; message from Old Testament – 87; taught compassionate righteousness of God – 87; reform of socio/political structures – 87; stewardship issues most common teaching – 88; disparity between rich and poor – 89; Teaching – wealth = spiritual danger – 92; broke rules and stereotypes – 94-95; teachings on the kingdom 97-102; Sermon on the Mount – 98-101; Blessings, Beatitudes – 99-100; Book of Mormon – ministry and the Golden Age that followed – 135-138; preacher of the kingdom – 139; central to prophetic restoration tradition – 201

Joshua leader of the first communities in the Promised Land - 41

Jubilee – 29-32; Isaiah – 63; Luke 4:18ff; synagogue's response to Jesus – 71; Jesus' answer to John, the tenets of Jubilee – 71-72; ministry of Jesus – 84; Sermon on the Mount, restatement of Jubilee – 100-101; sharing in apostolic church based on – 106; in gentile church – 113-115; Jesus' kingdom related to Jubilary obedience – 197

Judaism, a defined religion – 66; early church a movement within – 111; fall of Jerusalem,

289

adoption of church seal, visual theology depicting peace; - 178; church emphasis, 191; Call to build temple dedicated to – 193; Peace Colloquys, Temple Peace Center – 193; condition in Zion – 197

Peaceable Kingdom – 13-14; peacemaking and the kingdom – 100

Persecution – NT – 116; Book of Mormon – 129; Kirtland – 156; Expulsion order, continual persecution – 164; sue for peace – 165; moved to Far West – 168; extermination order – Saints leave MO or be killed – 168-169; Haun's Mill massacre, loss of property – 169; church petitioned federal government for redress of wrongs – 169; murders of Joseph and Hyrum Smith – 172

People of the land – 80-81

Pharisees - 80

Poor people – 26; 28; 30-31;Jubilee – good news to the poor 32; genuine need – fault of the distribution system – 34; food for everyone – right of community membership – 35; king to be their protector – 45; Zion as a refuge for the poor – 53; prophets spoke against oppression of – 56; sins against the poor, disobedience to God – 57; commandment to care for – 60; see people of the land; purity laws – 82; Jesus' teachings restate OT

92; love of – 92;
apostolic church'
teaching – 106-109;
Book of Mormon
Golden Age,
common possessions
– 135-138; early
Restoration
teaching, Kirtland –
153-156; possessions,
theology of
consumption,
materialism –
demonic forces that
threaten
Christianity – 200

Poverty, a permanent
class - 47

Praise and
thanksgiving, role of
– 21

Private property –
meaning of – 35

Prophets – 55-
59;prophet's hope
for Jubilee – 71;
time of the,
messianic age - 82

Rabbinic Judaism – 67-
69

Reciprocal texts – 22

Reorganization – 173-
179; 1852 – initial
conference – 173;

Repentance – part of
the meaning of
shalom – 10;
prophet's message –
58

Resident – 17

Restoration movement –
importance of
community see part
IV, 140-203; NT
Primitivism – 139;
Christianity began
as – 139; communal
groups, Kirtland –
153-156

Revelation – continuing
in relationship to
Torah – 25;
importance of place
where revelation
was received – 26;
important part of
Restoration
movement – 145;
anticipation of
future answers being
given, more light
and truth – 161

Sin – began as
dissatisfaction,
denial, doubt,
suspicion,
selfishness, pride –
11; essential nature
of sin – brokenness
of relationships – 12;
confession or
acknowledgment –
13; prophet's
confrontation of –
58-59
Slaves – Hebrew,
Sabbatical year – 35-
36; children of - 36
Smith, Frederick M.,
prepared for
leadership – 180;
passionately believed
in Zion – 180-181;
leadership problems,
"Supreme
Directional Control"
– 181-182; Great
Depression – church
financial problems –
183
Smith, Israel A., -
concerned with
spiritual issues, Zion
was first of all
spiritual – 185-186
Smith, Joseph II, world
of, early influences -
142-143; influence
of, theology – 158;
trauma survivor –
169-170; changes in
leadership style –
171-172; murder of
– 172
Smith, Joseph III –
assumed leadership
of church – 1860,
reformer,
moderating
influence – 173;
guidance in
formation of Lamoni
176-178;
Smith, W. Wallace
–religious and social
change, including
difficult issues – 189;
position on Zion
clarified – 189
Smith Wallace B., -
theological issues –
191; issue -
ordination of women
– 191;
Sojourner – 16

300

was first of all a spiritual issue – 185-186; postwar, gospel into diverse cultures, message of Zion had to be changed, importance of Jesus Christ stressed – 187-188; Zion became a principle of all of Christian life, rather than a real community – 188; 1966 statement on Zion – 189; hastening time – stewardship is required – 190; question former assumptions about – 195; Zion is concerned with salvation for people – 196; demonstration community involved in all areas of life – 196; grace and justice linked, conditions of righteousness, unity, love and peace with no poor – 197; the way things are done – 197; holistic approach to environment, health, education, social relationships – 198; integral part of salvations for humans and the earth – 199; stewardship, necessary for Zion – 201; call to inclusive 21st century global community - 201